# ARBITRATION 1982
## CONDUCT OF THE HEARING

# ARBITRATION 1982
# CONDUCT OF THE HEARING

---

## PROCEEDINGS OF THE THIRTY-FIFTH
## ANNUAL MEETING
## NATIONAL ACADEMY OF ARBITRATORS

Washington, D.C.                          May 25–28, 1982

*Edited by*
### James L. Stern
*Professor of Economics*
*The University of Wisconsin*

*and*

### Barbara D. Dennis
*Editorial Associate*
*The University of Wisconsin*

The Bureau of National Affairs, Inc.                  Washington, D.C.

Copyright © 1983
The Bureau of National Affairs, Inc.
Washington, D.C. 20037

**Library of Congress Cataloging in Publication Data**

National Academy of Arbitrators. Annual Meeting
(35th:1982:Washington, D.C.)
  Arbitration 1982.
  Includes index.
  1. Arbitration, Industrial—United States—Congresses.
I. Stern, James L. II. Dennis, Barbara D. III. Title.
KF3424.A2N36 1982     344.73'0189143     83-3885
ISBN 0-87179-411-X     347.304189143

Printed in the United States of America
International Standard Book Number: 0-87179-411-X

# PREFACE

Despite the large turnout at the 35th Annual Meeting of the Academy in Washington, D.C., the format of the proceedings provided ample opportunity for members and guests to meet in small groups to discuss the conduct of the arbitration hearing. The essence of these half-dozen or more simultaneous discussions of the admissibility of evidence and procedural rulings during the hearing is contained in Chapters 5 and 6 of this volume. Ted St. Antoine, the Program Chairman for the Annual Meeting, is to be thanked for the many hours he spent in the summer, fall, and early winter of 1982 extracting the highlights from the tapes of all the individual sessions.

Ted Jones's Presidential Address was warmly received by his fellow members who found in it support for their "own brand of industrial justice." Feelings of the advocates in the audience were assuaged by Ted's assurance that the arbitrator's "brand" was extracted from the wisdom he gained from the parties. Harry Edwards gave further support to arbitrators and the arbitral process by expressing a strong preference for arbitration rather than the courts as the best forum for resolving conventional disputes about personnel and industrial relations issues. This is high praise from a former arbitrator turned Federal Appellate Court judge.

Ben Aaron set forth, and defended ably, a comprehensive role for the arbitrator in ensuring that the arbitration process would be fair. The commentators, Andrea Christensen and Judith Vladeck, representing the management and union point of view, respectively, took issue with Ben about the extent to which the arbitrator should set ground rules for ensuring fairness and, along with Ben and many members of the audience, debated this question at some length. Portions of that discussion are included in Chapter 3.

Dick Mittenthal and two advocates—Stuart Bernstein for management and Sam Camens for unions—presented their views about the art of opinion-writing. Although there was general agreement that arbitrators should state matters clearly, precisely, and succinctly and should refrain from writing suspense stories, there was, as can be gleaned from the discussion in Chapter 4, some disagreement about the approach the arbitrator should take in developing his opinion and what should and should not be included in it.

The editors wish to express the appreciation of the officers and members of the Board of Governors of the Academy to the Program Committee and to Nick Zumas, the Arrangements Chairman, and his committee for the work that went into making the meeting so successful. The editors are grateful to the authors for getting their papers in promptly, and apologize to the members of the Academy for the somewhat lengthy gestation period required to get this volume into print. We will try to do better next year!

James L. Stern
December 1982 Barbara D. Dennis

# CONTENTS

CHAPTER 1

# A MEDITATION ON LABOR ARBITRATION AND "HIS OWN BRAND OF INDUSTRIAL JUSTICE"

EDGAR A. JONES, JR.*

The scriptural reading for our meditation on this occasion is a familiar one. It presents us in three sentences with a riddle enfolded in a paradox. It reads as follows:[1]

"[A]n arbitrator is confined to interpretation and application of the collective bargaining agreement: *He does not sit to dispense his own brand of industrial justice.* He may of course look for guidance from many sources, *yet his award is legitimate only so long as it draws its essence from the collective bargaining agreement.* When the arbitrators' words manifest an infidelity to this obligation, courts have no choice but to refuse enforcement of the award."

The "his own brand" phrase has gained currency,[2] first, in petitions by losing parties to vacate awards on the ground that some hapless arbitrator has flunked the *Enterprise Wheel & Car* "essence" test; and second, in the opinions of judges who vacate the award, thereby transforming the contractual winner into a judicial loser.[3]

---

*President, National Academy of Arbitrators; Professor of Law, University of California, Los Angeles, Calif.
[1]*United Steelworkers* v. *Enterprise Wheel & Car Corp.,* 363 U.S. 593, 597, 46 LRRM 2414 (1960).
[2]There are several perspectives from which one might view the import of that protean phrase: the Supreme Court that uttered it, the appellate courts that superintend its applications, the trial courts that vacate or confirm arbitral awards in its name, the arbitrators who do the awards, and the collective bargainers who create the office of arbitration and jointly select the persons to sit as arbitrators to hear and decide their disputes. The central role of the collective bargainers in selecting *their* own brand of industrial justice has not been sufficiently remarked. It is the focus of this address.
[3]*See, for example, Safeway Stores, Inc.* v. *Machinists Lodge 1486,* 534 F.Supp. 638 (D. Md. 1982); *United States Postal Service* v. *Nat'l Rural Letter Carriers Ass'n,* 535 F.Supp. 1034 (N.D. Ohio 1982). *See also F. W. Woolworth Co.* v. *Warehousemen's Local 781,* 629 F.2d 1204, 104 LRRM 3128 (7th Cir. 1980) (reversing district court's vacation of arbitral award); *Smith Steelworkers, DALE 19806* v. *A. O. Smith Corp.,* 626 F.2d 596, 105 LRRM 2044 (7th Cir. 1980) (reversing district court's vacation of arbitral award); *International Brotherhood of Firemen and Oilers Local 935-B* v. *Nestle Co.,* 105 LRRM 2715 (6th Cir. 1980) (vacating arbitral award that had been confirmed by district court); *Johnson Bronze Co.* v. *United Automobile Workers.* 621 F.2d 81, 104 LRRM 2378 (3d Cir. 1980) (reversing district court's vacation of arbitral award). *Also see* Philadelphia cases cited, *infra,* at note 6. *See* Kaden, *Judges and Arbitrators: Observations on the Scope of Judicial Review,* 80 Col. L. Rev. 267 (1980).

1

The paradox inherent in the Court's "essence" test in those three sentences is that it created a semantic slipnoose around the exercise of arbitral judgment and committed its use to what the Court itself characterized as inexperienced and uninformed judges.[4] At the same time, throughout the three opinions of the *Steelworkers Trilogy*, the Court convincingly detailed the functional necessity for chosen arbitrators rather than imposed judges to resolve collective bargaining grievances.[5]

That distinction was realistic and remains valid. It is based on the realization that arbitrators and judges look to different resources of judgment and tend to think differently about them in deciding issues arising out of collective bargaining.[6] The Court ac-

---

[4]For example: "The lower courts in the instant case had a like preoccupation with ordinary contract law. The collective agreement requires arbitration of claims that courts might be unwilling to entertain. In the context of the plant or industry the grievance may assume proportions of which judges are ignorant." *United Steelworkers* v. *American Mfg. Co.*, 363 U.S. 564, 567, 46 LRRM 2414 (1960). ". . . The courts, therefore, have no business weighing the merits of the grievance, considering whether there is equity in a particular claim, or determining whether there is particular language in the written instrument which will support the claim. The agreement is to submit all grievances to arbitration, not merely those which the court will deem meritorious. The processing of even frivolous claims may have therapeutic values of which those who are not part of the plant environment may be quite unaware." *Id.* at 568. "The labor arbitrator performs functions which are not normal to the courts; the considerations which help him fashion judgments may indeed be foreign to the competence of courts." *United Steelworkers* v. *Warrior & Gulf Navigation Co.*, 363 U.S. 574, 46 LRRM 2416 (1960). "The ablest judge cannot be expected to bring the same experience and competence to bear upon the determination of a grievance, because he cannot be similarly informed." *Id.* at 582.

[5]". . . The question is not whether in the mind of the court there is equity in the claim. . . . The function of the court is very limited when the parties have agreed to submit all questions of contract interpretation to the arbitrator. It is confined to ascertaining whether the party seeking arbitration is making a claim which on its face is governed by the contract. Whether the moving party is right or wrong is a question of contract interpretation for the arbitrator. In these circumstances the moving party should not be deprived of the arbitrator's judgment, when it was his judgment and all that it connotes that was bargained for." *United Steelworkers* v. *American Mfg. Co.*, 363 U.S. 564, 567–568, 46 LRRM 2414 (1960).

[6]For an example of the significantly different analytical approaches of a conceptually minded judge and a pragmatically inclined arbitrator, compare *Western Airlines, Inc.*, 37 LA 700 (Edgar Jones 1961) with *Trans World Airlines, Inc.* v. *Beaty et al.*, 402 F.Supp. 652 (S.D.N.Y. 1975), *aff'd by oral op.* 542 F.2d 1165, 94 LRRM 2125 (2d Cir. 1976) (begging question whether court-enforced company policy was itself contractually sustainable as "just cause" for discharges under "grandfather" provisions insulative of Flight Engineers—and therefore arbitrable).

A graphic example is presented by several cases that arose out of one labor dispute involving several Philadelphia supermarkets in which a federal district judge's preoccupation with an inapposite legal concept manifestly caused the court not to comprehend the collective-bargaining reasoning of two successive arbitrators. The distinction was not lost on the Third Circuit, however, which reversed both of the district court vacations of the arbitral awards at issue. *Philadelphia Food Store Employers' Labor Council* v. *Retail Clerks*, 453 F.Supp. 577, 98 LRRM 3225 (E.D. Pa. 1978) (Troutman, J., vacating award of Arbitrator Lewis Gill against employer), *rev'd*, 87 CCH L.C. ¶11,593 (3d Cir. 1979) (per curiam, unpublished op.); *Acme Markets, Inc.* v. *Local 6, Bakery Workers*, 470 F.Supp. 1136, 101 LRRM 2575 (E.D. Pa. 1979) (Troutman, J., vacating award of Arbitrator Robert Koretz against employer), *rev'd*, 87 CCH L.C. ¶11,768 (3d Cir. 1980); compare *Warehouse Employees Local 169* v. *Acme Markets, Inc.*, 473 F.Supp. 709, 105 LRRM 3206

cordingly concluded that judges should exercise considerable restraint to refrain from interfering with the bargaining processes
of which arbitration is an integral part.[7] Otherwise, for lack of
understanding, they may unwisely alter the evolution of the private bargain and exacerbate conflict. Adherence by employers
and unions to voluntarily fashioned conditions of employment
and production leads to stability and productivity.[8] The Court
saw that to be the central goal of national labor policy.

Seemingly recoiling somewhat from the implications of its
construct of arbitral independence, however, the Court created
the paradox of the "essence" test. It did so by joining conceptually what are functionally incompatible. First, it said that judges
must not allow arbitrators to stray beyond the parameters of the
essence of collective agreements. But second, it also said that
the parties' chosen arbitrators are more aware than are judges
of the parties' intent and needs which are constitutive of that
"essence."[9] Thus, as written, the "essence" test is simply unworkable.

In turn, the riddle of "his own brand" inheres in the unworld-
liness of the declaration that an arbitrator "does not sit to dispense his own brand of industrial justice." Several examples
should suffice.

---

(E.D. Pa. 1979) (Broderick, J., dismissing union petition to vacate Arbitrator Buckwal-
ter's award in favor of employer).

See Jones, *The Name of the Game Is Decision—Some Reflections on "Arbitrability" and "Authority" in Labor Arbitration*, 46 Tex. L. Rev. 865 (1968); Jones, *Power and Prudence in the
Arbitration of Labor Disputes: A Venture in Some Hypotheses*, 11 U.C.L.A. L. Rev. 675 (1964)
(comparing conceptual and pragmatic patterns of decisional thinking, at 715 passim).

[7]". . . The court should view with suspicion an attempt to persuade it to become
entangled in the construction of the substantive provisions of a labor agreement, even
through the back door of interpreting the arbitration clause, when the alternative is to
utilize the services of an arbitrator." *United Steelworkers* v. *Warrior & Gulf Navigation Co.*,
363 U.S. 574, 585, 46 LRRM 2416 (1960).

[8]"Arbitration is a stabilizing influence only as it serves as a vehicle for handling any and
all disputes that arise under the agreement." *United Steelworkers* v. *American Mfg. Co.*, 363
U.S. 564, 567, 46 LRRM 2414 (1960). "The Judiciary sits in these cases to bring into
operation an arbitral process which substitutes a regime of peaceful settlement for the
older regime of industrial conflict." *United Steelworkers* v. *Warrior & Gulf Navigation Co.*,
363 U.S. 574, 585, 46 LRRM 2416 (1960). "The refusal of courts to review the merits
of an arbitration award is the proper approach to arbitration under collective bargaining
agreements. The federal policy of settling labor disputes by arbitration would be under-
mined if courts had the final say on the merits of the awards. . . . [T]he arbitrators under
these collective agreements are indispensable agencies in a continuous collective bargaining process. They sit to settle disputes at the plant level—disputes that require for
their solution knowledge of the custom and practices of a particular factory or of a
particular industry as reflected in particular agreements." *United Steelworkers* v. *Enterprise
Wheel & Car Corp.*, 363 U.S. 593, 596, 46 LRRM 2423 (1960). ". . . [T]he question of
interpretation of the collective bargaining agreement is a question for the arbitrator. It
is the arbitrator's construction which was bargained for; and so far as the arbitrator's
decision concerns construction of the contract, the courts have no business overruling
him because their interpretation of the contract is different from his." *Id.* at 599.

[9]*See* note 4, *supra.*

An arbitrator is asked to decide whether an employer's disciplinary response to a grieving employee's conduct was contractually allowable under the otherwise undefined criterion of "just cause." There are thousands of these cases each year that are submitted to arbitrators. Where lies the "essence" from which to deduce what discipline is, and what it is not, for "just cause"?

A dozen employees work under an incentive system; they become dissatisfied with new piece rates set by the employer; they complain to no avail but they do not file a written grievance. Instead, they reduce their output from their usual average of 150 percent over the contractual minimum to, but not below, the 100 percent floor for the basic wage rate. Have they engaged in a contractually prohibited "slowdown," as the employer argues, or are they entitled to forgo reaching for the carrot that has become unpalatable?[10] Whence comes the "essence" from which to distill the solution to that problem?

A supermarket employer is a member of a multi-employer bargaining unit with agreements with four unions that represent their craft employees in the stores. The contract with one of the unions expires. The union strikes one of the employers; its members continue to work for the other employers. The contracts of the other three unions with the employers remain in effect. Each agreement contains a no-strike, no-lockout provision. One for all and all for one, all of the employers close down all of their stores. The Labor Board and the courts would characterize that lockout as "defensive" and therefore not a violation of Section 8(a)(1) and (5) of the NLRA, were the unions to file charges with the Board.[11] But they grieve instead. In arbitration, may the nonstriking unions get cease-and-desist orders and back pay for their members from the unstruck stores that shut down?[12] Where does one find the "essence" from which to

---

[10]The facts are drawn from *Charlton Furniture Co.*, an unpublished case heard by the author. For similar problems of "essence" and alternate decisional tangents, *see Bethlehem Steel Corp.*, 81-1 ARB ¶8036 (Edgar Jones 1980) (Where the collective agreement mandates that overtime is voluntary, does a refusal to continue work into overtime by several disaffected drydockmen during the operation of the drydock constitute a contractually prohibited refusal to work?); *Elevator Manufacturers Ass'n v. Local 1, International Union of Elevator Constructors*, 534 F.Supp. 265 (S.D.N.Y. 1982) ("Is the Union on strike when it refuses overtime work? . . . If I were to decide the issues presented, I would be making a finding which the parties bargained to have an arbitrator decide.").

[11]*See American Ship Building Co. v. NLRB*, 380 U.S. 85, 58 LRRM 2672 (1965); *NLRB v. Brown*, 380 U.S. 278, 58 LRRM 2663 (1965); *Weyerhaeuser Co.*, 166 NLRB 299 (1967). *See* Bernhardt, *Lockouts: An Analysis of Board and Court Decisions Since Brown and American Ship*, 57 Corn. L.Q. 211 (1972).

[12]*See* the Philadelphia cases, *supra* note 6. Two arbitrators held the actions of two of the employers to be violative of the collective agreement; a third arbitrator, unpersuaded

extract the collective bargaining wisdom to resolve that dispute?

If the arbitrator in these cases "does not sit to dispense his own brand of industrial justice," what other brand is available for him to dispense? The given answer is, "that of the parties." If that be so, where does the arbitrator locate it when they have not set it out in words in the agreement?

Now his award has been issued and is challenged in court. How does the court tell whether the award he has issued was "his own brand" rather than the parties' own brand? The given answer is that the Supreme Court has laid it down that his award must either draw its "essence" from their agreement or a court must refuse to enforce it.[13] That of course closes the loop of the paradox, which is—how may a court, from its resources and experience, be expected to make the necessary sensitive assessments of "essence" in these cases? Whether the court recognizes the situation or not, petitions to vacate awards usually arise out of the more difficult and divisive of the disputes that are heard by arbitrators. Yet the Supreme Court made a finding of fact that the ablest judge is not institutionally competent functionally and experientially to engage in that kind of probing of the soul of collective bargaining.[14] Most of them, in their days of practice as lawyers, have had no professional involvement with labor disputes.

The federal courts of appeals have mostly succeeded nonetheless in breaking out of the constraints of the circular "essence" test and of the "his own brand" riddle. They have done this by judicial fiat, compelling unwilling lower court judges to toe the line of imposed judicial restraint, however painful and unaccustomed an experience that does seem to be for some judges.[15]

---

by the decisions of the other two, thereafter upheld one of the employers; a federal district judge vacated the two awards for the unions; the federal court of appeals for the Third Circuit reversed the two district court decisions and reinstated the two arbitral awards. Net quantification of "essence": two enforced awards—with certified "essence" —struck down the actions of two employers, and one unchallenged ("essence"?) award sustained the actions of the third employer; *ergo:* one contractual source, two countervailing "essences."

[13]*See* text at note 1, *supra.*
[14]*See* note 4, *supra.*
[15]*See* notes 3 and 6, *supra.*

In the course of reversing and remanding a federal district court's vacation of reinstatement awards of two employees that had offended the "his own brand" sensibilities of the district judge, Fifth Circuit Judge John R. Brown observed, "Proving again that the infusion of judicial enthusiasm for arbitration in labor relations does not always keep the Judiciary out of the act . . . the District Court, performing a Solomonic role, declined to deny enforcement as such, denied enforcement of the back pay award, dismissed the Employer's complaint, but declared that if the two discharged employees extended an appropriate written apology to the employer, he would order reinstatement as to the

The courts of appeals have done that by interpreting the "essence" rationale in such a manner as to implement the determined effort of the Supreme Court to surround labor arbitration and the parties' collective bargaining agreement with the strongest possible measure of insulation from the displacing intrusions of courts. Yet they have not wholly precluded access to the ultimate constitutional safeguard of judicial review. It cannot otherwise be accomplished. It is semantically impossible for the Supreme Court or anyone else so to define the "essence" of a collective agreement as to enable a reviewing court to differentiate between the proscribed brand and the allowable brands available.

Although the Court did not remark the fact in the *Trilogy,* it is significant that the run-of-the-bench judges, from the least to the most competent, are selected to sit in judgment on a case by processes that are almost wholly depersonalized. That is in marked contrast to how the run-of-the-shop arbitrators are chosen. From the ablest to the least able among them, the process of their selection is highly personalized and individually focused. A trial or appellate judge on a multijudge court draws an assignment to hear or to review a case by the turn of some sort of rotation wheel or the direction of a presiding judge. The decision of whom to place in the seat of judgment in the courtroom is not controlled by the disputants; sovereign prerogative makes the choice. In contrast, collective bargainers are in complete control of the process for seating their arbitrators.[16]

The crucial difference between the selection procedures for judges and those for labor arbitrators is dramatized by a federal judge's rejection of a proposal for enabling peremptory challenges of federal judges in civil and criminal cases.[17] A bar association committee became concerned about "bad temper, intellectual mediocrity, or bias in a particular kind of case" on the federal bench in New York. They wish to avoid having a person judged by a judge who "has a personal bias" or whose "impartiality might be reasonably questioned." Under present

---

future." *Dallas Typographical Union No. 173* v. *A. H. Belo Corp.* 372 F.2d 577, 579 (5th Cir. 1967). The case is discussed in Jones, *The Name of the Game Is Decision—Some Reflections on "Arbitrability" and "Authority" in Labor Arbitration,* 46 Tex. L. Rev. 865, 877–879 (1968).
[16]"But precisely because dispute resolution in this setting involved as much rule-finding and rulemaking as rule-applying, recourse to the courts invites too narrow a view of the problem. . . . And the parties have too much at stake to entrust the contours of their relationship to whatever judge happens to come along next on the assignment list in the computer." Kaden, *supra* note 3, at 275.
[17]Bartels, *Peremptory Challenges to Federal Judges: A Judge's View,* 68 A.B.A.J. 449 (1982).

procedures, recusal (removal of a judge) seldom occurs because specific facts must be established supportive of disqualification.

Federal District Judge John R. Bartels has attacked the recommended peremptory procedure as "not the answer because it is not addressed to the bias or impartiality of a judge but simply permits the expression of the subjective feeling, whim, and reaction of a litigant or his attorney. No judge should be disqualified without some factual basis being set forth in an affidavit or otherwise." The judge set forth some of the reasons which have been held by courts to be *insufficient* for involuntary recusals of judges. They include:[18]

> "the preferences of one party for another judge; displeasure with the judge's performance in prior proceedings; preference for a judge possessing plaintiff's philosophy; previous expression by the judge on a particular point of law; prior adverse judicial determinations involving the same issue; and a judge's judicial philosophy or prior rulings of law in general."

Now substitute, if you will, "arbitrator" for "judge" in that recital and you will immediately recognize this as a litany of reasons commonly cited among parties for not selecting particular labor arbitrators.

However constituted may be the brands of judicial justice being dispensed in our courtrooms, and whatever one may think of the quality of the respective brands available, their components assuredly are not being predetermined by contesting litigants to accord with their perceived self-interests. Labor arbitrators, however, have for decades lived under that kind of subjective dispensation by the parties and their lawyers. Indeed, they have readily accepted their own dispensability in the selection process as indispensable to collective bargaining.

Before the parties join to select the person to "sit" to "dispense" whatever it is that will end up being dispensed, the individual they ultimately choose to arbitrate is just another person with some ideas and the presumed potential for some more. But he has no commission to do anything for or to anyone else, let alone for or to these collective bargainers. The office of arbitrator is entirely of their own creation; government does not compel it. It is wholly up to them whom they may choose in this process of comparative selection. The process is governed by the perceptions of self-interest of each of the bargainers as they

---

[18]*Id.* at 450.

try to identify, each in his own way, that individual arbitrator whose personal characteristics make it at least likely, if not certain, that the resultant award in the case will be favorable. Government does not tell them whom they must choose, nor what must be the components of his judgment.

Once appointed, however, the parties have placed their conflicting bets on this individual, whatever may be their respective reasons. In this second phase of the process of appointment, collective bargainers universally expect tough-minded integrity; they view any signs of subservience to one or the other with suspicion and disdain. So it is that some persons who would welcome careers as arbitrators fail in their ambition because they do not evidence in their conduct that they meet the common expectation of the parties that arbitrators will conduct themselves with visible independence of judgment before and after their appointment, true to the self that the parties have perceived and, for whatever reason, have selected.[19]

It would be astonishing if employers and unions were not to pay considerable attention to the personal characteristics of the individual whom they winnow out of the pack of available arbitral brands of industrial justice. This scrutiny of the collective bargainers is far from casual, particularly when lawyers are involved. The selection of an arbitrator is seen as central to the tactical problem of getting a favorable decision. Courtroom litigants may lack any effective control over the components of judgment of whoever will sit as judge in deciding their dispute. But collective bargainers always have the opportunity to analyze, compare, and prescribe the specific elements constitutive of the brand of industrial justice they respectively seek, each in his own hopeful way.

Those brand-name elements commonly examined by the parties include at least the following: experience, education, *past decisions on point*, temperament, fairmindedness, *past decisions on point*, skepticism, insight, *past decisions on point*, intelligence, articulateness, and, finally, *past decisions on point*. These judgmental elements are identified in the relative mix that appears desirable in a particular case. Each advocate sorts through the roster of available arbitrators very purposefully. Each looks for the particular composite of judgment on the shelf of arbitral availability

---

[19]*See* Loewenberg, *An Arbitral Timebomb?* 37 Arb. J. 50 (1982), discussing the dearth of, and the need for, empirical research to develop realistic profiles of participants' perceptions of arbitration and arbitrators.

that it deems most suitable to obtaining a favorable decision.

There have always been available aids of various sorts in that culling process. For decades, of course, there have been the two information networks operated by employer advocates and by union advocates. Accumulated hearsay and direct observations flow over the networks (horror stories predominate, naturally) detailing the varying perceptions of the rationalities and irrationalities of individual arbitrators. Those perceptions, realistic or fanciful, have become encrusted on reputations and are seen to be part of "his own brand."

The commercial marketplace of data about labor arbitrators includes looseleaf periodic subscription services that reproduce current arbitral decisions essentially on a sampling basis; well under 10 percent of the annual output of arbitrators gets into print. Computer programming has also now been introduced in an effort to gather into one repository the decisional output of all active labor arbitrators.

One marketer has gathered awards of more than 2,300 arbitrators. Its sales brochures headline the availability of "Your Own Private Arbitration Tracking System." It poses the question: "Have you ever needed to make a quick decision on which arbitrator to choose for a case?" Offered is "a comprehensive computer search of over 40,000 arbitration awards." Its "entire data base" can be searched by arbitrator name, union, employer, subject, or any combination, resulting in a computer printout listing all of an arbitrator's awards, designating the employer or union as "winners." Its brochure reads: "Our computer search is particularly useful in choosing an arbitrator, i.e., when a list is received from AAA or FMCS, just call us with the names and we will send back a list of all the cases we have from the arbitrator, listing: employer and union names—dates—subjects—who won—and citations to summaries or full text."

Another service sells lists of accumulated published and "private" awards of individual arbitrators, together with "management reaction" comments which record "approvals" and "dissents" by employer respondents. Its reports disclose the extent to which collective bargainers seek to calibrate the quantity and quality of past decisions and the quirks and fancies of individual arbitrators. The approach and data are quite typical of all such evaluative services, whether manual or computerized. Here is the way the several dozen respondent employers polled by this service described the brand of industrial justice of one busy

Academy member whom we shall call *Brand A* (some of the employers would prefer *Brand F* as his name, as you will see):

> "Conducts orderly hearing; does not permit introduction of irrelevant data (22 dissents); grasps issues readily (1 dissent); gives no indication of bias during hearing or in award (16 dissents); does not compromise or split awards (14 dissents); does not put burden of proof improperly on employer (20 dissents); respects contract language (17 dissents); gives weight to past practice when contract is ambiguous (10 dissents); confines himself to terms of submission agreement (1 dissent); adheres to the record (16 dissents). *Views his authority as broad* (3 dissents). *Recognizes reserved rights doctrine* (some dissent). *Requires due process in disciplinary cases and favors progressive penalties.* Top-notch arbitrator, who is more conservative than many others. . . . Relatively unqualified, particularly for contract technicalities and job evaluation issues. . . . Allow him to be judge and be somewhat beholding to him in your approach.

> "*Consensus:* Qualified with reservations, particularly in discharge cases. . . . A restrictive submission agreement, a transcript and post-hearing brief are recommended. Must be restricted to avoid displeasing results. . . . Qualified for clear-cut cases."

In addition to those subjective and varying appraisals of the conduct and attitude of each arbitrator whose name appears in this service's data packet, there is a personal resume of education, prior employment, professional memberships, umpireships, panels (AAA, FMCS, state and local governments), and the per diem fees charged. The bulk of each individual report is comprised of an extensive listing on several pages of the arbitrator's past decisions with citations to the publications in which they may be found (a few are recorded simply as "private"). Each case citation is accompanied by several words describing the subject matter, and the cases are listed under one of two headings, either "to employer" or "to union." Our *Brand A* arbitrator's total published output comprised 272 citations, 144 "to employer" and 128 "to union." He has probably decided about 2,500 cases in his arbitral career.

Lest it be thought that only private-sector employers and unions seek this kind of appraisal data for individual arbitrators, consider the following advice from the State of Michigan Office of the State Employer to its labor relations staff concerning 16 named arbitrators, several of whom are Academy members:

> "Examination of numerous awards, as well as extensive discussion with other management representatives, indicates that the following arbitrators should be avoided to the maximum extent possible. This

Office strongly recommends that Departmental Labor Relations Liaisons categorically reject the following individuals should they appear on a AAA, MERC, or FMCS panel:

[4 women's and 12 men's names are listed.]

"Reasons for exclusion include: arbitrator continually exceeding authority; demonstrated bias against employers; substitution of judgment where employer's discretion is authorized; refusal to confine the *dicta* and the award to the record; napping during hearing."

Public and private employer and union advocates alike sniff out that kind of information like a bear in a berry patch!

One may question the usefulness of such an assortment of information as that which was supplied the employer subscribers interested in choosing among the arbitrators surveyed. The point, however, is not whether the parties are wise or foolish in the criteria they use for their selections; it is that they are thorough and calculated in their appraisals and resultant appointments. Indeed, wise or foolish, information (or misinformation) identical to that which I have just read to you about our *Brand A* arbitrator is bandied about in the corridors of each annual meeting of this Academy, at bar association meetings, and at cocktail parties and dinners throughout the country throughout the year. When a brand-name arbitrator has been selected by the parties, the assumed components of expected judgment and hearing conduct have been carefully remarked and evaluated.

Of course, each of the advocates in any case hopes that the mindset of this one who is now chosen has been profiled accurately enough to make it reasonable to predict to a "yes"-needing client that *Brand A,* when applied to the facts of the case at hand, will disclose that a "yes"-saying arbitrator has been named—even as an advocate for the "no"-needing client is assuring *his* client that a comparative analysis of the brands available indicates that a "no"-saying arbitrator has been chosen.

Later, after the award in the case has been issued, it is inevitable that the "yes"-needing or "no"-needing losing party will discover to its disappointment, or even dismay, that it has miscalculated or somehow been misled about the components of *Brand A.* But in this process of competitive selection, *"his* own brand" was analyzed and adopted as *their* own brand, whatever may have been their respective expectations and however deeply felt may be the loser's resentment at the loss. Whatever may be the content or import of the award, and however it may otherwise be described, the brand of industrial justice dispensed in that challenged award is the precise brand that they assessed and agreed to purchase, eyes open, for better or for worse, for richer or for poorer.

A court should give short shrift to those plaintive cries of surprise and outrage from the party who now discovers that it has lost its taste for the brand it had investigated and then bought.[20] Both parties knew, going into the arbitration, that sooner or later, coming out, one of them would have to swallow hard. They knew that, and they accepted it, when they appointed their *Brand A* arbitrator rather than one of the many others available. Courts should be most reluctant to override the earlier commitment of both parties to select this particular arbitrator as the articulator of their contractual obligations in order now to relieve one party from the unwelcome result of that purposeful choice.

There may be reasons for a court to vacate that award. It may be contrary to a public policy which the court must protect from encroachment.[21] It may be the product of fraud or of improper conduct serious enough to warrant judicial intervention. But if the sole basis of the petitioner for setting the award aside is that it allegedly conflicts with some express or implied term of the contract, the court should inquire further. If the contract is *that* clear, was not the prospect for improper interpretation evident from the outset? Should not the party now urging vacation more properly have refused to arbitrate in the first place? If the contract explicitly conferred on the supermarkets the right to close down their entire operations if one rather than all of them are struck by a union, the matter is simply not arbitrable, foreclosed as it is by express language—and so said the Supreme Court.[22] But when the "essence" is not expressed, the courts will order

---

[20]*See, for example, Louisiana-Pacific Corp.* v. *IBEW Local 2294,* 600 F.2d 219, 102 LRRM 2070 (9th Cir. 1979) (One employer with two separate collective bargaining agreements with two unions; disputed work; two bilateral arbitrations; two conflicting awards, one for Union A, another for Union B; district court held each had "essence," confirmed each, Union A's for future work, Union B's for 585 hours of pay for past deprivation; 9th Circuit affirmed: "At several stages the Company made choices as to collective bargaining and litigation strategies. It must now abide the consequences of these choices.").

[21]*See, for example, Local No. P-1236* v. *Jones Dairy Farm,* 519 F.Supp. 1362 (W.D. Wis. 1981) (award sustaining employer's disciplinary action for complaint to U.S.D.A. inspectors, vacated as contrary to public policy which encourages disclosure of unsanitary conditions).

[22]"A specific collective bargaining agreement may exclude contracting out from the grievance procedure. Or a written collateral agreement may make clear that contracting

the matter arbitrated because it is the manifested will of the parties to submit such disputes to arbitration.[23] Why should it be viewed any differently once the award has issued? Why should not the party now seeking court intervention be deemed to have waived any right it may have had for that intervention once it elected to submit to arbitration?

Interestingly, a court intervening to rearrange these contractual circumstances to suit its own view of contractual propriety brings itself into conflict with the Supreme Court's decision in *H. K. Porter, Inc.* v. *NLRB.* [24] (That was a decision, incidentally, that was widely acclaimed by management advocates because of its emphasis on freedom of contract and its disapproval of governmental intervention to impose terms not freely bargained for by the collective bargainers.[25] Ironically, it is true that the bulk by far of petitions to vacate arbitral awards originate from employers.) In *H. K. Porter* the Court ruled that government (the NLRB in that instance, the vacating court in this one) is without power to compel an employer *or a union* to agree to any substantive contractual provision of a collective bargaining agreement. In the name of a "fundamental" statutory policy of "freedom of contract," the Court declared in *H. K. Porter* that to allow the Board—and assuredly a court—"to compel agreement when the parties themselves are unable to do so would violate the fundamental premise on which the Act is based—*private bargaining* under governmental supervision of the procedure alone, without any official compulsion over the actual terms of the contract."[26] If that insulation from government dictate holds for employer bargainers, as it does, it assuredly does also for union bargainers.

What could be more central to "private bargaining" and to the daily search for consensus by an employer and a union than

---

out was not a matter for arbitration. In such a case a grievance based solely on contracting out would not be arbitrable." *United Steelworkers* v. *Warrior & Gulf Navigation Co.*, 363 U.S. 574, 584, 46 LRRM 2416 (1960).

[23]"Apart from matters that the parties specifically exclude, all of the questions on which the parties disagree must therefore come within the scope of the grievance and arbitration provisions of the collective agreement." *United Steelworkers* v. *Warrior & Gulf Navigation Co.*, 363 U.S. 574, 581, 46 LRRM 2416 (1960).

"In the absence of any express provision excluding a particular grievance from arbitration, we think only the most forceful evidence of a purpose to exclude the claim from arbitration can prevail, particularly where, as here, the exclusion clause is vague and the arbitration clause quite broad." *Id.* at 584–585.

[24]397 U.S. 99, 73 LRRM 2561 (1970).

[25]*See, for example,* Swerdlow, *Freedom of Contract in Labor Law: Burns, H. K. Porter, and Section 8(d)*, 51 Tex. L. Rev. 1 (1972).

[26]*Supra* note 24, at 108 (emphasis added).

is the competitive process whereby they select that brand of industrial justice by which they agree to be governed in resolving disputes? When a court intervenes to set aside that award, it is bending governmental power to aid one party to default on the agreement to submit the issue for decision by that person. Stripped of its hortatory rhetoric, the petitioner is doing so because it has now lost its freely undertaken wager on the probability of success that it made when it agreed to go with the *Brand A* arbitrator rather than with *Brand B, Brand C,* or some other brand on the shelf of availability.

That is indeed a strange cause for a court to embrace in the name of justice and contractual "essence." Instead, the court should decide whether there did exist a contractual commitment to arbitrate. If it finds it, it should then leave the parties to their own consensual devices. It was, after all, their freely undertaken contractual obligation to designate some person to be their arbitrator and then, win or lose, right or wrong, to abide by that arbitrator's resolution of their dispute, as final and binding on both of them.[27]

One characteristic of collective bargaining is that agreements are made for relatively short terms—one, two, or three years. It is the usual expectation of bargainers that an occasional aberrant arbitral decision will be returned to the same process of negotiation by which the parties created the arbitrator's authority in the first place. It is common for vexatious awards to be

---

[27]"The premise of the *Steelworkers Trilogy* is that the court should allow the parties to a collective bargaining agreement containing a binding arbitration clause to receive the benefit of the bargain—*binding* arbitration on contract disputes. Professor St. Antoine recognized the soundness of this doctrine when he wrote:

'Put most simply, the arbitrator is the parties' officially designated "reader" of the contract. He (or she) is their joint *alter ego* for the purpose of striking whatever supplementary bargain is necessary to handle the anticipated unanticipated omissions of the initial agreement. Thus, a "misinterpretation" or "gross mistake" by the arbitrator becomes a contradiction in terms. In the absence of fraud or an overreaching of authority on the part of the arbitrator, he is speaking for the parties and his award *is* their contract.'

St. Antoine, *Judicial Review of Labor Arbitration Awards: A Second Look at Enterprise Wheel and Its Progeny,* 75 Mich. L. Rev. 1137, 1140 (1977). This Court has followed this doctrine time and again." *Boise Cascade* v. *United Steelworkers,* 588 F.2d 127, 128–129, 100 LRRM 2481 (5th Cir. 1979).

*See also* Kaden, *supra* note 3, at 275: "The parties' stake in arbitral finality, then, exists not so much because the arbitrator has special competence, experience, or understanding, or even because sometimes he may be filling in gaps in the agreement, making rather than applying rules. Instead, the parties have an institutional stake in finality because the arbitrator is their creation; he functions by their consent and at their sufferance, and his powers and roles can and should be molded by them to suit their own purpose. That they freely do so is evident in the wide variety of arbitration procedures, selection mechanisms, and individual umpires selected in major collective bargaining agreements."

modified or vacated in the next negotiations. It is also common for the sense of immediate outrage at a resented award to dissipate and the ruling to be left intact. But if an award proved egregiously upsetting to the functioning of the workplace, or to the sense of propriety of the losing party, once again experience indicates that midterm negotiation will take place and relief will be bargained for and reached.

Those various bargaining responses to resented awards routinely occur. They do, that is, unless misconceived judicial intervention unwisely displaces them with adjudicative processes. True enough, negotiation is a more difficult and frustrating course of action than simply turning to a court with a petition to vacate an award that has lost its "essence." But as the Supreme Court emphasized in *H. K. Porter*, negotiation and compromise, without governmental dictate, is the essence of free enterprise.

As an arbitrator, I have no problem whatsoever with the prospect of an attorney petitioning a court to vacate an award of mine or of some other arbitrator, whatever may be the reason advanced, including that it has no "essence" (or, perhaps, to his nostrils, too much essence). The problem of disruption of the bargaining relationship that is entailed is not created by petitioning employers or unions. It is created by courts that encourage the practice of petitioning to vacate resented awards by their willingness to muster governmental power to override the voluntarily undertaken contractual commitment by collective bargainers to arbitral finality.

Why should a court intervene to set to naught that mutual conference of confidence in that person,[28] chosen for those reasons, by the collective bargainers as *their* arbitrator, as *their* brand of industrial justice?

---

[28]"The labor arbitrator is usually chosen because of the parties' confidence in his knowledge of the common law of the shop and their trust in his personal judgment to bring to bear considerations which are not expressed in the contract as criteria for judgment." *United Steelworkers* v. *Warrior & Gulf Navigation Co.*, 363 U.S. 574, 582, 46 LRRM 2416 (1960).

# CHAPTER 2

# ADVANTAGES OF ARBITRATION OVER LITIGATION: REFLECTIONS OF A JUDGE

HARRY T. EDWARDS*

## I. Introduction

Some of you may recall that during the 1980 meeting of the Academy, in Los Angeles, Tom Roberts was planted as a "voice from the audience" to engage in a dialectical discussion with Mickey McDermott during the presidential address.[1] I want to make it clear that I have no such collaborator in this audience. I should also advise you that, fearing the worst from some notable and devilish pranksters, such as Jim Hill, Lew Gill, Tom Roberts, Arnold Zack, and Richard Bloch, I have instructed the hotel security guards to arrest anyone who rises or motions as if to speak during my talk.

Seriously, I am truly delighted to be here today to see so many old friends and esteemed former colleagues from the labor relations community. When Professor St. Antoine called to invite me to speak, I accepted without hesitation and with a feeling of honor. Even though a number of you have warned me that our friendships will suffer if I talk too long, I still relish the opportunity to share some time and a few thoughts with so distinguished an audience.

## II. The Life of a Federal Appellate Court Judge

When Rolf Valtin and I met to discuss my proposed speech, he asked me to share with you some of my experiences as a judge, especially in comparison with some of my professional

---

*Member, National Academy of Arbitrators; Circuit Judge, United States Court of Appeals for the District of Columbia Circuit, Washington, D. C.

[1]McDermott, *The Presidential Address—An Exercise in Dialectic: Should Arbitration Behave as Does Litigation?* in Decisional Thinking of Arbitrators and Judges, Proceedings of the 33rd Annual Meeting, National Academy of Arbitrators, eds. James L. Stern and Barbara D. Dennis (Washington: BNA Books, 1981), 1 [hereinafter "McDermott"].

pursuits as an arbitrator. After much deliberation, I finally decided that the best way for me to address Rolf's request would be to indicate to you some of the benefits that are lost when one leaves arbitration to become a judge. For example,

1. As a federal judge, my earnings capacity has been reduced.
2. In addition, I can no longer claim a tax deduction for an "office" at home.
3. I have no opportunities, like Richard Bloch and Arnold Zack, to produce commercial movies.
4. Unlike Ted St. Antoine, I have never had my picture in *Sports Illustrated.*
5. And, I will never have a chance, like Tom Roberts, to travel widely at home and abroad to sample the fare at the world's best hotels.

As a judge, I am the beneficiary of life tenure and a guaranteed pension, in return for which I am required to perform in a hot robe, write long opinions with numerous footnotes, speak to no one about my work (save my judicial colleagues and my law clerks), avoid political issues, and make routine public disclosures of all of my associations and earnings. In a sense, being a judge is like being imprisoned in a cage with steel bars in the middle of Times Square in New York City. You can see and hear all that is happening around you, but your participation in those events is seriously circumscribed.

Actually, much of what I have just said is offered with tongue-in-cheek. I have truly enjoyed my time as a judge, notwithstanding some feelings of isolation. The work load is incredibly heavy, but it is made tolerable because of the invaluable assistance that I receive from two secretaries, three law clerks and, occasionally, a legal intern. In my most weary moments, my chambers staff gives me strength through their youthful energy, extraordinary intelligence, loyalty, and constant devotion to the public responsibility inherent in their jobs. They are also interesting and fun people to have around, so the office has been a pleasant place to be during my first two years as a judge.[2]

In addition to the joys of working with my personal staff, I have gained the great rewards associated with good relations

---

[2]Edwards, *A Judge's Views on "Justice, Bureaucracy, and Legal Method,"* 80 Mich. L. Rev. 259 (1981).

with some brilliant colleagues on the bench. I have found that the challenge to produce truly quality legal opinions is sometimes raised to euphoric heights when I have worked on difficult and critically important cases with my fellow judges on the D.C. Circuit.

I have also found that the supposed cloistered life of a judge is tempered by opportunities to teach, lecture, write, and participate in various public endeavors. Indeed, in some ways I felt more cloistered as an arbitrator than I do now as a judge. As an arbitrator, I rarely received any direct feedback on my opinions. As a judge, however, I get constant feedback from the comments or dissents of my colleagues, in petitions for rehearing filed by attorneys on the losing side of a case, in published articles in the law reviews and, occasionally, even in a decision by the Supreme Court.

I would not trade my life as a judge for any other at this time. However, I must tell you that my work as a judge has caused me to more fully recognize the extraordinary skills possessed by an untold number of labor arbitrators in this country. It has also helped me to better understand the fundamental significance of the arbitration process in the administration of justice. With these insights in mind, I come here today first and foremost to sing your praises.

### III. The Advantages of Arbitration Over Litigation

My basic message to you today is actually quite simple. It is this: If I were employed in a job from which I could be fired, and if I did get fired and had a right to challenge my discharge in a forum of my choice, *I would rather be in arbitration than in court.* Having served as an arbitrator and as a judge, and having worked as an advocate in each forum, I am now of the view that arbitrators are nonpareil as "judges" in a wide variety of cases involving personnel and labor relations matters. I concede that what I am saying is merely impressionistic and is born out of my own professional experiences. Nevertheless, I would like to pursue my thinking with you, albeit briefly, both to discard certain ideas to which I have previously subscribed and to raise some questions and suggestions for your digestion. Along the way, I will attempt to explain the bases for my impressions.

## 1. The Hays Assault on Arbitration

Probably the best place for me to start is with a historical reference to an opinion about arbitration that is plainly at odds with my own view. The senior members of the Academy will no doubt recall that, in 1964, Judge Paul Hays, a former arbitrator and labor law professor, launched a massive attack on the entire institution of labor arbitration.[3] I was only a senior in law school when Judge Hays gave his infamous Storrs lectures at the Yale Law School; therefore, I have no clear recollection of the arbitration profession about which he spoke. Nevertheless, I was truly astonished by the viciousness of the Hays assault, especially given the conspicuous absence of analytical and empirical support for many of his assertions.[4] A few short excerpts will highlight Hays' principal theme:

> "[L]abor arbitration has fatal shortcomings as a system for the judicial administration of contract violations. . . . An arbitrator is a third party called in to determine a controversy over whether one of the parties to the collective bargaining agreement has violated that agreement . . . he does not in fact have any expertise in these matters and is not actually expected to have any, since it is expected that he will listen to the evidence presented by the two parties and decide on the basis of that evidence whether the charge of contract violation is or is not sustained. For his task he requires exactly the same expertise which judges have and use every day. . . .
>
> "There are only a handful of arbitrators who, like Shulman and Cox, have the knowledge, training, skill, and character which would make them good judges and therefore make them good arbitrators. . . . A system of adjudication in which the judge depends for his livelihood, or for a substantial part of his livelihood or even for substantial supplements to his regular income, on pleasing those who hire him to judge is per se a thoroughly undesirable system. . . .
>
> "I believe that the courts should not lend themselves at all to the arbitration process. Labor arbitration is a private system of justice not based on law and not observant of law. There is no reason why it should be able to call upon the legal system to enforce its decrees. . . . We know that a large proportion of the awards of arbitrators are rendered by incompetents, that another proportion, we do not know how large but are permitted by the circumstances to suspect that it is quite substantial, are rendered not on the basis of any proper

---

[3]Hays, *The Future of Labor Arbitration*, 74 Yale L.J. 1019 (1965) [hereinafter "Hays"].
[4]*See* Meltzer, *Ruminations About Ideology, Law, and Labor Arbitration*, in The Arbitrator, the NLRB, and the Courts, Proceedings of the 20th Annual Meeting, National Academy of Arbitrators, ed. Dallas L. Jones (Washington: BNA Books, 1967), at 2–7 [hereinafter "Meltzer"].

concerns, but rather on the basis of what award would be best for the arbitrator's future."[5]

My research indicates that the response to Judge Hays was both swift and effective in denouncing the attack. For example, the inimitable Bernard Dunau tersely observed,

> "It is unfortunately true that the level of judging, whether judicial, administrative or arbitral, is in the overall quite mediocre, but for those who have worked in all three forums, the arbitrator does not suffer by comparison."[6]

Saul Wallen[7] and Bernie Meltzer[8] both successfully refuted Hays' claim that arbitrators' economic self-interest, linked with future acceptability, will distort adjudication. As Professor Meltzer aptly noted:

> "[T]he principal question for an arbitrator, assuming for the moment that he is ruled by a greedy desire for more customers, is how to reduce the risk implicit in the fact that one party generally will lose. I can think of no better answer to that question than conscientious workmanship, for such workmanship appears to be the best protection against the veto that labor and management will each be able to exercise in the future. The need for future acceptability would thus appear to bring the arbitrator's self-interest and disinterested adjudication into harmony rather than conflict. Consequently, even if one accepted a devil's view of arbitrators as a group ruled by love of money, it would not follow that the pressure for future acceptability would corrupt the decisional process."[9]

Probably the clearest indictment of the Hays critique has been history itself. One need only consider the growth of the Academy since 1964, the founding of the Society of Professionals in Dispute Resolution (SPIDR), the expansion of the FMCS and the AAA, the widespread adoption of both interest and rights arbitration in the public sector, the use of arbitration in the federal service, and the employment of arbitration techniques in the resolution of international disputes, small claims matters, and a variety of malpractice and commercial issues, in order to fully understand the wholesale rejection of the Hays thesis. Arbitra-

---

[5]Hays, *supra* note 3, at 1034–35.
[6]Dunau, *Review of Hays, Labor Arbitration: A Dissenting View*, 35 The American Scholar 774–76 (Autumn 1966).
[7]Wallen, *Arbitrators and Judges—Dispelling the Hays' Haze*, in Labor Law Developments, Proceedings of the 12th Institute on Labor Law, Southwestern Legal Foundation (Washington: BNA, Inc., 1966), 159.
[8]Meltzer, *supra* note 4.
[9]*Id.* at 3–4.

tion has stood the test of time in a marketplace where the consumers have demanded effective and fair systems of voluntary adjudication. If anything, these past two decades have revealed certain fallibilities of our court system, not of arbitration, as an excessive caseload has more and more burdened the judiciary.

## 2. Why Is Arbitration Better?

As I suggested earlier, I would go one step further in my response to the Hays thesis. I not only believe that Judge Hays has been proven wrong, I also believe that arbitrators are unsurpassed as "judges" in cases involving personnel and labor relations matters. This is not just because arbitrators bring a special expertise to their work. Nor is it because arbitrators are smarter or more skilled than judges. In fact, it seems clear to me that there are many superb judges who would be equally good as arbitrators, and vice versa. I therefore conclude that if labor arbitrators are indeed nonpareil as "judges" in cases typically brought to arbitration, much of their success must be attributable to certain unique features of the *arbitration process.*

Before I continue, let me stress that, at this point, the only types of cases to which I am referring involve those that are routine fare for arbitrators. In particular, I have in mind disputes focused on employee and management rights in the workplace, in situations involving discipline, work assignments, pay and fringe benefit claims, creation or classification of new jobs, and application of principles such as seniority, merit, nondiscrimination and just cause. These cases generally involve interpersonal relations, straightforward contract claims brought by individuals or small groups of employees, and matters that usually can be heard within one day without significant discovery. This is not an all-inclusive list, but I think it accurately describes traditional labor arbitration practice.

Judges, like arbitrators, also decide *private law* cases of the sort heard in labor arbitration. However, judges are additionally required, on a routine basis, to hear and decide a host of *public law* cases involving criminal prosecutions, statutory enforcement, review of agency regulations, complex constitutional claims, and class action suits. Nothing that I say today is meant to suggest that our court system is inadequate to handle public law issues or that we should expand arbitration to encourage the development of public law in private tribunals. Arbitrators frequently must consider public laws in order to resolve private disputes. However, I do not consider this to be the same as arbitrators deciding cases brought pursuant to public law. On this point, I am inclined to concur in Ted St. Antoine's thoughtful analysis of the arbitrator as a "contract-reader:"

"[T]here [are] obviously . . . situations in which the arbitrator is entitled or even mandated to draw upon statutory or decisional sources in fashioning his award. That is when the parties call for it, either expressly or impliedly. If a contract clause . . . plainly tracks certain statutory language, an arbitrator is within his rights in inferring that the parties intended their agreement to be construed in accordance with the statute. Similarly, the parties may explicitly agree that they will abide by the arbitrator's interpretation of a statute whose meaning is in dispute between them. In each of these instances, I would say that technically the arbitrator's award implements the parties' agreement to be bound by his analysis of the statute rather than by the statute itself. . . .

"The treatment of an arbitral award by a reviewing court is also clarified by the notion of the arbitrator as a contract-reader. A 'misinterpretation' or 'gross mistake' by the arbitrator becomes a contradiction in terms. So long as he is dealing with a matter duly submitted to him, the arbitrator is speaking for the parties, and his award *is* their contract. . . .

". . . As between the parties themselves, I see no impediment to their agreeing to a final and binding arbitral declaration of their statutory rights and duties. Obviously, if an arbitrator's interpretation of an OSHA requirement did not adequately protect the employees, or violated some other basic public policy, a court would not be bound by it. But if the arbitrator imposed more stringent requirements, I would say the award should be enforced. . . .

"Whatever damage may be done to the pristine purity of labor arbitration by this increased responsibility for statutory interpretation, I consider an expanded arbitral jurisdiction inevitable. . . . [R]ecent statutes [such] as Title VII . . . are so interwoven in the fabric of collective bargaining agreements that it is simply impracticable in many cases for arbitrators to deal with contractual provisions without taking into account statutory provisions. . . . I conclude, in contrast to the forebodings of my friend Dave Feller, that we are actually entering a new 'golden age' for the arbitration process."[10]

---

[10]St. Antoine, *Judicial Review of Labor Arbitration Awards: A Second Look at* Enterprise Wheel *and its Progeny,* in Arbitration—1977, Proceedings of the 30th Annual Meeting, National Academy of Arbitrators, eds. Barbara D. Dennis and Gerald G. Somers (Washington: BNA Books, 1978), at 35–36 [hereinafter "St. Antoine"]. *See also* Bloch, *Some Far-Sighted Views of Myopia,* in *id.* at 233. In contrast to the views of St. Antoine and Bloch, *see* Feller, *The Coming End of Arbitration's Golden Age,* in Arbitration—1976, Proceedings of the 29th Annual Meeting, National Academy of Arbitrators, eds. Barbara D. Dennis and Gerald G. Somers (Washington: BNA Books, 1976), 97. For a time, many of my own views were quite similar to certain of the principal themes expressed in Professor Feller's *Golden Age* article. *See* note 21 *infra.*

Before trying to explain to you my views as to *why* arbitration may be better than litigation to handle cases of the sort normally brought in arbitration, I should first indicate to you the bases for my qualitative judgment. There are two factors that are clearly supported by objective evidence and there are two additional factors that are supported solely by the impressions that I have developed after working as an advocate and a decision-maker in the arbitration and litigation arenas.

As to the objective evidence, I would cite the factors of *speed* and *expense*. In a recent article published by the American Bar Association, it was reported that the average time to process a grievance to the arbitrator's award was approximately 250 days. The time is substantially less in expedited cases.[11] In-court litigation time in comparable cases is much longer. For instance, to offer a limited sample, I would cite three cases that I have heard during the 1981–82 term involving employee dismissals. In one case, an employee was fired from a government job in December of 1973 and the final judgment in the case—following the employee's second trip to the Court of Appeals—did not issue until January of 1982.[12] In the second case, a government employee was fired from his job with the Army as an alleged "security risk" in August of 1980. The final decision in his favor did not issue until almost two years after his discharge.[13] In the third case, yet another government employee was discharged in March of 1979 for alleged misconduct on the job. The case is still pending three years after the challenged action. In each one of these cases, the issues were complex, but not unlike those found in literally hundreds of cases that are satisfactorily and expeditiously decided by arbitrators each year.

As for the factor of expense, I think that no evidence need be cited to make the point that full-blown litigation, including discovery and appeals, is significantly more expensive than arbitration.

My final two points, indicating the bases for my view that arbitration is superior to litigation *in comparable cases*, raise two suggestions. First, I would argue that the *results* in arbitration are, on the average, qualitatively better than judicial decisions.

[11] American Bar Association, *A New Look at Methods, Procedures and Systems Designed to Expedite the Labor Arbitration Process*, in Section of Labor and Employment Law, 1981 Committee Reports, Vol. II (Chicago: ABA Press, 1981), 198.

[12] *Jolly* v. *Listerman*, 672 F.2d 935 (D.C. Cir. 1982). Three more months passed before the Court of Appeals decided not to hear the case en banc. *Id.*, 675 F.2d 1308 (D.C. Cir. 1982).

[13] *Hoska* v. *Department of the Army*, 677 F.2d 131 (D.C. Cir. 1982).

Second, I would contend that the adversaries in a case are generally more *satisfied* with arbitration opinions than with those issued by courts. It may be foolhardy for me to offer such sweeping conclusions based solely upon subjective impressions, but I think that the points are important and may be worth pursuing. I will leave it to others, at a later date and with better research, to dispel my impressions.

Having indicated how I believe that arbitration is better than litigation in comparable cases, let me now explain why I think this is so.

As a general proposition, I have found that the judicial process is heavily steeped in procedures. Many cases may be won or lost on "procedural" points that have nothing whatsoever to do with the merits of the case. These procedural rules often are vitally important to preserve the integrity of the judicial process, but they also may obscure the real dispute between the parties. In complex litigation, involving difficult public law issues, it makes good sense to channel a case pursuant to rigid rules of procedure. It is difficult, however, to explain to an individual complainant that his challenge to a work assignment, alleged underpayment, or discharge cannot be fully heard because of a procedural bar. Although procedural bars are recognized in arbitration, they are not nearly so pervasive as in litigation.

As a related point, I would suggest that, in comparable cases, there appears to me to be more evidence of "common sense" at work in arbitral proceedings and decisions than in judicial proceedings and opinions. This may be because arbitrators have a freer rein than do judges to exercise common sense. Mickey McDermott probably best highlighted what I mean during his 1980 presidential address to the Academy. When asked whether arbitrators should "ignore the rules of evidence in arbitration," he replied as follows:

"Just about—or better yet, develop a rather charitable sense of relevancy and then work out arbitration rules for deciding the proper weight to be given to evidence once it is in. That's what counts in any event. More often than not, at least in my experience, the opponent of the evidence is not really so concerned about the evidence's coming in. He is more concerned, should it come in, about the time he might have to spend and the lengths he might have to go to in order to dig up countervailing proof. Thus, if the doubtful evidence were admitted, the proponent would be satisfied, and if the opponent then were told that, although the evidence is in, it will carry almost no weight because it is only remotely relevant or because it is unpersuasive hearsay, then the opponent would be satisfied, too. If the proponent thereafter were not successful on the merits, he could blame it on the arbitrator's stupidity, but he could not say that the arbitrator did not even listen. And there is a world of difference between those two positions—between losing after full argument and losing after having been shut off from making any argument because of rules that are not fully understood even by all lawyers and surely not by very many employees or supervisors."[14]

As a third point, I would suggest that it makes a positive difference that arbitrators are selected by the parties. As Bernie Meltzer has correctly noted, the "acceptability" factor gives an arbitrator a strong incentive to produce high quality decisions. In addition, the parties to an arbitration, having participated in the selection of their judge, rarely believe that a case is won or lost on the "luck of the draw" of the decision-maker.

Finally, and possibly most importantly, I would cite the lack of appellate review as a critical factor in the success of arbitration over litigation in comparable cases. In papers recently presented to this Academy, Professors Ted St. Antoine[15] and Charles Morris[16] both have reported that, with rare exceptions, judicial review of labor arbitration opinions has remained narrow pursuant to the mandate of *United Steelworkers* v. *Enterprise Wheel & Car Corp.*[17] In my view, this is a salutary development that has helped foster the growth of arbitration in this country.

The problem with expanded judicial review is not necessarily the threat of "excessive intervention" by the courts.[18] Rather, in my opinion, the potential hazard of judicial review is that it will likely result in arbitrators deciding cases and writing opinions in such a way as to insulate their awards against judicial reversal. As a judge, I have already seen too many cases in which ALJs, agency officials, and judges in lower courts have written opinions with an eye toward appellate review but blind to the heart of the issues before them. Decisions in such cases often parrot appropriate statutory standards, usually in conclusory terms, but suffer from a lack of reasoned analysis.

Without the threat of appellate review, arbitrators have been free to focus solely on the case before them (rather than on the

---

[14]McDermott, *supra* note 1, at 17.
[15]St. Antoine, *supra* note 10.
[16]Morris, *Twenty Years of Trilogy: A Celebration,* in Decisional Thinking of Arbitrators and Judges, Proceedings of the 33rd Annual Meeting, National Academy of Arbitrators, eds. James L. Stern and Barbara D. Dennis (Washington: BNA Books, 1981), 331.
[17]363 U.S. 593, 46 LRRM 2423 (1960).
[18]Meltzer, *supra* note 4, at 12.

case as it might appear to an appellate court). In my experience as an arbitrator, I found that there was tremendous pressure to produce high quality opinions, not only to insure my future acceptability but also because I knew that I was the judge of last resort. In other words, arbitrators know all too well that a bad decision is costly because there is no appeal available to the parties; as a consequence, professional pride alone drives any good arbitrator to work extremely hard to avoid erroneous results. This is not to say that judges or ALJs indulge error; it is merely to suggest that they may sometimes focus on the wrong things because of the possibility—and in some cases, the inevitability—of judicial review.

## IV. Some Thoughts About the Future

### 1. The Problem of the "Magistrate Mentality"

In preparing for my talk today, I had occasion to read John Kagel's fine paper on "Grievance Arbitration in the Federal Service."[19] One thing in particular caught my eye in the Kagel article. In describing labor arbitrators in the federal service, John observed:

"A higher order of initial sophistication for the arbitrator will be needed to guide the parties to produce the relevant portion of regulations and statutes and administrative agency decisions, such as those of the FLRA, on which the arbitrator is to rely. For, quite clearly, the arbitrator, as the first link in one or more appellate chains, is serving as a magistrate in this regard."[20]

I hope that the Kagel thesis is wrong and that arbitrators in the federal service do not develop what I will call a "magistrate mentality." The courts generally do not look to arbitrators merely to create a record for appeal. Instead, the courts expect the arbitrator to fully consider and decide the case just as might be done in any other labor arbitration setting. Most appellate judges give great deference to the judgments of arbitrators and ALJs in personnel cases. Thus, if the arbitrator adopts a "magistrate mentality," and performs only as if he or she is "the first link in one or more appellate chains," then it is entirely possible

---

[19]Kagel, *Grievance Arbitration in the Federal Service: Still Hardly Final and Binding?* in Arbitration Issues for the 1980s, Proceedings of the 34th Annual Meeting, National Academy of Arbitrators, eds. James L. Stern and Barbara D. Dennis (Washington: BNA Books, 1982), 178.
[20]*Id.* at 192.

that no one will ever concentrate fully on the merits of the case. Indeed, if arbitrators in any sector begin to think of themselves as magistrates rather than arbitrators, the advantages of the arbitral process will be lost.

## 2. The Old Bugaboo About "External Law"

In the past, I have often expressed grave reservations about arbitrators deciding public law issues.[21] In the light of my experience on the court, however, I have found that my reservations have been significantly tempered. Like my colleagues, Judge Alvin Rubin[22] and Judge Betty Fletcher,[23] both of whom recently have addressed the Academy, I agree that

> "[a]s new issues and problems in improving employment conditions arise, and as we deliberate better ways to handle issues now being resolved only in the courts, we must consider seriously the possibility that some problems can best be resolved by giving a wider hand to collective bargaining and to resolution of disputes in arbitration."[24]

Judge Fletcher went so far as to suggest that, for individual claims,

> "arbitration in the context we know it . . . is the best tool we have, the best forum for the grievant. And I think arbitrators have it within their power and their grasp to improve the process in order to accomplish the goals of Title VII, in the context of the traditional forum. . . .
>
> "The advantage[] of relying on private arbitrators . . . [is] that . . . arbitration provides speedy dispute resolution by persons knowledgeable about the industry and the players, and persons who are skilled in resolving disputes in a way that does not disrupt ongoing relationships."[25]

---

[21]Edwards, *Arbitration of Employment Discrimination Cases: An Empirical Study*, in Proceedings of the 28th Annual Meeting, National Academy of Arbitrators, eds. Barbara D. Dennis and Gerald G. Somers (Washington: BNA Books, 1976), 59; Edwards, *Labor Arbitration at the Crossroads: "The Common Law of the Shop" Versus External Law*, 32 Arb J. 65 (June 1977); Edwards, *Arbitration of Employment Discrimination Cases: A Proposal for Employer and Union Representatives*, 27 Lab. L.J. 265 (May 1976).

[22]Rubin, *Arbitration: Toward a Rebirth*, in Truth, Lie Detectors, and Other Problems in Labor Arbitration, Proceedings of the 31st Annual Meeting, National Academy of Arbitrators, eds. James L. Stern and Barbara D. Dennis (Washington: BNA Books, 1979), 30 [hereinafter "Rubin"].

[23]Fletcher, *Arbitration of Title VII Claims: Some Judicial Perceptions*, in Arbitration Issues for the 1980s, Proceedings of the 34th Annual Meeting, National Academy of Arbitrators, eds. James L. Stern and Barbara D. Dennis (Washington: BNA Books, 1982), 218 [hereinafter "Fletcher"].

[24]Rubin, *supra* note 22, at 36.

[25]Fletcher, *supra* note 23, at 228.

I not only agree with these sentiments, but I believe that arbitration should be explored as a mechanism for the resolution of individual claims of discrimination in *unorganized,* as well as unionized, sectors of the employment market.[26]

As for concerns about the competence of arbitrators to hear such claims, I have no doubt that there are many highly qualified arbitrators who could easily be trained to deal with this limited category of public law issues. And as for the threat of public law issues being decided by private tribunals, I am now convinced that the most important public law issues inevitably find their way to the courts and as a consequence, the courts invariably take the lead in the development of controlling legal standards with respect to such matters.

## V. Conclusion

When the *Steelworkers Trilogy*[27] was decided by the Supreme Court in 1960, what the Court knew and implicitly praised about arbitration was that: (1) it was a relatively *speedy* system of justice; (2) it was mostly *informal;* (3) it was *therapeutic* in the sense that it allowed workers to "have their day in court;" (4) it was *voluntarily binding;* (5) it usually involved a judgment from someone who was well-known and well-respected by the parties; (6) it was relatively *cheap;* (7) it was a *flexible* process that could easily be changed to suit the parties; and (8) most importantly, it was an *extension of collective bargaining;* that is, a private system of jurisprudence, created by and for the benefit of the parties. The system of arbitration in America has continued to be a successful venture in dispute resolution because the traditional characteristics of the process have not been altered. So long as this remains true, arbitration should endure as superior to formal litigation as a method for dispute resolution in cases involving personnel and labor relations matters.[28]

---

[26]*See* Meacham, *Mediation and Arbitration in Employment Discrimination Disputes: A Feasibility Study,* prepared for the Ford Foundation (Employment Discrimination Dispute Resolution Project, NOW Legal Defense and Education Fund, May 1982). *See also* Clark, *The Legitimacy of Arbitrating Claims of Discrimination,* in Arbitration Issues for the 1980s, Proceedings of the 34th Annual Meeting, National Academy of Arbitrators, eds. James L. Stern and Barbara D. Dennis (Washington: BNA Books, 1982), 235.

[27]*Steelworkers* v. *American Mfg. Co.,* 363 U.S. 564, 46 LRRM 2414 (1960); *Steelworkers* v. *Warrior & Gulf Navigation Co.,* 363 U.S. 574, 46 LRRM 2416 (1960); *Steelworkers* v. *Enterprise Wheel & Car Corp.,* 363 U.S. 593, 46 LRRM 2423 (1960).

[28]This is not to suggest that there should be no further experimentation with alternative procedures for grievance handling. A number of interesting studies in the mediation of grievances and in expedited arbitration procedures have recently been published. *See,*

Furthermore, it is my belief that the labor arbitration techniques so well understood by members of this Academy may have broader applications in connection with dispute resolution in fields other than labor relations. The widely publicized National Institute for Dispute Resolution is nearly ready to launch a major project to consider alternative approaches to dispute resolution. It would seem to me that Academy members would have much to offer by way of counsel and advice to the leaders of any such project.

In conclusion, I would echo the words of Judge Rubin, given during his speech to the Academy at the 1978 meeting in New Orleans:

> "It seems to me that arbitration is not only a just means of resolving disputes, but that even the most formal proceeding is much faster, less expensive, and more responsive to industrial needs than the best-run courts available today. It is a myth that access to justice must mean access to the courts."[29]

Arbitration is not perfect; however, for the resolution of certain types of cases, we have yet to develop a better system of justice.

---

e.g., Goldberg, *The Mediation of Grievances Under a Collective Bargaining Contract: An Alternative to Arbitration* (Chicago: Northwestern University Law School, 1982); Goldberg and Brett, *An Experiment in the Mediation of Grievances* (Chicago: Northwestern University, 1982); American Bar Association, *A New Look at Methods, Procedures and Systems Designed to Expedite the Labor Arbitration Process, supra* note 11. It is hoped that such experiments will continue.
[29]Rubin, *supra* note 22, at 35.

# Chapter 3

# THE ROLE OF THE ARBITRATOR
# IN ENSURING A FAIR HEARING

Benjamin Aaron*

## I.

The topic of this session is not a new one; under various headings, it has been discussed repeatedly and exhaustively at the annual meetings of the Academy. Yet we recur to the subject as predictably, if not as frequently, as the swallows return to Capistrano. What impels us to do so?

I suggest the reason is that the guarantee of a fair hearing lies close to the heart of our arbitration system. Ralph Seward reminded us over 30 years ago that arbitration "is primarily important because of its nature as a *process.*" It is, he said, "a *method* of settling disputes [that] . . . derives its importance and its lasting effects from its characteristics as a *method.*"[1] Arbitrators may make bad decisions without seriously damaging the process, but if arbitration hearings are widely perceived to be unfair, or—to state the same thing in different words—to be lacking in due process, the system cannot endure. The periodic reexamination of the requirements of a fair hearing is necessary if only because it compels us to rethink our basic premises, to question the validity of established practices—in short, to strive to add depth and clarity to our notions of fair procedure in the arbitration of labor disputes.

My problem, however, is not to explain the importance of the topic; rather, it is to say something new about it. Virtually every luminary of the Academy has addressed himself or herself to one or another aspect of the subject at some time during the past 35

---

*Member, National Academy of Arbitrators; Professor of Law, University of California, Los Angeles, Calif.

[1]*Arbitration in the World Today,* in The Profession of Labor Arbitration, Selected Papers from the First Seven Annual Meetings of the National Academy of Arbitrators, 1948–1954, ed. Jean T. McKelvey (Washington: BNA Books, 1957), 66, 69. Italics in original.

years, and one of our most distinguished former colleagues, Willard Wirtz, came about as close to presenting a definitive summation of the principal problems involved as anyone is likely ever to achieve.[2] I note, parenthetically, that although Wirtz presented his paper in 1958, the problems he addressed are still with us and encompass most of the important elements of a fair hearing. It behooves me, therefore, to state at the outset that little, if anything, I shall have to say is new. The best I can do is to crochet a little around the borders of the principal themes previously emphasized by others.

## II.

Before getting down to specific situations, however, I want to raise a preliminary question. In discussing the arbitrator's role in ensuring a fair hearing, we must ask ourselves: fair in respect of whom or what? I suggest that fairness is owed not only to the grievant, but also to the parties and their representatives, as well as to the arbitration process itself. The views of the various participants in the arbitration process as to what constitutes the appropriate degree of fairness in each case are likely to cover a broad spectrum. No one can hope to pinpoint a fixed spot along that continuum as "correct"; the most one can do, it seems to me, is to find a reasonably narrow range that excludes insufficient safeguards, on the one hand, and unreasonable expectations, on the other.

There is a natural tendency to focus one's attention on fairness to the grievant—the person who has been discharged, disciplined, denied a promotion, refused a transfer, and so forth, although, as I shall seek to show a little later, there are many cases—perhaps a majority—in which principles of fairness alone do not seem to require his or her presence at the arbitration hearing.

I draw a distinction between the parties to the collective agreement and their representatives because, although lack of fairness to the latter is concededly an offense of equal magnitude against the former, representatives—especially lawyers—sometimes make procedural demands in the name of their clients that in my judgment do not rise above the level of indul-

---

[2]*Due Process of Arbitration,* in The Arbitrator and the Parties, Proceedings of the 11th Annual Meeting, National Academy of Arbitrators, ed. Jean T. McKelvey (Washington: BNA Books, 1958), 1.

gence of their personal preferences. Such claims may safely be denied without prejudicing the fairness of the hearing.

The requirement of fairness to the arbitration process itself is, of course, a catchall, in the sense that any unfairness to the grievant, the parties, or their representatives does harm to the entire process. What I have in mind, however, is something else: the duty not to use the arbitration process for purposes for which it was not intended and which it cannot fulfill.

## III.

Let us return now to the matter of fairness to the grievant. Whenever I ask my students what are the key elements of fairness, the first response is usually that the grievant must be given adequate notice of the time and place of the arbitration hearing and must be allowed to attend. That practice is observed under many procedures, but in many others it is not. It may be persuasively argued, of course, that allowing a grievant to attend the arbitration hearing is worthwhile, not only for its educational value, but also because in witnessing the employer's representatives being compelled to justify their behavior to a neutral party, in the course of which they may be subject to searching and often embarrassing cross-examination, the grievant experiences a kind of catharsis that helps to make even eventual defeat acceptable. As I have already suggested, however, there are a great many cases in which the grievant's presence at a hearing is certainly not required by law. Remember that the decision to process a grievance through the grievance and arbitration procedure is within the union's sole discretion, always assuming that it acts in full compliance with its duty of fair representation.[3] Thus, the union is free initially to reject a grievance as being without merit, to settle it on a compromise basis at some stage of the grievance procedure, or to refuse to appeal it to arbitration in the good-faith belief that the claim will not be sustained. In the frequent instances when the issue is one of contract interpretation and the relevant facts are not in dispute, a fair arbitration hearing can be held even if the grievant is not present.

Traditionally, the concern about providing a fair hearing to the grievant has focused on two types of cases. The first of these

[3]*Vaca v. Sipes,* 386 U.S. 171, 191, 64 LRRM 2369 (1967). *See* Aaron, *The Duty of Fair Representation: An Overview,* in The Duty of Fair Representation, ed. Jean T. McKelvey (Ithaca, N.Y.: Cornell University, 1977), 8.

is one in which two or more employees claim the right of promotion to a higher-rated job, the employer appoints one, and the union appeals the claim of someone else to arbitration. The second is one in which the grievant has been disciplined or discharged for some alleged misconduct. In both types of cases the grievant has a personal stake in the matter that must be recognized in addition to the union's interest in protecting the integrity of the collective bargaining agreement, but the requirements of a fair hearing in the two paradigms invoke differing considerations.

### A.

Let us take the promotion case first. Typically, there is a provision in the collective agreement that says that as between rival candidates for the promotion, if skill and ability are substantially equal, the one with the most seniority shall be promoted. The employer promotes X, who has less seniority than Y. Y grieves, on the ground that his skill and ability are equal or superior to that of X. The union appeals Y's grievance to arbitration. Y appears and testifies at the hearing; X, now the incumbent of the disputed job, is not present. In order to remove any issue involving the union's duty of fair representation prior to the arbitration hearing, I shall assume that both X and Y are union members in good standing, and that before deciding to process Y's grievance the union had interviewed both employees, had carefully evaluated their respective records, and had concluded in good faith that Y's claim to the promotion was well founded.

Previous surveys of arbitral opinion as to whether fairness requires X's presence at the arbitration hearing have revealed a broad variance of opinion among arbitrators.[4] Some argue that given the assumptions I have made, the union has no obligation to call X as a witness or even to invite him to attend the hearing. Inasmuch as the union has satisfied its duty of fair representation toward X and has concluded in good faith that Y has a better claim to the disputed job, they feel that X has no right to participate further in the case, unless, of course, the employer calls him as a witness. Others are content to rely upon the assumption that

---

[4]E.g., Fleming, *Due Process and Fair Procedure in Labor Arbitration,* in Arbitration and Public Policy, Proceedings of the 14th Annual Meeting, National Academy of Arbitrators, ed. Spencer D. Pollard (Washington: BNA Books, 1961), 69, 70–78; Wirtz, *supra* note 2.

whatever rights or interests X may have will be fully protected by the employer, which must defend its appointment of X to the disputed job. Still others, uncomfortable with the idea that X's right to remain in the disputed job will be attacked in a hearing at which he is not present, insist on calling him as their own witness, if both parties fail or refuse to do so.

This last approach is the one I follow, although I concede that it may do more to quiet my own squeamishness than to increase objectively the fairness of the arbitration hearing. I say that not because I think X will be fully and fairly represented by the employer; in fact, I believe that to be a very shaky assumption indeed. The employer will represent its own interests, and will do so with varying degrees of competence. Moreover, in advancing its own cause, it may make arguments or concessions that compromise X's legitimate claims. It seems to me, however, that if the union has met its duty of fair representation to X in the preliminary stages of the case, and fully explains at the arbitration hearing the basis of its decision to support Y's claim rather than that of X, fairness does not require that X be given another chance personally to argue the merits of his case to the arbitrator. The difficulty is that the arbitrator cannot always be sure that the union has dealt fairly with X prior to the arbitration— hence my practice of routinely calling X as my witness.

Another practical reason for protecting X's interests in the arbitration hearing is the sensitivity of the courts to issues of this kind, which has resulted in some rather bizarre and mischievous opinions in a long series of cases from *Clark* v. *Hein-Werner Corp.*[5] to *Smith* v. *Hussman Refrigerator Co.*[6] To ensure that the arbitration award, should it be in Y's favor, will not be vacated on review, I think the union would be well advised to include in its opening statement something on the order of the following:

> "The union has carefully reviewed and compared the seniority, skill, and ability of both Y (the grievant) and X (the incumbent). In our judgment Y's skill and ability is at least equal to that of X; therefore, Y, rather than X, should have been promoted to the disputed job, because Y has greater seniority than X.
> "Accordingly, the union does not intend to call X as a witness. Should the arbitrator have any doubts as to the relative skill and ability of X and Y, however, the union urges the arbitrator to call

---

[5]8 Wis.2d 264, 99 N.W.2d 132, 45 LRRM 2137 (1959), *rehearing denied,* 100 N.W.2d 317, 45 LRRM 2659 (1960).
[6]619 F.2d 1229, 103 LRRM 2321 (8th Cir. 1979), *cert. denied sub nom. Local 13889, United Steelworkers* v. *Smith,* 449 U.S. 839, 105 LRRM 2657 (1980).

X as his (or her) witness, subject to the right of both parties to cross-examine X."

Such a statement will not only support the union's claim that it acted in good faith, but will also prompt the arbitrator to do that which he probably ought to do routinely in this type of case.

## B.

I turn next to the matter of ensuring a fair hearing for the grievant in a case involving discipline or discharge. This situation may give rise to a great many questions involving the fairness of the hearing, and time does not permit me to deal with all of them. Accordingly, I shall confine my discussion to those that seem the most important.

It has been many years since I have heard a disciplinary case in which the grievant was not present at the hearing or had not at least been given ample notice and the opportunity to be present. I believe it is now almost the universal practice to have the grievant present in such cases, but I remind you that the Chrysler-UAW Umpire System, over which our late colleague, David A. Wolff, presided so successfully, provided for two final appeal board steps without the presence of any witnesses—the appeal board members and, if necessary, the impartial chairman relying upon written statements rather than oral testimony.[7] Be that as it may, I believe that fairness requires that the grievant in a discipline or discharge case be given due notice of the hearing and the opportunity to be present. On the other hand, I do not think the arbitrator need refuse to proceed with the hearing in the grievant's absence, provided that there is satisfactory evidence that the necessary notice has been given and no timely or acceptable reason for the grievant's failure to appear has been presented.

Suppose, however, that the grievant is present. The employer presents its case first, and begins by calling the grievant as a hostile witness. The union objects and asks the arbitrator to uphold the grievant's right not to testify. Again, one finds a wide range of arbitral opinion on this question. Some arbitrators argue that the objection must be sustained in order to protect the grievant's asserted privilege against self-incrimination; oth-

---

[7]Wolff, Crane, and Cole, *The Chrysler-UAW Umpire System,* in The Arbitrator and the Parties, *supra* note 2, at 111. This practice was abandoned in 1963 with the mutual consent of the parties.

ers maintain that the employer should first be required to put on its "own" witnesses before calling the grievant; still others think that to uphold the objection would unfairly interfere with the presentation of the employer's case.

The first two positions seem to me to lack merit. An arbitration hearing is not a criminal proceeding, so the privilege against self-incrimination is not available, even assuming that the necessary state action is involved, which is rarely the case in the private sector. Requiring the employer to put on its case before calling the grievant as a witness is justified by its proponents on the ground that the employer should not be permitted to prove the existence of just cause out of the mouth of the grievant. Thus, the alleged justification is merely a restatement of the self-incrimination argument. Moreover, it ignores the very point at issue, because the grievant's testimony is very much part of the employer's case; indeed, it may be the whole of it.

The third position strikes me as being the only tenable one of the three, but I dislike it because allowing the employer to proceed is likely to create a good deal of bad feeling between the parties, as well as some disenchantment on the union's side with the arbitration process, whether or not such feelings are justified. In such a situation my preference is, first, to inquire whether the union intends to call the grievant as a witness. If the answer is yes, I then ask the employer not to call the grievant, pointing out that it can elicit the same testimony on cross-examination. This usually is satisfactory to the employer.

If, however, the union should indicate that it does not intend to ask the grievant to testify, other problems arise and will be handled by the arbitrator according to his notions of the purpose of the arbitration hearing. Mine are briefly stated. I believe that the purpose of an arbitration hearing is to come as close to the "truth" about the matter in dispute as is possible for fallible human beings to achieve in the circumstances. The word "truth" must be enclosed in quotation marks, for I follow Justice Holmes in asserting that the truth is only what I can't help believing, and I don't suppose that my "can't helps" are necessarily shared by others.[8] Having this point of view, I reject the

---

[8]"[W]hen I say that a thing is true I only mean that I can't help believing it—but I have no grounds for assuming that my can't helps are cosmic can't helps—and some reasons for thinking otherwise." Howe, ed., 2 Holmes-Laski Letters, 1916–1935 (Cambridge, Mass.: Harvard University Press, 1953), 1124.

idea of an arbitration hearing as just another adversary proceeding, although adversarial elements are inevitably present. Thus, when advised that the grievant will not be called by the union to testify, I am likely to observe that I shall feel free to draw unfavorable inferences from the grievant's silence, unless the evidence overwhelmingly supports one side or the other.

There are, I know, some risks in this approach. The grievant may, for example, be a person of so volatile a temperament, so inarticulate, and so excessively timorous or belligerent that his testimony will work to his serious disadvantage and at the same time fail to contribute materially to the evidence that the arbitrator must consider. I like to think that I will not be unduly influenced by such characteristics, should the grievant elect to testify, but I suppose that this is merely one of the delusions suffered by those of us who are of relatively advanced age and have had many years of arbitration experience. At any rate, in this instance, running the risk of prejudice to the grievant's case seems justified in order to be faithful to what, to me, is the higher obligation to serve what I have defined as the purpose of the arbitration hearing.

## C.

Quite a different set of problems is presented by the attempt of either side to introduce written statements by parties who, for one reason or another, are not available to testify. In my own experience, such questions have most frequently involved reports of undercover agents, such as "spotters" in retail establishments or on streetcars or buses, and doctors' letters recounting diagnosis and treatment of grievants. The usefulness of undercover agents is automatically terminated once their identity is disclosed; employers who use them argue, therefore, that they should not be compelled to testify or, sometimes, that they be allowed to testify in camera, with only the arbitrator present. It has been my custom to reject both of those suggestions on the ground that to do otherwise would be to deny the grievant a fair hearing. The written reports of undercover agents, some of whom are really *agents provocateurs*, are notoriously unreliable, and without the supporting testimony of the writer, they are, in my opinion, entitled to no probative value. Usually, however, disciplinary action against a grievant based on such reports is predicated on a series of them submitted over time rather than on just one. If it turns out that none of them has been revealed to the grievant at the time it was placed in his file, the union may rightly protest against them on those grounds, and the issue of the nonappearance of the undercover agent then becomes moot.

In my experience, doctors' letters are likewise of dubious value. On the relatively infrequent occasions when doctors have appeared to testify before me, I have been impressed by their poor performances as witnesses, particularly under cross-examination. Nevertheless, it often happens that both sides agree to submit such letters, and in those circumstances I think it improper for an arbitrator to refuse to admit them. Like the postnegotiation recollections of witnesses as to what the parties intended or actually agreed to, however, the medical evaluations of employers' and unions' doctors tend to cancel out each other.

## D.

Another problem that arbitrators face—with increasing frequency, I suspect—is what to do when a grievant, either prior to or at the time of the hearing, requests the right to have his case presented by a representative of his own choosing rather than by a union spokesman. The usual justification for such a motion is that the union is hostile to the grievant and that it cannot or will not present his case honestly and effectively. In my experience, both the union and the employer have usually opposed the grievant's request.

From a purely legal point of view, the problem is not a difficult one. As the exclusive bargaining representative, the union is in full control of the grievance. The grievant has no legal right to bring in someone else to handle his case; if the union fails to represent him fairly, his remedy is to bring an action against the union and the employer under Section 301 of the Taft-Hartley Act.[9] The arbitrator is thus justified on legal grounds in denying the grievant's motion for separate representation. I suggest, however, that the arbitrator's dilemma is not so easily resolved, for he has a duty to try to make the grievance and arbitration procedure work for the benefit of all those involved. This is

---

[9]*Vaca* v. *Sipes, supra* note 3; *Humphrey* v. *Moore*, 375 U.S. 335, 55 LRRM 2031 (1964).

particularly true when he has reason to suspect that the union does not intend to present an effective case in support of the grievant. Suppose, for example, he is confronted with a situation similar to that in *Soto* v. *Lenscraft Optical Corp.*, [10] in which the grievants had been discharged for engaging in a wildcat strike that arose out of their activities on behalf of an outside union. The incumbent union's attorney had represented the employer in the latter's successful effort to have the strike enjoined. The grievants, who were guilty of treason in the eyes of the incumbent union, quite naturally had no confidence that its attorney would represent them fairly in the arbitration proceeding. When their request to be represented by their own attorney (who, coincidentally, was also the attorney for the outside union) was denied by the arbitrator, the grievants refused to participate in the hearing. Counsel for the incumbent union offered no defense on their behalf, and the arbitrator sustained their discharges. The grievants then brought suit to vacate the arbitrator's award. A lower court decision in their favor was reversed on appeal, on the dubious ground that because the grievants were not legal parties to the arbitration, they had no standing to challenge the award.

If the identical case were to arise today, I assume that the ultimate decision would be for the plaintiffs, but at the moment I want to focus on the arbitrator's role in such a situation. Although he would be justified in denying the grievants' request to be represented by their own attorney, I suggest that it would be equally proper and clearly desirable for the arbitrator to point out to the incumbent union's attorney that he could not represent the grievants fairly, and to propose to him that they should be allowed, on a nonprecedential basis, to use their own attorney. The effect of this would be to deprive the grievants of a claim that they were not fairly represented, and also to permit the incumbent union to remain silent, or perhaps even to support the employer's position on the merits of the dispute. Of course, the union or employer might reject the proposal, and the arbitrator would hardly be in a position to insist upon it, but at least he would have satisfied his responsibility of trying to make the arbitration process work.

---

[10] 137 N.Y.L.J. 6 (April 12, 1957), 7 App. Div. 2d 1, 180 N.Y.S.2d 388, *reversed sub nom.* Matter of Soto, 7 N.Y.2d 397, 165 N.E.2d 855 (1960).

*E.*

I shall conclude my discussion of the arbitrator's role in ensuring a fair hearing for the individual grievant with some remarks about "rigged" or "prejudiced" cases. The former term relates to those grievances which the union and employer have secretly agreed should be decided against the grievant and as to which they seek the arbitrator's equally secret concurrence; the latter refers to instances in which a representative of either the employer or the union, but most often the latter, lets the arbitrator know that he neither expects nor desires to win the case, but does not communicate that information to either the grievant or the opposing party. I am familiar with both types of situations, but the number of times I have experienced either one in over 30 years of practice as an arbitrator is so small that I sometimes wonder whether the magnitude of the problem has been exaggerated. Even so, that it exists at all should be of grave concern to all participants in the arbitration process.

The rigged award is the more reprehensible of the two types because it necessarily involves collusion between both parties and the arbitrator. The practice has occasionally been defended on the ground that the arbitrator is the mere "creature" of the parties and has no function other than to do their bidding when they are in agreement. This view is likely to be supported by the rationalization that the parties know much more about the case than does the arbitrator, and that it is safe to assume that if they are in agreement, they are acting in the best interests of the labor-management relationship. To me, at least, such arguments are totally unconvincing and morally unacceptable. Unaccustomed as I am to associating myself with any of the observations of the late Judge Paul R. Hays in his celebrated polemic against labor arbitration,[11] I must concur with his denunciation of rigged awards as "so vicious that no system including such a practice can have any proper claim to being a system of justice."[12] The Code of Professional Responsibility for Arbitrators of Labor-Management Disputes, although perhaps not quite as explicit on this point as one might wish, can certainly be read as condemning the practice.[13]

---

[11]Labor Arbitration: A Dissenting View (New Haven: Yale University Press, 1966).
[12]*Id.*, at 113.
[13]The following paragraphs of the Code are relevant: [11] "Essential personal qualifications of an arbitrator include honesty, integrity, impartiality and general competence in labor relations matters."

The incidence of unilateral attempts by one party or the other to prejudice a case is not only probably more frequent than that of rigged awards, but also infinitely more troublesome. The arbitrator asked to participate in a rigged case has a clear obligation to decline and to withdraw immediately from the situation. What his or her obligations are after hearing a prejudicial comment, however, is a much-vexed question. It is clear that an arbitrator ought, in the words of Sir Matthew Hale, a seventeenth-century Lord Chief Justice of England, "[t]o abhor all private solicitations in matters depending,"[14] but sometimes the solicitation is made before the arbitrator can prevent it. The Academy's Committee on Professional Responsibility and Grievances wrestled with this problem for two years before handing down an advisory opinion that represented a compromise of varying views among the committee members, all of whom, however, eventually endorsed the opinion. The facts before the committee were as follows:

> "Prior to the start of a discharge hearing, the Union representative approached the arbitrator and remarked, out of earshot of the Company representative: 'I've got a loser. I don't expect to win this one.' The arbitrator admonished him that he had misbehaved, and that his remarks could prejudice the grievant's rights. The arbitrator stated that he would excise the remarks from his evaluation of the dispute and would decide the case on its merits without regard to them. Before the hearing began, the arbitrator disclosed to the Company the Union representative's remarks and the arbitrator's response. Neither the Company nor the Union interposed any objection to the arbitrator's continued service in the case."

Some committee members thought the arbitrator had no choice but immediately to withdraw from the case; others felt

---

"[18] An Arbitrator must uphold the dignity and integrity of the office and endeavor to provide effective service to the parties."

"[26] Such understanding [of the significant principles governing each arbitration system in which he or she serves] does not relieve the arbitrator from a corollary responsibility to seek to discern and refuse to lend approval or consent to any collusive attempt by the parties to use arbitration for an improper purpose."

"[65] Prior to issuance of an award, the parties may jointly request the arbitrator to include in the award certain agreements between them, concerning some or all of the issues. If the arbitrator believes that a suggested award is proper, fair, sound, and lawful, it is consistent with professional responsibility to adopt it."

"[66] *Before complying with such a request, an arbitrator must be certain that he or she understands the suggested settlement. . . . If it appears that pertinent facts or circumstances may not have been disclosed, the arbitrator should take the initiative to insure that all significant aspects of the case are fully understood. To this end, the arbitrator may request additional specific information and may question witnesses at a hearing.*"

[14]*Things Necessary to Be Continually Had in Remembrance*, Bartlett, Familiar Quotations, 12th ed. (Boston: Little, Brown, 1948), 1039.

that the arbitrator was under no duty to disclose the incident to anyone and could properly continue to serve, so long as he felt that his judgment had not been affected; still others believed the arbitrator was bound to disclose the incident to the grievant, to the employer, or to both; and the views of some members embodied variations of these main themes. Although the opinion is too long to be quoted in full, I shall summarize the main points. The first duty of the arbitrator is to determine whether a remark of the type cited in the example does or does not reflect an effort by the union to induce the arbitrator to sustain the discharge. If he concludes that it does manifest such an effort, he should not continue to serve without the informed consent of the discharged employee. The arbitrator's second duty is to decide whether he can disregard the remark and render a fair decision in spite of it. If he concludes that he can, he may continue to serve; if he has any doubt about his ability to do so, he must withdraw. Those duties are the same for ad hoc arbitrators and permanent arbitrators.

Whether the opinion correctly states the full dimensions of the arbitrator's responsibility in this type of situation remains a matter for consideration. Although, as a member of the Academy committee that issued that opinion, I supported it, I have never felt entirely comfortable with it. Can an arbitrator who has heard the manifestly improper comment by the union representative ever erase the incident from his subconscious? Suppose that rather than being influenced against the grievant as a consequence, he leans over backward to be fair: is he any less biased in his judgment? On the other hand, would he always be justified in disclosing to the grievant and to the employer an ill-advised remark that might poison the relationship between the parties for years to come? Could he not better serve the parties and the process by remaining silent but subsequently impressing upon the offending representative the seriousness of his misconduct? Or suppose the arbitrator feels that he must withdraw: should he, nevertheless, in the interest of protecting the integrity of the arbitration process, inform the grievant and the employer of the union representative's remark, or would this be an act of officious meddling? Inasmuch as I cannot resolve these questions to my own satisfaction, I can hardly presume to do more than leave them with you without further comment.

## IV.

I should like to turn now to the arbitrator's duty of fairness to the parties and their representatives, bearing in mind the distinction between the two groups I mentioned earlier.

*A.*

There is, or should be, no need to dwell in detail on the points emphasized in the Code of Professional Responsibility, but it may be useful to comment briefly on the following two paragraphs of the Code:

> "[106]a. Within the limits of [the] . . . responsibility [to provide a fair and adequate hearing], an arbitrator should conform to the various types of hearing procedures desired by the parties.
> . . .
> "[108]c. An arbitrator should not intrude into a party's presentation so as to prevent that party from putting forward its case fairly and adequately."

I cite these provisions not because I disagree with them but because I think they do not reach certain related and more troublesome problems. Particularly in the case of relatively new collective bargaining relationships, the parties are not sure what kind of hearing procedure they want, and often they look to the arbitrator for guidance. In my view, the arbitrator has the obligation to provide such guidance rather than to sit back and allow the parties to flounder. Surely one of the most valuable services an arbitrator can perform is to cut off irrelevant or superfluous testimony, and to refuse to accept evidence he knows he will not credit, rather than to admit it "for what it's worth."

One does not frequently hear of incidents in which an arbitrator prevented a party from "putting forth its case fairly and adequately," but what about the situation in which a party gives ample demonstration of its inability to present its case in a competent or even intelligible manner: is it the arbitrator's duty to remain silent while a grievant's complaint or an employer's response is butchered beyond repair? I think not. Indeed, I believe an arbitrator has a duty to intervene—either by examining witnesses or calling additional witnesses—whenever it appears that this is necessary to develop the relevant facts and to get at the "truth." I am aware that many parties' representatives, especially lawyers, object to this point of view; I suspect it is because they regard arbitration as a purely adversarial exercise in which the only reasonable goal is winning the decision. With respect, I disagree and prefer to think of arbitration as a cooperative effort not only to get at the "truth," but also to find an appropriate solution to a problem. I hope it isn't necessary to add that by "appropriate solution" I do not necessarily mean a compromise, but rather one that is reached through a process that helps to develop acceptance on the part of the losing party.

A somewhat touchier aspect of the intervention question concerns the arbitrator's suggestion of arguments not advanced by either party. My rule of thumb has been to confine myself to inquiries about the relevance of provisions in the collective bargaining agreement which seem to bear upon the issue, but which have not been cited by either side. Most parties agree that the entire agreement is applicable to any issue, and I seldom encounter any more the argument that because the union has rested its case on an alleged violation of Article Y, the arbitrator must decide the issue on that basis, even when it's obvious that Article Z, not Y, is involved. I do not favor suggesting arguments on external common or statutory law or administrative regulations, because I feel strongly that the arbitrator's job is primarily to interpret and apply the collective bargaining agreement even when, in his judgment, it is contrary to external law.

In any event, if an arbitrator does propose arguments not advanced by either party, he is obligated to do so in the presence of both. The cardinal sin is to base his decision upon a theory not relied upon by either party and not presented by the arbitrator for their consideration at the hearing. If the arbitrator decides, subsequent to the hearing, to base his decision on a theory not raised or argued by either side, he is obligated to disclose it to the parties and to allow them to present their views, either at a reconvened hearing or in briefs. In general, however, I think arbitrators would be well advised to avoid such situations except in especially compelling instances.

Fairness to the parties' representatives assuredly requires courtesy in allowing them to put on their respective cases with a minimum of interference, so long as they stick to the issues. Some representatives, however, whether legally qualified or not, have a habit of dragging out the presentation to unreasonable lengths, punctuating it with requests for unnecessary recesses, continuing with cross-examination long after it has ceased to be productive, burdening the record with superfluous evidence, and constantly interrupting the presentation by the opposing party with technical objections. The arbitrator may firmly put a stop to such tactics without fear of prejudicing the right to a fair hearing.

*B.*

Under the heading of miscellaneous instances of an arbitrator's violation of the parties' right to a fair hearing, a particularly egregious example is the arbitrator's announcement, after he has agreed to set aside at least one day for a hearing, that he must leave by noon, and his insistence that the parties' presentations be shortened on that account or that an additional day of hearing be scheduled. I was recently informed of such an instance in which the arbitrator not only refused to stay for the extra few hours that would have been required to complete the hearing, but gave as his reason that he had scheduled another hearing for the afternoon, on the assumption that the first would have been concluded by lunch! The mounting costs of arbitration have become a matter of general complaint. Although I believe that arbitrators' fees usually represent only a modest proportion of those costs, I also think that the arbitrator's duty to ensure a fair hearing includes the obligation to avoid the unnecessary extension of hearing time. The arbitrator's conduct in the instance just described seems to me a gross violation of the Code of Professional Responsibility.

*C.*

The remaining issue I shall consider under the heading of the arbitrator's duty of fairness to the parties and to their representatives concerns a challenge to the arbitrator's qualifications to serve in a particular case. Such a challenge may rest on solid or on quite insubstantial grounds. An example of the former would be the arbitrator's financial interest in the employer's business, whether or not disclosed by him; an example of the latter would be that the arbitrator had previously decided an issue on all fours with the one presently under consideration in a totally unrelated case. The problem, of course, is with situations falling somewhere in between the obvious cases at one or the other end of the spectrum.

The Code of Professional Responsibility deals with some aspects of the problem and makes the arbitrator responsible for disclosure of circumstances not expressly mentioned therein if he thinks they might have a bearing on his acceptability to one or both of the parties.[15] Although I have never been asked to recuse myself and cannot speak from experience, my inclination would be to accede to any request that has even a slight color of validity. It frequently happens, for example, that one of the advocates appearing before me is an old acquaintance. Although I am convinced that this circumstance will not affect my judgment, I can appreciate that counsel for the other side may not share this conviction. Should he ask me to withdraw for that reason, I would be prepared to do so.

A more troublesome question is when to disclose the relationship. Often one does not know until one shows up for the hearing who will be representing the parties. My practice is to mention it at the hearing, before the proceedings begin.

Some arbitrators feel that if a party does not wish them to serve, however objectively groundless the reason, they should withdraw. One can understand and sympathize with this feeling without agreeing with it. In such situations, the arbitrator should remember that he has a duty of fairness to both sides. Recusing oneself for an obviously insufficient reason advanced by one party is unfair to the other. It may needlessly extend the duration of the case and result in extra expenses to the parties. To withdraw under those circumstances seems to me as wrong as to refuse to do so for good cause shown.

## V.

I come finally to the arbitrator's duty of fairness to the arbitration process itself which, as I have previously suggested, includes the obligation not to permit it to be used for purposes for which it was not intended and which it cannot fulfill.

### A.

Perhaps the principal example of what I have in mind is an attempt by the arbitrator, *without the consent of the parties*, to mediate a dispute submitted to him for decision. The qualifying phrase is critical; the last thing I intend is to revive the sterile debate over whether it is ever appropriate for an arbitrator to

---

[15]See "Required Disclosures," paragraphs 27–38, relating generally to disclosures to the parties and appointing agencies of personal relationships and pecuniary interests.

mediate. That matter was settled long ago, and the Code of Professional Responsibility recognizes the propriety of an arbitrator mediating at the request, or with the consent, of both parties.[16]

The distinction between arbitration and mediation is clear, however, and in the great majority of cases involving ad hoc arbitrators, the parties do not want the arbitrator to mediate. If he insists upon trying to do so against their wishes, he is violating his obligation under the Code and is doing a great disservice to the arbitration process. The case of an impartial umpire is different only in the greater likelihood that the parties may desire him to mediate in at least some of the cases coming before him. If they do not clearly indicate that preference, however, the umpire has no greater warrant to mediate than has the ad hoc arbitrator.

### B.

In recent years there has been an increase in the number of requests by the parties that arbitrators render so-called bench awards, by which is meant an oral decision delivered immediately after the conclusion of the hearing. Such a procedure has a number of clearly discernible advantages: it saves considerable delay in the resolution of the grievance, as well as the added expense of paying for the time spent by the arbitrator in studying the record and writing his decision and opinion. It also obviates any need for posthearing briefs. The resort to bench awards also has equally apparent disadvantages. Of necessity, the arbitrator's decision will be less well considered than if he had more time to reflect upon it. The procedure is obviously unsuited for complex cases in which, if I may use myself as an example, the arbitrator may not finally decide how to rule until after he has written down a summary of the facts and of the parties' arguments. It is also arguable that the parties may lose something valuable when they dispense with a formal written opinion that analyzes their respective positions and explains in greater detail than would ordinarily be possible in a bench opinion why the arbitrator decided the way he did—but that choice, after all, is one they are entitled to make for themselves.

However an arbitrator weighs the arguments in favor of or

---

[16]*See* "Mediation by an Arbitrator," paragraphs 53–58.

against bench awards, his primary obligation to the arbitration process, in my view, is to do the very best job he can, and if he feels uneasy or insecure about issuing bench awards, he should so advise the parties, even if this means that they will turn to someone else. If the arbitrator has some sort of continuing relationship with the parties, the problem can be rather easily resolved. He and the parties can agree on guidelines for resort to bench awards, thus permitting the arbitrator to use that procedure in the kinds of cases in which it presents no difficulties for him, while reserving his right to prepare written decisions and opinions in the more complex matters.

## VI.

In the course of paying his profound disrespects to members of a calling which he himself had long pursued before he was elevated to the federal bench, Judge Hays branded all but a "handful" of arbitrators "wholly unfitted for their jobs" and lacking "the requisite knowledge, training, skill, intelligence, and character."[17] Basing his indictment "upon observation during twenty-three years of very active practice in the area of arbitration and as an arbitrator, and upon the hints I pick up in the literature here and there,"[18] Hays proceeded to paint a picture of arbitrators and the arbitration process that calls to mind the revelations of Jimmy (the Weasel) Fratiani about the folkways of organized crime. In one of his more restrained comments, Hays observed:

> "The literature of arbitration today, and it is among the dullest and dreariest, consists almost entirely of subjective discussions of arbitration written by arbitrators, who are likely to know very little about arbitration outside their own experience—and about their own experience are not inclined to frankness."[19]

As a remedy, he recommended "frank and thoughtful studies" of the arbitration process by its "clients."[20]

With the rise of a new literature of "critical labor law theory" by a small group of talented legal thinkers on the Left,[21] we can expect further criticism of the arbitration process, although one

---

[17]*Supra* note 11, at 112.
[18]*Id.*, at 111.
[19]*Id.*, at 38
[20]*Ibid.*
[21]*See, e.g.*, the Forum devoted to this subject in 4 Ind. Rel. L.J. 449 (1981).

hopes it will be more carefully researched than was Hays's irresponsible diatribe. Meanwhile, those of us who still believe that, despite its faults, our grievance-arbitration system is a praiseworthy and successful social invention ought to make sure that we are not deluding ourselves, and that our perceptions are true reflections of reality. Exercises of the type we are engaged in this morning are useful; they also support an observation I made some years ago that no other group of specialists seems "to take such perverse delight as do arbitrators in examining their own real or imagined deficiencies in private sessions and inviting criticisms by others in public meetings."[22]

It must be admitted, however, that we usually end up giving ourselves passing grades. Perhaps the time has come for the Academy, in company with other organizations, to sponsor a searching and objective inquiry into the arbitration process, with special emphasis upon the conduct of arbitration hearings. The research team should include persons having no connection with arbitration. Such an inquiry should provide us with valuable information—some of it probably unpleasant—about how arbitration actually works, and it would give us, in the words of the poet, the priceless gift

"To see oursels as others see us!
It wad frae monie a blunder free us,
An' foolish notion."[23]

## Comment—

ANDREA S. CHRISTENSEN[*]

Issues relating to the duty of fair representation and conduct of the hearing are generally viewed as primarily union concerns. But if an arbitration award is challenged, the issue of the underlying fairness of the hearing becomes equally important to the employer. Thus, if the arbitrator fails to conduct what is perceived by any of the participants to be a fair hearing, the company will normally become a participant in any subsequent court challenge. The costs related to any rehearing that may result

[22]Aaron, Book Review (Hays, Labor Arbitration: A Dissenting View), 42 Wash. L. Rev. 976, 978 (1967).
[23]Burns, "To a Louse" (1736).
[*]Kaye, Scholer, Fierman, Hays & Handler, New York, N.Y.

from an unenforceable award as well as the costs of any court litigation will be borne equally by the employer. If the award is overturned, the employer stands liable for any back pay, damages, or remedial action that is ordered by the court.[1] Some courts have also directed that the company pay or participate in the payment of the challenger's legal fees and costs.[2] Cases have also been remanded to arbitration before a new arbitrator where the original arbitrator's decision cast doubt upon his impartiality toward the contested terms of the collective bargaining agreement.[3] It is, therefore, of critical importance to a company representative that the conduct of an arbitration hearing be perceived by all participants as being fair and in compliance with fundamental principles of due process.

In preparing for this presentation, I have reviewed various state and federal judicial and administrative decisions that have been critical of, or have vacated, arbitration awards on the grounds that the conduct of the hearing was procedurally defective. Increasingly, the losing party in an arbitration proceeding is resorting to the courts to try again. In order to avoid multiple hearings on the same issue, we must become sensitive to what courts believe to be a fair hearing and under what standards the courts will enforce an award as having emanated from a fair arbitral proceeding.

An area of increasing concern to the parties, the courts, and Professor Aaron is the role of the grievant and/or his personal representative at the arbitration hearing. Not only because of its cathartic effect but also because of the likelihood that the process will be better served, I believe that a grievant should be asked to attend the hearing. In cases where the grievant has a personal stake in the outcome, I, as an employer representative, would object to the commencement or continuation of a hearing if the grievant were absent. Most arbitrators with whom I have worked have agreed with me. Not only does the grievant's presence at the hearing eliminate one ground for subsequent challenge, but even though the grievant may not be convinced of the correctness of the result if he loses, there is a faint hope that his observation of, and particpation in, the hearing may persuade

---

[1]*Grane Trucking Co.*, 241 NLRB 133, 139, 100 LRRM 1624 (1979).
[2]*Holodnak* v. *Avco Corp.*, 381 F.Supp 191, 206–207, 87 LRRM 2337 (D. Conn. 1974), *aff'd in part, rev'd in part on other grounds*, 514 F.2d 285, 88 LRRM 2950 (2d Cir. 1975), *cert. denied*, 423 U.S. 892 (1975).
[3]*Grand Rapids Die Casting* v. *Local 159*, 111 LRRM 2137 (6th Cir. 1982).

him of its inviability. Therefore, absent extraordinary circumstances, the arbitrator should decline to open the hearing in the absence of a grievant who will be personally affected by the decision.[4]

The issue as to whether a grievant should be called as the employer's first witness, or as any witness for the employer, is not a concern of mine, since I view such activity to be unnecessarily abrasive and foolhardy. It has not been my experience that witnesses who are hostile to your point of view provide helpful or predictable testimony for your case. If the union elects not to call the grievant as a witness, that carries its own message.

In the case where the interests of the grievant and union diverge or where they are two union employees with conflicting interests, I have found it to have a salutary effect (albeit expensive) for the union to provide counsel for both employees.[5] Alternatively, a request can be made of the second concerned employee (if he is not the one the union is currently representing) to intervene in the proceedings. It has been held by one federal court that an arbitrator's refusal to permit such intervention rendered the award unenforceable.[6] Questions then arise as to whether the intervening employee should be represented by his/her own counsel. Due process would seem to require it since the union has already stated that it does not represent the individual's interests, and obviously the arbitrator cannot represent the individual.

The alternative proposed by Professor Aaron of calling the individual employee as his own witness has several practical drawbacks. Most significant is the obvious discomfort of the employee who is called out of the plant without notice and without preparation and is expected to testify as to matters on which his recollection may be weak and which may be very complicated and difficult to articulate. This individual's testimony will be pitted against that of other witnesses who, at a minimum, have a representative at the hearing and most likely have been prepared for their testimony. The end result may well be the same as if the nonrepresented employee had never been asked to testify.

---

[4]*Grane Trucking Co.*, *supra* note 1, at 137–138.
[5]*See, Russ Togs, Inc.*, 253 NLRB 767, 106 LRRM 1067 (1980).
[6]*Sedita v. Board of Education*, 82 Misc.2d 644, 371 N.Y.S.2d 812 (1975). *aff'd in part*, 53 A.D.2d 300, 385 N.Y.S.2d 647, 93 LRRM 2467 (1976), *rev'd on other grounds*, 43 N.Y.2d 827, 402 N.Y.S.2d 566 (1977).

The issue of whether the grievant should have his own lawyer at the hearing and, if so, what role the lawyer should play during the hearing is not a problem that generally concerns management. I have never objected to the presence at the hearing of the grievant's personal lawyer. In my view, if the grievant is represented by his own lawyer instead of the union, the grievant assumes the risk that his retaining personal counsel may affect the arbitrator's view of the case.

Where the grievant's lawyer is not permitted to participate actively in the arbitration proceeding, the arrangement has the salutary effect of reducing the length of the hearing, but there is the possibility that the grievant's lawyer will subsequently challenge the award on the ground that the union's lawyer failed to represent the grievant properly. Obviously, lawyers are adept at finding fault in the trial techniques of their colleagues.

One alternative used by some arbitrators is to ask the grievant's lawyer, at the conclusion of the hearing, to state his views as to the fairness of the hearing vis-à-vis his client. This is a novel approach, but offers the lawyer something of a Hobson's choice since he has to choose between offending the arbitrator before a decision is rendered or creating a record that would defeat a subsequent challenge under a duty of fair representation claim.[7]

Another area of concern to the courts, and I am sure to arbitrators as well, is the one in which an arbitrator's intervention in the hearing has led to a challenge of the result. Thus, questions have been raised where arbitrators have cross-examined witnesses too vigorously at the hearing, a technique that also has the drawback of unnecessarily prolonging the hearing.[8] Also suspect are arbitral comments at the hearing as to a witness's credibility and instances where the arbitrator is openly critical of the contractual procedures negotiated by the parties or where he gratuitously advises the parties as to revisions that should be made in their contract language. In one case the court found the arbitrator's comment that the contractual procedures "shocked his conscience" raised serious questions as to whether the final award was dictated by his personal bias against the contractual procedures or by the merits of the case. Absent other independent grounds to sustain such an award, it would be vacated.[9]

---

[7]*Liotta* v. *National Forge Co.*, 473 F.Supp. 1139, 1145, 102 LRRM 2348 (W.D.Pa. 1979), *aff'd in part, rev'd in part on other grounds,* 629 F.2d 903, 105 LRRM 2636 (3d Cir. 1980), *cert. denied,* 451 U.S. 970 (1981).
[8]*Holodnak* v. *Avco Corp., supra* note 2, at 198–199.
[9]*Grand Rapids Die Casting* v. *UAW Local 159, supra* note 2 at 1156.

In another case an arbitrator stated in his award that he was unable to make any credibility findings because he found that none of the witnesses had clean hands; he refused to make any factual findings and, instead, referred to the critical facts in the case as "alleged incidents"; and he noted that he would put the case in his files under the caption "Swiss Cheese" because it had so many holes in it. Though the arbitrator may be praised for his candor in chastising the parties' representatives, the result was an award that was viewed as unacceptable by the NLRB.[10]

Arbitrators should try to advise the parties as to their understanding of the evidence that has been presented and should, where appropriate, outline the parties' respective positions without commenting on their validity. On the other hand, any comment an arbitrator makes at the hearing that can be interpreted as critical of one side's position forces that party to scurry around to find additional witnesses or documents to shore up what he believes to be a weakened case.

An arbitrator's brief questions to clarify factual issues are helpful to the parties, but he/she should raise new contractual arguments not mentioned by the parties only after notice to, or consultation with, both representatives. The arbitrator need not agree with the parties, but he/she should be aware of their respective positions before launching into uncharted waters in the parties' agreement. Indeed, in any case where an arbitrator is concerned as to whether one side's case is being properly presented, the arbitrator can speak privately, in camera, to the representatives and should do so before jumping into the fray, with the resulting risk of appearing partisan.

Although an arbitrator's refusal to admit relevant evidence will constitute reversible error, arbitrators should not seek refuge by admitting any evidence proffered "for whatever it's worth." Particularly troublesome to the process are the massive exhibits that have not been marked by the party introducing them for specific areas of interest and which normally the arbitrator has no intention of considering in the final award. If the arbitrator is going to accept such exhibits, he/she should notify the parties whether or not he intends to look at them and, if so, what significance he thinks the exhibits might have. Otherwise, the opposing party may feel compelled to create competing and

---

[10]*Triple A Machine Shop, Inc.*, 245 NLRB 136, 102 LRRM 1559 (1979).

equally voluminous exhibits that will ultimately be totally irrelevant to everybody. It is understandable that arbitrators will continue to admit the "kitchen sink" since courts are more likely to vacate an award where evidence has been excluded than where it has been unnecessarily admitted.

In my research, I found that arbitrators have tripped over a variety of what would appear to be obvious procedural hurdles to the point where their awards have been rendered unenforceable. The following are some examples of what may not be normal arbitral practices, but which have occurred with disturbing frequency.

In one case an award was vacated where the arbitrator disregarded the testimony of an eyewitness on the grounds that the testimony should have been provided as part of the employer's case in chief and not as rebuttal testimony.[11] Citing favorably Professor Aaron's view that an arbitrator will accept any information "that adds to his knowledge of the total situation," the court found that the employer had been denied a fair hearing since the arbitrator had not announced in advance, and the collective bargaining agreement did not specify, that strict courtroom rules of evidence would be applied. The court also seemed dismayed that the arbitrator had not been called to testify at the trial—presumably unaware of the possibility that the American Arbitration Association and the arbitrator most likely would have opposed any such appearance.

Although normally it is the practicing lawyers who represent the parties in arbitration hearings who have been accused of burdening the process with technicalities, their brethren who sit at the head of the table have also been found guilty of insisting upon the observance of hypertechnical rules of evidence and procedures,[12] or enforcing strict rules of evidence with which at least one of the parties is unfamiliar.

An arbitrator's refusal to grant an adjournment when the employer's chief witness became ill at the hearing, and where the employer and his remaining witnesses thereafter walked out, rendered unenforceable the arbitrator's award of $100,000 damages to the union.[13] Though the arbitrator was understand-

---

[11]*Harvey Aluminum, Inc.* v. *Steelworkers*, 263 F.Supp. 488, 64 LRRM 2580 (C.D. Calif. 1967).

[12]*Western Electric* v. *Communication Equipment Workers*, 554 F.2d 135, 95 LRRM 2268 (4th Cir. 1977), *aff'g*, 409 F.Supp 161, 91 LRRM 2621 (D. Md. 1976).

[13]*Allendale Nursing Home* v. *Joint Board*, 377 F.Supp. 1208, 87 LRRM 2498 (S.D.N.Y. 1974).

ably irritated by the numerous delays occasioned by the parties, his peremptory conduct was viewed as "overkill." Similarly, an arbitrator's refusal to accept one party's reply brief where the controversy had been submitted by briefs was grounds for vacating the award and directing that the case be heard by another arbitrator.[14] In still another case, an arbitrator's failure, because of multiple hearing dates, to allow cross-examination of a critical witness rendered the proceeding unfair and subject to rehearing, in the NLRB's view.[15]

An arbitrator's award was overturned on the grounds of bias in a case where the arbitrator questioned a union dissident as to his political and personal views and badgered him to the point where he finally admitted that he now supported the union.[16] The announcement by the union at the outset of the hearing that they did not represent the grievant and the subsequent failure of the arbitrator to provide any procedural safeguards for the grievant resulted in an unenforceable award.[17] Finally, where an arbitrator failed to issue his award for six years after the close of the hearing, a federal court ordered the arbitrator removed, directed him to return all exhibits, and enjoined him from collecting any fee for his services.[18]

Although, obviously, some of these cases are dramatic aberrations, it is still clear that as losing parties discover that courts will be sympathetic to their challenges of arbitral results, the challenges will become more frequent and the grounds for them more sophisticated.

## Comment—

JUDITH P. VLADECK*

To take issue with Ben Aaron is a formidable, intimidating process. Respect for him as an outstanding scholar and practitioner in the world of labor arbitration is inhibiting. Of equal, or perhaps more, concern is that, in challenging his views about

---

[14]*Green-Wood Cemetery* v. *Cemetery Workers*, 82 LRRM 2894 (N.Y. Sup. Ct. 1973).
[15]*Versi Craft Corp.*, 227 NLRB 877, 94 LRRM 1207 (1977).
[16]*Holodnak* v. *Avco Corp.*, supra note 2, at 198–199.
[17]*Russ Togs, Inc.*, supra note 4, at 767.
[18]*Local 508, Graphic Arts International Union* v. *Standard Register Co.*, 103 LRRM 2212, *motion denied*, 103 LRRM 2214 (S.D. Ohio 1979).
*Vladeck, Waldman, Elias & Engelhard, P.C., New York, N.Y.

"The Role of the Arbitrator in Ensuring a Fair Hearing," one is required to quarrel publicly with expressions of support for fairness, truth, and due process. One might as well say harsh words about motherhood and the flag. But, with due respect to Professor Aaron, and due process, I am obliged to dissent.

I start with an area of agreement. The subject of fair hearing and the arbitrator's role has been well and fully debated in prior meetings of this body. Reading the 1958 Willard Wirtz paper and that of Robben Fleming in 1961,[1] as well as the comments that followed them, makes one aware that arbitrators and representatives of the parties have struggled with these questions for decades and anticipates many of the issues that Ben has addressed.

So what is new? What is new is that today we are dealing with an institution that is sufficiently mature to warrant a fresh analysis. It behooves us to keep examining and reexamining the process because whatever disagreements we may have—the arbitrators and the "clients"—the consensus remains firm: the labor-arbitration system is useful. It deserves to be nurtured and kept alive.

I suggest that in the new examination, we should focus on the following:

1. Is the view, expressed by Professor Aaron, that the arbitrator is concerned with balancing the interests of *three* parties—the employer, the union, and the grievant—correct? Or is it an arbitrator-created fiction?

2. Is the purpose of an arbitrator hearing, as Professor Aaron described it, "to come as close to the 'truth' about the matter in dispute as it is possible for fallible humans to achieve in the circumstances"?

3. Is the view of fairness in the arbitration context as requiring the equivalent of "due process" correct, or is fairness in the arbitration context something else?

## I.

In addressing these questions, it is my view that we mouth, but fail to hear, the basic principles that underlie the process: that

---

[1] Wirtz, *Due Process of Arbitration*, in The Arbitration and the Parties, Proceedings of the 11th Annual Meeting, National Academy of Arbitrators, ed. Jean T. McKelvey (Washington: BNA Books, 1958), 1; Fleming, *Due Process and Fair Procedure in Labor Arbitration*, in Arbitration and Public Policy, Proceedings of the 14th Annual Meeting, National Academy of Arbitrators, ed. Spencer D. Pollard (Washington: BNA Books, 1961), 69.

grievance arbitration is a method of settling disputes, that it is the result of a voluntary agreement of the parties in a collective bargaining relationship, that it is an extension of that relationship, and that the arbitrator is a creature of the parties. We forget what we once all knew: the process is an integral part of the collective bargaining relationship of the employer and the union, adopted by them to serve as a terminal point in their grievance procedure. It can be as broad or limited as they choose—who the arbitrator is, what issues he may hear, what remedies he may award, how his decision shall be treated. All of these are for the parties to determine.

I believe that in the past two decades the process has been subverted, taken away from its creators, and is being made into some bastardized version of what was intended—now neither fish nor fowl nor fine red herring.

The departure from its essential characteristics was signaled in the Wirtz article, where Wirtz said he was prepared to argue for the proposition "that the discharge of the arbitrator's function of determining the ground rules for the arbitration proceeding requires a broad balancing of interests, including recognition of independent individual interests even where this means . . . piercing the institutional, representative veil."[2]

Wirtz acknowledged that this was a view not shared by many of his colleagues, and he cited Harry Dworkin, Herbert Blumer, Philip Marshall, and others. Indeed, Wirtz quoted Dworkin who had said:

> "Arbitration usually results from a voluntary agreement of the parties in which they bind themselves in advance to observe the terms of the award. Thus, whether the results be good, bad, or indifferent . . . such effects are calculated risks which the parties have seen fit to assume. . . . The decision is not unfair where it results from the application of standards agreed to by the employee's duly authorized collective bargaining agent. . . . Everything has been handled according to due process, including the award in which the employee is 'thrown to the wolves' since it results from the employee's voluntary action."[3]

The Wirtz view of arbitration as involving three parties, with the arbitrator in the paternalistic position of protector of the individual grievants, has, by passage of time, and with the tacit or passive acquiescence of the real parties, appeared to have acquired legitimacy. If unchecked, I predict it will kill the pro-

---

[2]Wirtz, *supra* note 1, at 35.
[3]*Id.*, at 4.

cess. Professor Aaron does not question the proposition. He assumes it, saying, for example, that in promotion or discipline cases, the grievant has a personal stake that must be recognized in addition to the union's interest in protecting the integrity of the collective bargaining process. This is a backward proposition if ever one was uttered, since the grievant has no personal stake *without* collective bargaining.

As a practical matter, what difference does it make if the arbitrators who now adopt such an approach as a given differ with the views of the union "client"? To me, the difference is fundamental. Governed by such an unstated rule, the arbitrator no longer acts as an umpire, serving to resolve issues between the actual parties—the union and the employer—but, instead, is a surrogate representative of the grieving employee, skewing the hearings to achieve what he considers fairness for the individual. Apart from the offense implicit in the arbitrator's notion that he can and will do a better job for the workers than their union, it disserves the fundamental purpose—the extension and preservation of the collective bargaining process.

The arbitrator who sees the individual grievant as having a "personal stake" as separate from his union, and for humanitarian reasons elevates the grievant's "interests" to that of a contending party, risks the ultimate destruction of the union, without which no worker in the plant will have any right.

We cannot for one moment afford to forget—without unions, workers have no due process in their employment. Workers leave their constitutional rights at the factory gate. From the moment they enter, they may be searched, spied upon, eavesdropped on, photographed, interrogated, subjected to lie detector tests and psychological exams, fired without cause, or sometimes even worse, fired for having exercised a constitutional right. Only if the union is the representative of all of the members of the unit, and only if it speaks for them in one voice can it be effective. No one questions the authority of the management spokesman to speak authoritatively for the employer; only the same acknowledgement of the union as representative will preserve the status of the parties to the collective bargaining process as coequals in that process.

I suggest that arbitrators have unwittingly tread where Congress and the NLRB have not. In collective bargaining, the union has the legal power and authority, as well as the duty, to serve as the exclusive representative. In those circumstances in which the courts or the Board may find that the union has not fairly represented the member, the remedy is with the courts or the Board. The arbitrator should not arrogate to himself the authority to create his own duty of fair representation jurisprudence.

## II.

Stemming from the confusion engendered by the Wirtz view that the arbitrator should be endowed with "the obligation and authority to look, in the protection of certain individual interests, to standards that are unaffected by the individual's election of representatives and by the actions of those representatives," we have come to the Aaron view of the arbitrator as activist, an independent pursuer of truth, regardless of what the parties present to him. This thinking is expressed in three suggestions made by Professor Aaron:

1. That an arbitrator is free to draw a negative inference from the union's decision not to call the grievant as a witness (or perhaps worse, to voice such an intention during the hearing).

2. That in cases where he "suspects that the union does not intend to present an effective case in support of the grievant,"[4] it would be desirable for the arbitrator to recommend to the union attorney that he cannot fairly represent the grievant and to propose that the grievant be permitted to choose his own counsel.

3. In a promotion case where the grievant has been passed over for someone less senior, where the union does not do so, that the arbitrator should (and Aaron says he does) call the employee who was promoted as the arbitrator's own witness.

Professor Aaron explains that this is necessary because the arbitrator "cannot always be sure that the union has dealt fairly with the promoted member in explaining why it is supporting the challenge to the company's decision to promote him."

For those who are caught up in the notion that they have been appointed as independent searchers for the truth, and who are not acquainted with it, I recommend a brilliant disquisition on the subject of the search for truth in another forum—Judge Marvin Frankel's great essay, "The Search for Truth, an Umpirecal View."[5]

Judge Frankel seems to suffer from the same pangs that afflict

---

[4]*Id.,* at 5.
[5]Frankel, 123 U. Pa. L. Rev. 1032 (1975).

Professor Aaron, "that our system of justice, adversary as it is, rates truth too low among the values that institutions of justice are meant to serve."[6] (I do not accept Professor Aaron's disclaimer that labor arbitration is not an adversary proceeding.)

Judge Frankel explains that the process is not designed to ferret out truth by pointing out that in our judicial system an advocate's prime loyalty is to his client and not to the truth as such—that in the last analysis, truth is not the only goal. If it were, he suggests, there are other more efficient methods of pursuing it, for example, as with research in medicine or history.[7]

Judge Frankel addressed proposals for controlling adversary excesses in the trial process which are relevant to our discussion: intervention by the judge, and better training and regulation of counsel. I will not address his second point since, in my view, the parties to the labor arbitration process have the right to choose their own representatives, at whatever level of competence, just as they have the same right in choosing their arbitrators.

But his examination of the intervention by judges deserves substantial attention from those arbitrators who have decided, in their quest for the truth, that they may call witnesses, interrogate those called by the parties, and in other ways insist on controlling what evidence is presented to them by the parties.

Judge Frankel starts his discussion with my favorite lines. Referring to the statement that in a trial in the federal courts, the judge is not a moderator, he says: "It is not inspiring to be a 'mere' anything. The role of moderator is not heady" (p. 1041). He goes on to say:

> "The fact [is] that our system [which prohibits a judge from investigating or exploring the evidence before the trial] does not allow much room for effective or just intervention by the trial judge in the adversary fight about the facts. The judge views the case from a peak of Olympian ignorance. His intrusions will in too many cases result from partial or skewed insights. He may expose the secrets one side chooses to keep while never becoming aware of the other's. He runs a good chance of pursuing inspirations that better informed counsel have considered, explored and abandoned after fuller study. He risks at the minimum the supplying of more confusion than guidance by sporadic intrusions.
>     . . .

---

[6]*Id.*, at 1036.
[7]*Id.*, at 1042.

"Without an investigative file, the American trial judge is a blind and blundering intruder, acting in spasms as sudden flashes of seeming light may lead or mislead him at odd times."[8]

While Judge Frankel raises the question of whether the virginally ignorant judge is always to be preferred to one with an investigative file, at least in our larger system of justice, these questions are asked. It is not assumed that they may be definitively answered by the judges.

## III.

"Due process" is used loosely in our discussion. Due process is not an abstract doctrine: it varies with the subject matter and the situation; it depends on the circumstances. If we mean the right to be heard, we should say so. If we mean those elements which have been considered as part of due process in a criminal case—presumptions of innocence, right of confrontation—we should say so.

In labor arbitration, your notion of due process and mine may differ. We are bound by the rules of law—in New York there are statutory requirements—and, generally, we are bound to the rules of the agency administering the process.

But let us not trade charges of lack of due process, or denials, without more care. If we believe that the parties may develop their own procedures, then we have to concede that absent any statutory or tribunal rules, the parties are free to decide what is fair. Arbitrators may not, I submit, select blindly, and at random, from rules developed for other procedures and other forums, those parts of due process they prefer.

Philip Marshall, who was also quoted in the Wirtz paper, said, and I agree:

"The fundamental question is what the parties expect of the arbitration process. I believe that they have the right to get what they expect and that if what they expect does not conform to the niceties of 'due process,' it is not the arbitrator's function to alter their voluntary arrangement in the absence of any applicable law which demands otherwise."[9]

If what I have said is heard as reducing the arbitrator's role to "mereness," I do not so intend it.

---

[8]*Id.*, at 1036.
[9]Wirtz, *supra* note 1, at 4, n. 4.

You may ask what it is I want of arbitrators. In general, I hope for intelligence, integrity, impartiality, sufficiently secure egos so that they do not need the process as a vehicle for self-promotion. Sufficient kudos will come to those who can serve the function for which they have been named.

What is a fair hearing in my view? It is not bits and pieces of what in the trial courts we call due process, but it has the same root—a fair-minded trier, an opportunity to be heard, to be listened to, to be judged without fear or favor.

The particular kind of hearing is within the control of the arbitrator—we take our chances with his personality. It will be long or short, formal or relaxed, largely as a result of what he or she prefers at the moment.

But what I want is someone who, in his or her own style, knows what the process is, knows what his place in it is—someone who will not try to do my job for me or tell me how to do it. I don't want someone who thinks he is there to police my conduct or, indeed, that of the employer, except to the extent that we ask him to do so.

This is not a *mere* cipher's job. It is vastly important to the peaceful, orderly relationship of the parties to the agreement. The arbitrator is indispensable; his judgment is what is bargained for and relied upon.

As a final point, to bolster an unpopular position, I rely on a higher law, the Torah, which reminds us: "Each was given a task, for each individual will not find the center of gravity of the universe within himself, but in the whole of which he is an essential part."

## Discussion—

MR. AARON: I hadn't intended to make an instance-by-instance reply to the various points being made, but I feel that I have been negligent in not making it very clear at the outset that I assumed everybody realized that the expression of these views is inevitably idiosyncratic. I am not trying to say what every arbitrator should do. I indicated what I thought was comfortable for me, and I tried to explain, in giving my examples, that the spectrum of views on this subject was very, very broad. If you happen to disagree with the suggestions I made and what I said I would do, you have a perfect right to do so. Although I am full of admiration for Judith's excellent presentation, I must say that I am totally unconvinced. I adhere to the views that I expressed, and I really feel, in some respects, that we are talking about quite different things. I don't think the arbitrator is like a judge. I don't think an arbitration hearing is like a judicial trial. For that reason, there are a lot of things about her presentation that seemed to me to indicate that we are sort of passing each other in the night rather than meeting head on on certain of these problems.

RALPH SEWARD: In spite of Ms. Vladeck's well-taken reminders that arbitration should be a process created by the parties, but that it often is not, what is being discussed today should be issues less for arbitrators than for labor and management, because it is for them to decide what kind of arbitration they want, to what extent grievants, if necessary, should have separate representation, whether or not independent counsel can be invited and under what conditions, and to what extent an arbitrator should have investigative powers. Many arbitrators have been granted investigative powers by their parties. I think that the extent to which these issues are being discussed as though they were primarily for arbitrators to decide represents what is unfortunately a great vacuum in the field that should be filled by joint decisions of labor and management.

NEIL BERNSTEIN: Related to what Ralph has said, I think one of the strengths of the arbitration process is the great diversity of arbitrators and arbitrators' philosophies that are available. Those parties who want an activist arbitrator can find activist arbitrators all over the country who will come in and take over a hearing for them and show them how a case should be handled. Those who want something closer to a mere moderator can also find plenty of arbitrators who will serve according to that model. I would suggest that the parties who do have strong feelings as to what they want or don't want from an arbitrator should take that into account in making their selection, and those arbitrators who are too far out of line in their images will find that the marketplace will take care of them in due course.

J. E. ISAAC: I find myself completely on Professor Aaron's side, as I view it very much in the context of the arbitration system as it operates in Australia, which is a compulsory arbitration system concerned with interest as well as grievance disputes. It seems to me that the difference between Professor Aaron and Ms. Vladeck may be given some solution if, so to speak, it's borne in mind that my acceptance of Professor Aaron's position is based on the view that an arbitration process is concerned not only with the parties before the arbitrator, but also with the public interest, which is the basis on which the Australian public arbitration system operates. The question, therefore, is whether a collective bargaining agreement can or should ignore the public interest or should be more narrowly based on the immediate interests of the parties concerned.

WILLIAM SIMKIN: I would like to ask Ms. Vladeck to comment on this problem. I think I can state with fair accuracy that all of us who have been around for a while get a sizable proportion of grievances submitted by unions where the responsible union officials desperately want to lose, but where they feel forced to bring a case to arbitration either for internal political reasons or in reaction to some of what I think is unfortunate legislation that has been enacted in recent years. If that is the case, would you comment on the arbitrator's problem in that kind of situation, assuming that he is able to detect it.

Ms. VLADECK: Of course we have cases such as that. You have them. We have them. The arbitrator has to be guided by some conscience. I don't ever ask any arbitrator to stultify himself. I think the arbitrator, as a realist, takes into account the environment in the shop, and if he knows that the person whose case is being brought is a problem, it may well affect his judgment—but I'm not asking that it do so. That's his problem. I give it to him. That's why I have an arbitrator.

MR. SIMKIN: I shouldn't add any more, but I've always felt that one of the greatest crimes an arbitrator can commit is to let a union win a case that they want to lose. There is some kind of crazy psychology in labor relations where if a union loses an arbitration case that they desperately want to win, when it comes to the next negotiation, they have a chance to get their rights through negotiations, whereas if they win a case they desperately want to lose, they are almost disbarred from getting that corrected in the next negotiation.

PETER SEITZ: We've heard a great deal to our advantage and profit about truth. Of course we all search for it, and we hardly ever get a piece of it ourselves. Arbitrators pursue truth perhaps no more than others in the population, or attorneys for management or union. I'm sure that Judith Vladeck doesn't want to put us in the position of Pontius Pilate who is alleged to have said, "What is truth?" and stopped not for an answer. But we're not here to look for truth, and I think that she misconstrued Ben Aaron's remarks when he talks about the search for truth. We're there to make a decision, and we hope that the decision will be a correct and fair one. We are doing it frequently under extremely difficult circumstances where the level of advocacy unfortunately can be quite low. When the arbitrator sits there and has to make decisions on credibility and decisions on facts, he's not looking for truth, he's looking for accuracy. He has to make findings. I think a great deal of the difference between Mr. Aaron and Ms. Vladeck is related to a failure to recognize that distinction.

BEN FISCHER: I've been sitting next to Dave Feller and, modest fellow that he is, he didn't take issue with the misinterpretation of the Court decisions known as the *Trilogy.* We know, of course, that the *Trilogy* said that arbitration does not carry with it some obligation to protect the public interest. I think our friend from Australia really did well by this proceeding by pointing out what they have in Australia because it illustrates what we do not have here. I don't think the arbitrators have any interest in protecting the public interest except as citizens, nor do they have an obligation to do for the parties what the parties are so incompetent in doing. I am sympathetic with their problems, but nevertheless I think arbitration must resist trying to correct the inadequacies of collective bargaining or trying to defend individual workers through a process that is not designed to do that. As Judith has pointed out, it is designed as an extension of the collective bargaining procedure. It is part of that procedure, and it seems to me that Ben Aaron's philosophy—the notion that an arbitrator somehow has to protect the individual's interest—can really destroy the whole process. That's not what it's for *unless* through legislation or other means we decide on a whole new system of labor-management relations. I think that Ben's point of view is entirely respectable, but it is not the one we have, and it seems to me that we have to proceed with what we have. What we have is not arbitration as protector of the public interest or of the individual's interest.

ARCHIBALD COX: It seems to me that it is a matter of degree. As an arbitrator, I don't believe that I'm there in some independent role as the guardian of individuals or of the public. But if the parties want my name on a piece of paper, there are certain things that I think I owe to myself, and to some degree to the process, not to do. There are some things that the parties ought to do themselves, by collective bargaining. If these things are out of the range of what I regard as reasonably fair and decent, they can't ask me to take the responsibility. But if they are within that circle, which is awfully hard to define abstractly, then I think my philosophy would call on me to help. I think Ben's case about the leaders of the wildcat strike is one where it is very tempting to say to the union counsel, "You have a right to drop these grievances, but if you really want to go through a process of having what purports to be an independent decision as to whether the grievants were fairly treated, the only way we'll get that is to have the grievants' lawyer, if they want one, present their case. You can do it the way you want, but I don't think I want to be part of the charade that, in a sense, is going to deceive them and the rest of the world." But I don't know. The other half of me says that maybe counsel for the union are being very responsible, and I confess that I would be influenced by who they were.

MR. AARON: I realize that I am having more than equal time, but I would like to tie together what I understand to be the main drift of the discussion. Lest I seem to be donning the guise of a wild man who's recommending that the arbitrator take over every hearing and tell the parties what they can and cannot do, I should like to reassure you on that point. Going back to the point Ralph Seward made, it seems to me that if the parties really want to keep control of the proceeding down to the last detail, they can agree on their procedural rules. Then, if the arbitrator is unhappy with these rules, he ought to withdraw. He should not override what the parties have agreed they want to do. These problems arise only because the parties haven't done that, and it is therefore up to the arbitrator to decide what to do in the absence of any specific rule to the contrary. Judith and Ben Fischer express a basically different philosophy, and to me it is just a different aspect of the whole problem we had when we got the first interpretation of Section 301 of the Taft-Hartley Act. There were those, like Harry Shulman, who argued that the courts shouldn't have anything to do with the arbitration process, that arbitrators' decisions ought not to be enforceable in the courts, and that the need to enforce them meant that there had been a breakdown in the process—that it wasn't serving the function for which it was intended. That meant that the only way you could enforce an award, if it was in favor of the union, was by strike and other means of self-help on the part of the parties.

That was it. Well, the courts decided otherwise. Now we have statements that the arbitrators ought to do simply what they're there to do—what the parties want them to do. They're not to exercise any independent initiative except to reach a decision, which is what the parties want; everybody else should leave them alone, and the idea that there is some broader public policy at work here is wrong, contrary to the situation in Australia. But the courts have decided otherwise. Now when we come to the question of what is the future of the arbitration process, Judith says that if it proceeds along the way that she thinks my ideas will lead, the process will collapse. My perception is that if the arbitrator is the mere creature of the parties and no attempt is made to take into account the interest of the individual employees, regardless of how that may jibe with your notion of what the collective bargaining process is about, then I think that the process is going to collapse or, what is perhaps worse, it will be made over by legislation or by judicial decision into something far less useful than it is today. I think that is the basic difference between us.

# CHAPTER 4

# THE ART OF OPINION WRITING

## I.

STUART BERNSTEIN*

This program offers the usual Academy format—one labor and one management representative and one arbitrator, presumably the neutral between the two. In this instance, however, no inference should be drawn that there are three or even two sides to the subject of this meeting. There is not a good, or artful, opinion for management and another for labor. Hence, I do not intend to offer a management view on this, but rather some comments on what I consider to be the requirements for or characteristics of a good opinion—for all sides.

At the outset, I offer a definition of a good opinion: it is where I expect to win, but I lose, and when I read the opinion I am satisfied that justice has been done.

The first inquiry might well be, why an opinion at all?

A lawyer friend who plows the same turf I do received the announcement of the Academy program. He told me he didn't find this topic particularly interesting because he never read arbitrators' opinions—only the bottom line. "All I want to know," he said, "is did I win, or did I lose."

I must confess that I, too, read the bottom line first. I am an advocate and winning is better than losing. But I do go back and read the opinion—with pleasure when I win and very carefully when I lose.

What purpose does the opinion serve?

There is, of course, no requirement that an arbitrator explain his award absent a contractual requirement to do so. This issue was recently considered by the Third Circuit Court of Appeals where the losing party to an award challenged the failure of the arbitrator to issue an opinion. Both the trial and reviewing court

---

*Mayer, Brown & Platt, Chicago, Ill.

found the arbitrator was under no legal or contractual obligation to provide an explanation.[1] The Court of Appeals cited the familiar passage from *United Steelworkers* v. *Enterprise Wheel and Car Corp.*[2] that "arbitrators have no obligation to the court to give their reasons for an award."

What is significant about the appellate court's decision for our purposes was its discussion of the utility of opinions. It observed that the losing party "makes an attractive argument in favor of the desirability of requiring arbitrators to write opinions." The court outlined these arguments:

> "[O]pinions would establish a general body of precedent to guide management in administering the contract, to guide unions in deciding which cases to bring to arbitration and to guide arbitrators in making further decisions; the requirement of arbitral opinions will help insure that an arbitrator will consider the opposing contentions and formulate a coherent resolution; . . . the need to articulate reasons may influence the arbitrator to consider the matter carefully; . . . the opinion would meet the salutary purpose served by all written opinions—explanation to the losing party why it lost and evidence that its arguments were considered."

As authority for these arguments, the court referred to Jules Getman's article, "Labor Arbitration and Dispute Resolution."[3] Similar reasons are found in Sylvester Garrett's presidential address to the Academy at its 1964 meeting.

Syl Garrett included a few more, less altruistic reasons, primarily concerned with increasing the arbitrator's study time and, hence, remuneration. He, of course, was not advancing this as a valid reason, but rather was describing the argument of those who favored no opinions.

To the general reasons favoring opinions—precedent for the parties and arbitrator, acceptability to the losing party, and discipline for the arbitrator—may be added another. That is, the impact of the arbitration in NLRB proceedings—the *Spielberg* and *Collyer* doctrine,[4] in Title VII litigation—the *Gardner-Denver* footnote,[5] and in fair representation cases—*Vaca* v. *Sipes.*[6]

[1]*Virgin Islands Nursing Ass'n Bargaining Unit* v. *Schneider*, 668 F.2d 221, 109 LRRM 2323 (3d Cir. 1981).
[2]363 U.S. 593, 598, 46 LRRM 2423 (1960).
[3]*Labor Arbitration and Dispute Resolution*, 88 Yale L.J. 916, 920–21 (1979). *See also* Syme, *Opinion and Awards*, 15 LA 953 (1950).
[4]*Spielberg Mfg. Co.*. 112 NLRB 1080, 36 LRRM 1152 (1955): *Collyer Insulated Wire*, 192 NLRB 837, 77 LRRM 1931 (1971).
[5]*Alexander* v. *Gardner-Denver Co.*, 415 U.S. 36, 7 FEP Cases 81 (1974).
[6]386 U.S. 171, 64 LRRM 2369 (1967).

There may be some differences of view among us as to the desirability of indirectly shifting to the arbitration process the resolution of questions of violations of statutory rights. My own bias is that one good bite is enough, and whether it has been a good bite cannot be determined from the award alone.[7]

In any event, I suppose it is a condition of this assignment and the premise of your attendance that opinions are clearly desirable or are so ingrained in the process that further speculation on whether the award should be explained is pointless. However, the reasons for opinions articulated by Garrett, Getman, and the court of appeals might be kept in mind as a benchmark against which to test quality.

As one more warm-up pitch, let me confess to a certain reluctance in holding myself out as an authority on arbitral opinion-writing, qualified to tell you how they should be written or what they should contain. I have written a few myself as the sole neutral—three to be exact—and compared to that task brief-writing is a snap.

Apart from its result, the opinion analytically has four parts: the issue in contention, the facts, the arguments of the parties, and the discussion or analysis. This is not to suggest that a particular format or sequencing is preferable. The statement of the issue usually comes first, but in many instances the issue cannot be adequately explained apart from the factual background, including relevant contract provisions.

Also, it is not necessary that in all instances the result be saved for the last paragraph. An opinion is not a who-done-it. Some read as though the arbitrator felt he would lose his reader if he gave any hint as to how it was all going to come out before the very end. Supreme Court opinions are usually more merciful. They tell you right at the beginning—judgment affirmed, judgment denied—and the reasons then follow.

I have nothing to contribute on the question of "style." Some

---

[7]Another argument favoring the writing of opinions is the issue of reviewability—a reason that arbitrators may not find very attractive. Unless the arbitrator is required to articulate reasons for the award, it may be impossible for a party to challenge or a court to determine whether the arbitrator has in fact gone beyond the limits of his contractual authority. The question of judicial review was discussed by the court of appeals in the *Nursing Association* case, but was found to be an insufficient reason to impose a legal obligation to issue arbitral opinions. The court distinguished the arbitral process from administrative proceedings where articulation of the decision is required. The court was unwilling to impose this formality upon the arbitration process, citing with approval commentators who argue that "the unique and continuing relationship between management and labor may at times be better served by maintaining the informality and flexibility that characterizes many arbitrations." *Supra* note 1, at 224.

people write well, some do not. Some write lyrically, others with cold prose. Nothing said here today will make good writers of poor writers, or discourage those who are now first-rate stylists. All I would suggest is that opinions be written so they can be understood. Sometimes one gets the impression that the arbitrator has dictated the opinion into a machine and never again looked at the product. They ramble, have no coherent organization, and are just bad writing. "Dictated but not read" is not acceptable.

To button this down—I don't believe arbitrators should get hung up on a particular format. Let that be determined by the case itself, not by a habit of form. Opinions should be at least intelligible even if not great literature.

A word on the issue: This is usually not much of a problem. The grievance papers make it clear or the parties stipulate. Occasionally there is a hang-up on this, particularly in contract-interpretation cases. There may be disagreement on which provision is to be interpreted, or each side may try to load the question in its favor. The arbitrator's responsibility where the parties do disagree on the issue, or where they leave it to him to formulate, is to set out clearly his understanding of the dispute. This sounds pretty fundamental, but sometimes it gets lost in the shuffle.

Incidentally, in preparation of this paper I sought the views of two of my favorite opponents, Lee Burkey and Gil Feldman. Both mentioned the problem of the lack of a clear statement by the arbitrator of the issue he is deciding.

The statement of the facts is, to my mind, the most critical part of the opinion. I put aside the interesting but mostly useless philosophical inquiry as to what is a fact—the distinction between subsidiary and ultimate facts, evidentiary facts, and conclusory facts with which law students are tortured.[8]

The difficulty about writing facts is not that we don't know what facts are, but the temptation to write the facts to support the conclusion. The brief writer faces this all the time and he does this quite deliberately. But the advocate cannot be faulted because that is his function. His job is to convince the arbitrator or the court, and if he does so by highlighting the facts favorable to his side or minimizing those that are unfavorable, that is

---

[8]This still goes on. *See Pullman-Standard* v. *Swint,* 456 U.S. 273, 28 FEP Cases 1073 (1982), where the Court discusses the kind of "facts" found by a trial court which can be reviewed by an appellate court.

acceptable. There is a limit, of course; he has an obligation not to dissemble, and he ought not be so obvious that his ploy becomes transparent.

But what is acceptable conduct for the advocate is not for the arbitrator. The arbitrator has an obligation to state the facts accurately and as fully as the case demands. He cannot avoid facts that do not fit his conclusion. Nobody would disagree that the arbitrator has this responsibility. The problem is, how does he fulfill it?

This raises the interesting question as to when the arbitrator reaches a decision. At what stage of the process does he know how the case is going to come out? Does he decide while taking evidence, or listening to oral argument, or reading the briefs, or reviewing the transcript, or writing the opinion?

Well, the answer you would undoubtedly give is that it all depends. Some cases are easy and the answer is apparent as soon as you hear the opening statements of each side—sometimes I think after hearing only one side. Others are complex and you have to reflect—the study-time syndrome.

I would hope that to the extent it is possible for any human to be objective and not influenced by little imps we hesitate to talk about—things like what my batting average is with these parties—that in a case of any complexity the arbitrator not make up his mind until after he has written the facts.

David Wolff used to do that with the United Pilots System Board of Adjustment. He would bring in a statement of the facts and ask the board members whether the statement was fair—was there anything omitted that any member thought should be included, or anything included that ought not be there? He would then adjourn the session and reflect on the decision. There was more to it, of course: listening to arguments, determining whether there was a consensus, discussing a tentative award. Also the environment of a tripartite board is not the same as that of a neutral acting alone. But the sole arbitrator should be able to discipline himself not to jump too fast.

One of the three famous cases I decided as a neutral involved a two-day suspension of an employee for insubordination in walking off the job. There were many little details—who was standing where, was the door open so that the corroborating witness really could have heard what was going on, was the supervisor's statement to the grievant a direction or only a hope? The supervisor was new on the job and, I felt, a bit too quick to assert his authority. I had been having trouble getting appointments because of my identity as a management advocate, and this was my chance to show how impartial I was. Here I could decide for the union and establish my credentials as a good guy.

When I wrote the opinion, it just would not come out right. I tried three different approaches to the facts, convinced it was my style and not my preconceived conclusion that was at fault. I finally realized what I had done to myself and then upheld the discipline.

Since that experience, I am sensitive to any symptom of premature mind-making-up by the arbitrator when I am presenting a case. If a completely objective person such as I could get caught in his own wishful thinking, what must this alleged neutral be doing to me right now when he furrows his brow, or when he asks my witness a tough question during the hearing?

Illustrations of fact-fudging to fit the conclusion are hard to come by unless based on first-hand knowledge. Reading a reported case doesn't reveal much; there is no way you can know whether the statement of facts is other than accurate and fair.

One of my colleagues recently ran into a beauty. An employee was terminated for performing manual labor for a third party while on sick leave and after having turned down light duty offered by his employer. There was dispute as to the fact of the outside work having been done, when it was done, and the nature of the work. Each side had support from witnesses who might be considered less than objective. However, the company succeeded in getting the supervisor of the other employer to testify that the terminated employee had in fact performed manual labor during the time he was on sick leave. The arbitrator nonetheless found for the grievant, describing the company case as being founded on surmise, suspicion, and conjecture. The problem of the testimony of the third-party supervisor was handled very simply. It was ignored. However, the opinion reads well, but it hardly inspired confidence and certainly failed to meet the test of acceptability.

There is another side to the coin. If an arbitrator does fairly state the facts, he has a correlative obligation to account for them somewhere in his opinion. A company closed shop in March 1980 after more than 30 years of dealing with the same union. The contract provided a June 1 vacation-eligibility date. The employer refused pro rata vacation pay on the ground that since the claimants were not employees as of June 1, they were not entitled to vacation pay for the preceding year. The employees made out a good equitable claim, and there was some ambiguity in the contract—so a not unreasonable interpretation could support the claim. However, in a prior negotiation the union had proposed, and the employer had successfully resisted, an amendment to the vacation article to provide that in the event the employer went out of business, pro rata vacation would be paid to the terminated employees. The union agreed that such a proposal had been made and had been rejected. This history clearly had some relevance to the dispute at hand.

The arbitrator included this bargaining history in his statement of the case, mentioned it in his discussion, but never disposed of it. What he said, in effect, was that but for his misgivings about the union's failure to persuade the employer to agree to pro rata vacation pay for employees terminated as a result of the employer going out of business, he would have no doubt as to the merits of the union's claim. He then concluded as a matter of general arbitral authority that vacation is deferred compensation and accrues with time, and he awarded pro rata vacation pay. There was no further discussion of his misgivings or any explanation as to why the particular bargaining history did not make this case somewhat different from those cited in support of the award.

I raise this example not because I felt the decision was wrong. In fact, I thought the result was right, but the opinion left me hanging. The arbitrator had an obligation to do something with the bargaining history. One footnote to this case might be that since the employer is gone, there is no problem of the future relationship between the parties or the acceptability of the arbitrator.

Neither of the arbitrators in these two examples is a newcomer. They both enjoy excellent reputations, and I would not hesitate to select either of them again. But they, like all of us, must be alert to the trap of the opinion being a rationalization of a preconception, not an explanation. It is in the handling of the facts that this issue is most sensitive.

That part of the opinion describing the respective contentions should be easier to handle. An occasional problem is the cop-out of an advocate who is on shaky ground and tells you and the opponent that his position is obvious and he won't belabor the point. The arbitrator should insist that the arguments be clearly stated, either by oral summation or by brief. Although somewhat tangential to the subject at hand, the advocate who is required to file a concurrent brief is entitled to know the arguments of the other side and, in the case of the employer, the relief being sought. Once the arbitrator has the contentions in hand, he should set them out in the opinion and should respond to them, particularly to the arguments advanced by the losing party.

Many of us believe that cases are overbriefed, but a recent experience has changed my view on this. The case was fairly straightforward; there was a transcript and oral argument, and I was satisfied that a brief would have been superfluous. When the opinion came down, it was clear that the arbitrator had forgotten what the argument was all about. He is a busy fellow, overloaded, and way behind in getting decisions out. I finally bugged him about the delay and got a quick answer thereafter. I am sure he didn't have time to reread the record before getting at the job, forgot what the argument was about, and let fly. The result was not a disaster, but the situation was awkward. I am not sure whether the lesson is that arbitrators should not take on too much work or that parties should not nag when the decision is long overdue.

I realize that the suggestion that briefs always be filed so that the arbitrator is clear on the arguments appears to disadvantage the nonlawyer advocate. But a brief need be no more than a statement of the party's perception of the issue and facts and why he believes he should win. The briefer the better, to which all the arbitrators here would, I am sure, say "Amen."

The guts of the opinion is obviously that part usually called the discussion, sometimes analysis, decision, or opinion. How much should be said? If one purpose of the opinion is to guide the parties in the future, is there not a responsibility to spell out clearly the guidance being offered? How do you convince the parties—particularly the losing party—that you understood his arguments and that you knew what you were doing? You know there is no possible road map on this. The danger lies more in saying too much rather than not enough.

I have tested my own views on this with my union friends whom I have mentioned earlier, and we are in substantial agreement. A good opinion answers the questions put—all of them and no others. It allows its lesson for the future to come from its result, not its pontification. It does not lecture; it does not offer gratuitous advice. It does not denigrate or embarrass. It does not say—in an attempt to mollify or to apologize—if you had only done this, or relied on a different contract provision, it might have come out differently. If you have reserved judgment on evidentiary objections, or said you "would take it for what it is worth," then give us the ruling on the objections and tell us what it was worth.

The opinion should not be a vehicle for the arbitrator's philosophy. It is primarily for the grievant, not the advocates. Write so the principals understand why you have found as you have. There is a difference between the sophistication and knowledge of the process that can be assumed of a college-teacher grievant and a punch-press operator. It is to them that you owe the explanation, not to me or my counterpart. And, lest this litany be taken as somewhat condescending, let me assure you of what you must know: There is usually far less sophistication sitting on the employer side than on the union side of the table.

Well, easily said—but how do you know when to quit writing, or when you are inadvertently salting an old wound? You don't. When you are sitting alone and deciding alone or writing alone, there is no way you can know. This is why the job is so tough and why it is amazing that there are so many of you who do it so well.

Here is a fellow who didn't do it well. This is an old but memorable decision. I read verbatim:

> "Therefore it is the finding of the Umpire that, according to the existing agreement, the adjusted base rate and the special day rate are not to increase five cents effective this August 1 and five cents August 1 next year. The Company is within the terms of the Contract not to grant this increase in pay.
> "However, to promote better employer-employee relationship and co-operation, the Umpire strongly urges the Company to grant these increases. . . ."

There are some devices for testing the opinion for inadvertent flaws before its release. The tripartite panel is one obvious vehicle. Too often the parties waive contractually provided boards in the interest of expedience. But when the arbitrator has some concern about the opinion, he might well request that the board convene solely for the purpose of advising him whether his words have created more problems than his award has settled.

One tripartite-board case in which I was involved concerned an interpretation of the agreement defining competing seniority rights arising out of a merger. The arbitrator got the award okay, but simply could not understand the terminology of the trade. His opinion was incomprehensible. The partisan representatives finally took over, rewrote the offending paragraphs, and had the arbitrator sign the award.

Other ways of getting at the problem were proposed by Syl Garrett in his presidential address to the Academy in 1964, reported in the Proceedings of its Seventeenth Annual Meeting. I have already referred to this in another context.

One was a variant of the tripartite board—informal consultation between the arbitrator and the parties. For success, this procedure would require, he said, "a rare combination of character, sophistication and insight in the parties' representatives who consult with the arbitrator." Apparently, this is a combination all too rare since I have not heard of any use of this procedure.[9]

Another of his suggestions was to follow the practice of some equity courts of issuing proposed findings, conclusions, and an order to which the parties could file exceptions. An alternate proposal would be for the parties to submit proposed findings to the arbitrator from which he would draw his findings and conclusions. These latter proposals are probably far too formalistic. They might be explored, however, in a case of sufficient complexity where the arbitrator has some concern over the content of the opinion, and of course, only with the concurrence of all hands.

A related issue, and one on which comment has been suggested, is that of the role of precedent in the process. Precedent in this context is an ambiguous concept. It may imply the extent to which an arbitrator should be bound by decisions of other arbitrators, or it may relate to the device of bolstering a decision by reference to what others have done in an effort to bestow respectability on the decision at hand. Or precedent may refer to the impact on the future relations of the parties themselves —a reason in favor of opinion-writing advanced by the court of appeals in the case referred to earlier.

A number of considerations are raised. The arbitrator is not bound by precedent as a lower court is bound by decisions of a superior reviewing court. Nonetheless there is obvious merit

---

[9]During the course of his presentation at this meeting, Sam Camens of the United Steelworkers of America advised this writer in particular and the audience in general that, in fact, this procedure is frequently used in the steel industry.

to the notion that like cases should be decided in like manner
—the element of predictability in helping to guide the conduct
of both parties to a collective agreement.

Precedent is not a straitjacket. The metaphor used by the
Supreme Court was "a new common law," the "common law of
the shop."[10] However, the common law is not static. The greatest common law judges are those who have gradually moved and
shaped the law through due regard to the past and recognition
of changing social needs and public acceptance. Allan Dash's
contribution to the common law of subcontracting is an example
of this development. The changing attitudes of society toward
hair and dress styles are reflected in movements in arbitral
awards. The gradual change in decisions on the acceptability of
polygraph evidence is another. The common law arbitrator, like
the common law judge, follows a little and leads a little.

The arbitrator who uses precedent to decide must be mindful
of the limitations. Predictability may be a key element in any
system of justice. But new ground must be broken occasionally
—one spadeful at a time.

Little purpose is served in citing precedent in opinions, however much it may have influenced the arbitrator in reaching his
decision. It too easily becomes a substitute for reason and is too
glib a way out of a tough situation. The arbitrator in my accrued-
vacation-pay case was, I believe, guilty of that. He had a tough
case—the equity was clearly with the employees, but the bargaining history went the other way. He ignored the tough part
and justified his actions on precedent not really applicable to the
case before him. But, as we say, bad cases make bad law.

One last comment on precedent, both as a decision-making
and opinion-citing device: Precedent implies that there is a body
of reported case law that reliably reflects the state of the common law. Given the current haphazard method of publication,
there cannot be a great deal of confidence that this is so with
arbitral decisions. As I read the reports, I have the uncomfortable feeling that publication is to a considerable extent a device
for gaining recognition for the arbitrator or the victorious lawyer, or the judgment of some editor as to what is significant.
Although there has been some easing of the problem recently,
there is still the subtle pressure from the arbitrator to get per-

---

[10]*United Steelworkers* v. *Warrior & Gulf Navigation Co.*, 363 U.S. 574, 579, 582, 46 LRRM
2416 (1960).

mission from the parties to publish before the case has been heard.

Perhaps the Academy might undertake to collect decisions of its members and establish a committee which could recommend for publication those decisions it considered significant. If permission were sought from the parties by such a committee, I am sure it would be readily forthcoming. And if the established services were not cooperative, you might start your own publishing venture.

Another thought: In the course of worrying about this presentation, it occurred to me that arbitrators generally do not know how tough it is to be an advocate, and advocates do not know how tough it is to be an arbitrator. The arbitrator's attitude is —you guys have it easy, you throw everything at us and hope some will stick, and then we are left with the problem of sorting it all out. The advocates' attitude is that the arbitrator has the easiest job in the world—just sit there and listen, then go home and write a decision. No fuss, no muss, no overhead.

An exchange of roles might be illuminating. At some time during his apprenticeship, the arbitrator should be required to try a few cases as advocate. He should interview and prepare witnesses, anticipate cross-examination, decide what exhibits he needs and how to present them, enjoy the pleasure of hearing something new and damaging the first time his witness is asked a question on cross, make an oral summation, and then write a brief. When he reads the opinion resulting from his efforts, he will have gained some new insights.

The advocate, in turn, should hear and decide at least one case. He will learn at first hand the loneliness of the long-distance runner. What does he do with this case, what is the approach, who overstated, are there any signals I am not getting, how much do I say in the opinion, how little can I say and still appear intelligent? And then, when the opinion is out, he can sit back and wait for the reaction.

It may not be possible to implement this in actual cases, but a well-constructed moot court model could serve as well. This is another project for the Academy. I think you would get better presentations by advocates, and arbitrators might be a bit more sensitive of the art of opinion-writing.

And now the last word: Lest you go away from this meeting with the notion that only arbitrators have problems with opinion-writing, let me read what Justice Powell had to say about an opinion Justice Blackmun wrote recently. The case concerned the constitutionality of a provision of the Illinois Fair Employment Practices Act that effectively foreclosed a remedy because of a slip-up by the Commission and through no fault of the complaining party. Justice Blackmun wrote two opinions: One, the Court's opinion, joined by four justices, held the provision to be a due-process violation; his other opinion, joined by four other justices, held it to be an equal-protection violation. Justice Powell, who joined the second opinion, filed a separate concurring opinion. He wrote, in part:

> "It is necessary for this Court to decide cases during almost every Term on due process and equal protection grounds. Our opinions in these areas often are criticized, with justice, as lacking consistency and clarity. Because these issues arise in varied settings, and opinions are written by each of nine Justices, consistency of language is an ideal unlikely to be achieved. Yet I suppose we would all agree —at least in theory—that unnecessarily broad statements of doctrine frequently do more to confuse than to clarify our jurisprudence. I have not always adhered to this counsel of restraint in my own opinion writing, and therefore imply no criticism of others. But it does seem to me that this is a case that requires a minimum of exposition."[11]

This is sound counsel for all opinion-writers—avoid unnecessarily broad statements, exercise restraint, and engage in a minimum of exposition. This is also good advice for writers of speeches as well as writers of opinions.

## II.

### SAM CAMENS*

The title of today's panel discussion, "The Art of Opinion Writing," is a nice noncontroversial topic and one that the Academy has discussed in prior sessions. In fact, 17 years ago in this very city, a most illustrious panel composed of Syl Garrett, Ben Aaron, Gerald Barrett, Tom Kennedy, and Herb Sherman devoted a half-day to the "Problems of Opinion Writing," expressing views that were alternately critical, constructive, and self-applauding.

As one reads those Proceedings of the 18th Annual Meeting

---

[11]*Logan* v. *Zimmerman Brush Co.*, 455 U.S.422, 28 FEP Cases 9 (1982).
*Assistant to the President, United Steelworkers of America, Pittsburgh, Pa.

of the Academy, it becomes evident that the problems of opinion-writing have not changed significantly. Thus, one of the
participants in those discussions made the profound observation that "opinions should be precise, direct and models of
clarity."

Hear, hear, I fully agree! And, if I had any good judgment I
would sit down while we are all in agreement.

I have to say in all honesty that there is little concern in labor
circles about the "Art of Opinion Writing" to the extent that the
word "art" refers to matters of form, style, literary value, or
format. What we are looking for is a decision that is factually and
contractually sound, supported by an opinion that is understandable, that supports the decision, and that hopefully im-
proves—but definitely does not worsen—the existing company-
union, employer-employee relationships. If the opinion does
not satisfy these simple requirements, it is of no value to the
parties and may well be counterproductive, no matter how well
written it may be.

In my view, which reflects long experience in steel arbitration,
it is impossible to discuss the "Art of Opinion Writing" in a
meaningful fashion unless it is done in the context of union-
management relations. The success or failure of the arbitrator
is dependent on his capacity to write an opinion that is in keeping with the relationship between the parties.

This, then, brings us to the types of cases in which the arbitration opinion is important and can have a significant impact on
the parties. Collective bargaining is a very delicate and precise
process. In many cases the parties are not willing or able to
reach agreement on every aspect of a subject, and yet the pressures or realities of the situation make it imperative that some
accommodation be reached. What do they do? They write language that is vague, imprecise, and subject to interpretation.
The lack of precision and clarity may be intentional, or it may
be the result of ineptitude. Whatever the reason, the arbitrator's
task is to write an opinion that will rationalize the language and,
in the process, stabilize the parties' relationship. This is where
opinion-writing becomes an art form.

George Taylor described this aspect of arbitration at the Second Annual Academy Meeting: "Grievance arbitration is an extension of the collective bargaining process. . . . Arbitration
should produce results consistent with the parties' agreements
in respect to detailed unanticipated problems which simply can-

not be treated specifically in negotiations." Harry Shulman provided a similar description when he said that a labor agreement ". . . is a generalized code to govern a myriad of cases which the draftsmen cannot wholly anticipate."

If there is any doubt that companies and unions do, indeed, accord such latitude to arbitrators, consider the following list of generalities that arbitrators are traditionally expected to apply to a multitude of different situations under agreements negotiated by the United Steelworkers of America:

relative (ability), orderly (procedures), highest level (employee performance), earliest practicable date, consistent (with safety and health), sustained effort, just cause, incidental, detailed (application), necessary (guideposts), existing rights and obligations, under similar circumstances, reasonable course, sufficient, significant, equitable earnings, the integrity of earnings.

In hundreds of carefully conceived opinions, arbitrators have perfected the meaning of words in various factual settings. The result is an artistic and brilliant patchwork of opinions which in context have given meaning and stability to our collective bargaining agreements.

The best example of this is the classic "2B" dispute in the steel industry. U.S. Steel and the United Steelworkers of America had agreed in 1947 to a provision which protected local working conditions and plant practices, and which is now known as the "2B" clause. The ink had barely dried on the agreement when the parties found themselves unable to reconcile major disagreements regarding the meaning and scope of the clause. It was Syl Garrett who undertook the truly difficult and unenviable task of reconciling the differences by setting the guideposts for such questions as what local working conditions are, what they may encompass, how they may evolve, and how new practices are created.[1]

This same 1947 U.S. Steel agreement with our union contained a new provision dealing with incentives. Again, it took a series of Syl Garrett's opinions to give guidance to the parties in order for them to be able to cope with the hundreds of newly created disputes dealing with "equitable incentive compensation" and "maintenance of required incentive changes." These most urgent opinions guided the parties through the stormy sea of industrial turmoil to a calmer bay of manageable waters.

---

[1]N-146:1953; USC-846:1959—Sylvester Garrett (U.S. Steel).

There are many other situations in which arbitrators have guided our union and companies to safe harbor. For example, Herbert Blumer, who probably is not remembered by many in this assemblage, wrote a historic opinion on February 19, 1946, in a U.S. Steel case, defining and shaping the parameters of the term "relative ability" as applied to seniority disputes. Another example arose following our most recent (1980) steel negotiations when Jim Jones (Approved by Al Dybeck)[2] and Bert Luskin[3] resolved disputes relating to a newly negotiated provision limiting the use of temporary foremen as witnesses in disciplinary cases, and thereby repaired a problem that was seriously eroding the relationship of the parties.

As we review the great impact that arbitration opinions have had on our relations, we cannot overlook the important opinions that filled the voids where specific language, in many areas, was not at the time included in the basic labor agreement. The most notable of these situations were the contracting-out disputes.

Every student of arbitration should be aware of the great legacy of court cases—that is, the *Steelworkers Trilogy*[4]—and arbitration opinions written by (to name the most notable, but not all) Seward, Garrett, Alexander, McDermott, Stashower, Cole, Platt, Valtin, and Shipman.[5] It was these timely, forceful, well-reasoned opinions that provided the great crutch that carried us over the critical days of conflict and total impasse to a mature and stable labor relations atmosphere resulting in contract language specifically dealing with contracting out.[6]

In the types of situations discussed above, the arbitrator's opinion is the critical element in providing guidance to the parties or in settling a contractual dispute on the basis of a rationale that helps to eliminate rancor and often contributes positively to the development of the relationship. A mere decision that one party is right and the other is wrong would not serve these larger purposes. Hence, the true "Art of Opinion Writing" is the ability of the arbitrator to write an opinion which is understandable and convincing and which manifests tolerance

---

[2]USS-17315:1981—James E. Jones, Jr. (Approved by Al Dybeck) (U.S. Steel).
[3]702:1981—Bert L. Luskin (Inland Steel).
[4]*United Steelworkers* v. *American Manufacturing Co.*, 363 U.S. 564, 46 LRRM 2414 (1960); *United Steelworkers* v. *Warrior & Gulf Navigation Co.*, 363 U.S. 574, 46 LRRM 2416 (1960); *United Steelworkers* v. *Enterprise Wheel & Car Corp.*, 363 U.S. 593, 46 LRRM 2423 (1960).
[5]Report of the Joint Steel Industry-Union Contracting Out Review Commission, November 7, 1979, Exhibit 1—Human Relations Committee Paper dated 10/24/62.
[6]1963 Experimental Agreement on Contracting Out between United Steelworkers of America and Basic Steel Industry.

and sensitivity for the position of each party. This, indeed, is the true test of a great arbitrator, and the ability of many arbitrators to do this is the reason that the arbitration profession has prospered and attained its current high status.

How do arbitrators attain that level of performance? Do the great arbitrators possess magical powers? No. In my opinion the great arbitrators are great because they work at the task of obtaining a total understanding of the industry, its plants, the workforce, the practices and the common law of the industry and plant, the economic situation of the industry and its changing technology. They also become totally aware of the sociological aspects of the relationship, including the personal and political factors at all levels of the company and the union. Finally, and most essential, is an intimate knowledge of the agreement and the history of collective bargaining.

It is amazing how fully the great arbitrators master these subjects. There are some who have become so knowledgeable that I sense they know more about us than we know about ourselves.

If you are saying to yourselves that only a permanent arbitrator can become this knowledgeable and informed, I am sure that is true. What about the vast majority of situations that involve ad hoc relationships? I believe that the ad hoc arbitrator should at least aim for a similar level of understanding. This can be done, I think, by addressing a few fundamental questions, the following being only my feeble attempt to provide illustrative examples: What do the parties want of me? What is the nature of the dispute and what effect will it have on their continuing relationship? How careful must I be about such matters? Can I write an opinion that contemplates such questions based on the record that has so far been made? Are there some missing facts? Do the tensions before me represent something deeper than I comprehend? Is there some other section of the agreement involved that has not been discussed?

Ask! Ask! No one can make the best decision or write the most appropriate opinion if he has doubts or some gnawing concerns. The arbitration process must be a problem-solving institution, not a "win at all costs" contest. The arbitrator must literally dig out the facts if the parties do not adequately present them.

Recognizing this need, my union and the steel companies have provided as follows in the Expedited Arbitration Procedure: "The Arbitrator shall have the obligation of assuring that

all necessary facts and considerations are brought before him by
the representatives of the parties."

Furthermore, the Academy's Code of Professional Responsibility states as one of the general principles of hearing conduct:

> "An arbitrator may: encourage stipulations of fact; restate the
> substance of issues or arguments to promote or verify understand-
> ing; question the parties' representatives or witnesses, when neces-
> sary or advisable, to obtain additional pertinent information; and
> request that the parties submit additional evidence, either at the
> hearing or by subsequent filing."

I realize that there may be a few labor agreements that seek
to limit independent inquiry by the arbitrator. But let me reem-
phasize that I, for one, feel it is your obligation to the parties to
pursue the facts. The future viability of the collective bargaining
relationship is, to a degree, involved in each arbitration case,
and this is no less true with respect to ad hoc relationships.

The basic labor agreement is not a static document. It is a
code of conduct, not unlike the Constitution of the United
States, that is affected and modified by changing social movements, mores, culture, economics, national politics, legislative
and judicial developments, governmental decrees and regulations, and many other social and economic factors. The arbitration opinion must also reflect those changes. One of the
clearest examples of how and why arbitration is influenced by
factors outside the collective bargaining agreement is in the
area of employee discipline where an elaborate common law of
due process and procedural rights has developed by reason of
arbitration opinions that have reflected the civil libertarian
movement of the past four decades and incorporated many of
the concepts enunciated by the Supreme Court during that
era.

On the other hand, I have a feeling that many opinions issued
during the last decade have not kept pace with sociological
developments. I sense a serious cultural lag, and perhaps even
an unconscious "new generation" bias. This is particularly evident when the ominous subject of marijuana and drugs is involved. The problem does not arise in the clear-cut cases, such
as the employee who is selling grass on the job or is under the
influence while at work. But I have seen too many arbitration
opinions in which the parties seem to have lost all perspective
in their zeal to prove that an employee is in possession of mari-

juana, where an individual's rights of privacy and due process have been trampled and justice has been denied based on insubstantial evidence and the uncorroborated accounts of paid informants.

The discipline and discharge procedures of American industry are unjust. This is so despite the fact that discipline is subject to severe restraints by reason of collective bargaining agreements and procedural and substantive protections accorded by arbitrators. While existing constraints are quite significant, the disciplinary system is nonetheless terribly unfair because it conflicts with the principles of justice in a democratic society under which a person is presumed innocent until adjudged guilty by a jury of his peers.

While there are a few exceptions, such as in the container industry where the USWA and several major can companies have negotiated provisions that enable most disciplined employees to remain on the job pending adjudication of their offenses, in most cases employees suffer the pain and indignity of a penalty before their guilt or innocence is determined. This undemocratic procedure is resulting in much resentment among our members, causing the entire process to be suspect —and this includes the final step, namely, arbitration.

There is a further element of unfairness in the system. This is the fact that, in order to find that a suspended or discharged employee was not disciplined for just cause, an arbitrator must not only make a finding of "not guilty," but must also take the difficult step of revoking a penalty already imposed. In many cases this involves thousands of dollars of lost time, thus creating at least the appearance of an added element of pressure motivating the arbitrator not to overturn management's action.

No arbitrator should make the mistake of treating a discharge as a "run of the mill" case. A discharge is the most important event in an employee's life, perhaps barring death or a similar catastrophe. Hence, the opinion in a discharge case must reflect much more than simply a finding of guilt or innocence; the opinion must be highly sensitive to the necessity that all concerned feel they have received their "day in court."

A major proportion of discipline cases involve conflicting testimony, which necessitates credibility findings. It does not help the arbitration process to see opinions (fortunately, they are few in number) in which the grievant's testimony is characterized as self-serving while reliance is placed on a foreman's testimony on the theory that the foreman had no reasonable motive to lie. In the mind of the worker this is tantamount to an arbitrator's finding that supervision or management is honorable and the worker is not.

Similarly, I occasionally see a close case that seems to turn on the time-worn issue of whether guilt beyond a reasonable doubt or preponderance of the evidence is to be the standard of proof. This sort of theorizing in an arbitration opinion does little to advance either a specific case or the arbitration process. More important, however, is the fact that when an arbitrator adopts a lesser standard of proof in his opinion, this necessarily reinforces the workers' feeling that he is being viewed as a lower-class individual.

It is these kinds of problems that contribute to the workers' suspicion that arbitrators possess a middle-class bias and suffer from a cultural lag and a generation gap. Add this to the existing antagonism which flows from the failure of the system to apply the common principles of democratic justice and one can readily see why discipline opinions are threatening the viability of the arbitration process.

Great social and cultural changes are taking place in America, and most certainly in the workplace. There is a new, younger workforce, made up of tens of millions of well-educated Americans—zealous in defense of their freedoms, demanding of their rights, motivated by new values, searching for self-identity, wanting to have personal pride in their own achievements, capable of becoming deeply involved in their work, and ready and able to expend a far greater effort if given the proper encouragement and opportunity.

This new generation, seeking a more enjoyable and purposeful life, is placing demands on all of us to democratize the workplace, improve the work environment, and open up the system so that they can become involved in all facets of their working life. In view of the stern realities of declining American industrial competitiveness, we can no longer avoid the obvious conclusion that outmoded management methods—autocratic rule enforced by harsh disciplinary practices—result in an alienated workforce, inefficient production, poor quality, and a restricted union-company relationship.

There are some encouraging joint union-company programs to forge new styles of participative management with employee

involvement in decision-making. In basic steel, these cooperative efforts arise under the 1980 Experimental Agreement which
provided for Labor-Management Participation Teams, more
commonly known as LMPTs. That agreement states in part:

> "Collective bargaining has proven to be a successful instrument
> in achieving common goals and objectives in the employment rela-
> tionship between steel labor and steel management. However, there
> are problems of a continuing nature at the level of the work site
> which significantly impact that relationship. Solutions to these prob-
> lems are vital if the quality of work for employees is to be enhanced
> and if the proficiency of the business enterprise is to be improved.
>
> "The parties recognize that a cooperative approach between em-
> ployees and supervision at the work site in a department or similar
> unit is essential to the solution of problems affecting them. Many
> problems at this level are not readily subject to resolution under
> existing contractual programs and practices, but affect the ongoing
> relationships between labor and management at that level. Joint
> participation in solving these problems at the departmental level is
> an essential ingredient in any effort to improve the effectiveness of
> the company's performance and to provide employees with a mea-
> sure of involvement adding dignity and worth to their work life.
>
> "In pursuit of these objectives, the parties believe that local union
> and plant management at the plant can best implement this cooper-
> ative approach through the establishment of Participation Teams of
> employees and supervision in departments or similar units at the
> plant."

In view of the demonstrated success of our LMPT programs,
I am tempted to bend your ears about the great potential of this
concept. Suffice it to say that I am convinced there will be profound changes in disciplinary systems and rules, work attitudes,
managerial prerogatives, union concern for quality and production, grievance priority vs. LMPT responsibilities, and the status
of management and workers. Moreover, these changes may well
take place without any significant change in the contract language.

As these new concepts unfold, many disputes will undoubtedly arise. Once again, arbitration opinions may be necessary to
help bridge the gap. This, in turn, will require that the arbitrator
understand what is happening in the workplace.

Let me conclude by observing that I assume that all who are
trying to break into the ranks of the arbitration profession can
write with clarity and logic. If not, they don't belong in this
league. As I have tried to demonstrate in various ways in this
paper, the key to writing a good opinion is being fully informed

as to the entire case, including the parties, the related problems, the underlying tensions, and of course, the facts and issues of the case at hand. Then all of this knowledge must be encompassed in an opinion, written so that the losing party can accept the decision and not feel that the system has let him down, and so that, in the process, the parties' abilities to improve their relationships are enhanced. This is the "Art of Opinion Writing."

## III.

### RICHARD MITTENTHAL*

The arbitrator's job is divided into three fairly distinct tasks: hearing the case, making a decision, and writing the opinion.[1] The hearing demands some rulings, perhaps clarification of the issue or the evidence, but our choices tend to be limited. Decision-making offers us more discretion, although here too we are limited to a considerable extent by the parties' arguments, by the way the issues have been framed. Opinion-writing, however, provides us with an almost limitless number of choices. Which arguments should we use? Which should we discard? What facts should we stress? Where is the ultimate reality in the dispute? The possibilities in drafting the opinion—from the standpoint of organization, content, style, language, overall tone, and so on—involve a feast of discretion.

Arbitrators spend more time writing opinions than doing any other part of their job. Yet the Academy has devoted practically no time at all to this subject. That may be because opinion-writing has always been regarded as a highly individualistic affair which does not lend itself to generalization. Or perhaps we simply do not wish to divulge trade secrets. Whatever the reason, I believe there are generalizations which can be drawn about *good* opinion-writing. That is the purpose of this paper.

Let me begin with a few basic propositions. How we prepare an opinion is influenced to some degree by the audience for whom we write. I think the primary audience should be those in the employment community out of which the grievance arose.

---

*Member, National Academy of Arbitrators, Birmingham, Mich.
[1]In the more difficult cases, decision-making and opinion-writing may merge and become a single exercise.

That would include the aggrieved employee, his union representative, supervision within his department, and labor relations personnel. These are the people who experienced the problem; these are the people who need to be persuaded that the arbitrator's solution is sound and sensible. Such an audience suggests that the opinion be written simply without resort to Latin phrases, legal maxims, arbitration precedents, and other useless baggage. Such an audience is more likely to be convinced by a straightforward analysis of the facts and of the contract. Should we write for a larger audience, for publication in BNA reports, or for gratification of our egos, we run the risk of saying far more than is necessary. The temptation then is to elaborate, to go beyond the instant case to hypothetical situations and general principles and thus raise new questions. This kind of mischief should be avoided.

How we write the opinion is influenced to an even greater degree by our view of the purpose of the opinion. Surely all of us would agree that our essential purpose is to make a clear, concise, and compelling statement of why we decided the case the way we did. But there is, I believe, a deeper purpose. That is to attempt to convince the losing party that it had to lose and thus set the underlying dispute to rest.

Certain opinion-writing behavior flows from acceptance of these purposes. Convincing the loser demands a strong argument. The opinion must focus on justifying a given result. It must persuade. It must have a point of view. It must be muscular, linear, and single-minded. It must carry the reader forward, point by point, through the puzzle so that he can see by the final sentence that the arbitrator had no choice but to rule as he did.

An example would be useful. Suppose the arbitrator is confronted by a dispute in which the merits seem evenly divided—the dreaded 50-50 case. A common approach is to prepare an opinion that expresses the closeness of the issue and the difficulties in reaching a decision. Such baring of the soul, however, is not conducive to persuasion. The more committed the arbitrator is to the 50-50 scenario, the more likely his decision will appear to have turned on some relatively inconsequential factor. The arbitrator will have needlessly placed in the parties' minds the image of a coin being flipped in the air. The loser is likely to feel that if another arbitrator heard the case, or if the arbitrator who actually heard it had gotten out of bed on the other side the morning he made his decision, the result would have been different.

The better approach is that the arbitrator, once having arrived at a decision, should forcefully argue for his position. He should not dwell upon how troublesome the issue was. It may have been a 50-50 case when he began to study it, but by the time he makes his decision, he has transformed it into a 55-45 proposition at the very least.[2] There is no need to detail in the opinion the struggle the arbitrator experienced in moving from his initial 50-50 impression to his final 55-45 view. That would serve no useful purpose. The opinion should simply make clear that one party does have the better argument and the reasons why. Perhaps this requires some dissembling—that is, making it appear as if the case were easier to decide than it actually was. But I believe that such dissembling does the parties a service by increasing the arbitrator's chances of persuading the loser and thus increasing the possibility of setting the dispute to rest.

I recognize that the parties are not always concerned with winning and losing. They sometimes care less about the result than they do about the arbitrator's analysis. They simply seek direction. Here, too, the arbitrator's ability to persuade is vital. His views are far more likely to be heeded if his opinion is compelling, if he can show that his solution to the problem is sensible. There is no substitute for a tightly reasoned and well crafted opinion.

Obviously, what the arbitrator says is critical, but what he avoids saying may be more critical. Opinion-writing demands self-restraint. One must constantly be on guard, in reviewing a draft opinion, for the sentences and phrases that have a potential for trouble-making. The danger is not that the arbitrator will say too little but rather that he will say too much. Some arguments should not be made in an opinion because they are certain to invite new controversies. Some should be omitted because they raise matters that have not been mentioned by the parties.[3] Some should be ignored because they constitute dicta —that is, authoritative pronouncements on questions not before the arbitrator for decision. The arbitrator must apply his red

---

[2]From the arbitrator's perspective, there is no such thing as a 50-50 case. We are obligated by our job to convince ourselves that one party or the other has more than 50 percent of the merit on any issue before us. That exercise, in occasional cases, probably involves an element of self-deception.

[3]This restraint can and should be ignored on occasion. For example, where the parties fail to argue the case properly and ignore crucial points, the arbitrator may have no choice but to explore matters not covered by the parties in an attempt to provide a sensible answer to the dispute. I explore this problem further later in this paper.

pencil to more than argument. He must also ferret out irrelevancy, redundancy, unsupported statements, gratuitous advice, and idle philosophizing. A good motto for this kind of pruning is: If in doubt, leave it out.

Dicta pose a special problem. Most arbitrators agree that dicta should be avoided to the maximum extent possible, but there are cases where the use of dicta is almost unavoidable. Sometimes, for instance, it may be difficult to explain what a contract clause means without first stating what it does not mean. Or it may be difficult to explain what a contract clause means without first stating what some other related clause means. Sometimes the issue is presented in such broad terms that it cannot be discussed sensibly without first drawing some firm conclusions about matters not before the arbitrator for decision. In these and similar situations, dicta may have an irresistible appeal. Caution is nevertheless appropriate. The arbitrator should employ dicta only when his opinion would not otherwise be sufficiently strong. If he can write a persuasive opinion without resort to dicta, he should do so.[4]

One of the worst examples of lack of self-restraint can be found in opinions that seek to curry favor with the parties. The benign form of this disease is the act of applauding the rhetorical skill of the parties' spokesmen. The malignancy occurs when, as the saying goes, the arbitrator "throws a bone to the loser."[5] I refer to the arbitrator who goes out of his way to express agreement with one or more points made by the loser even though such agreement has absolutely no bearing on the rationale for the decision. This kind of opinion-writing is deplorable.

Another fundamental problem, closely related to self-restraint, arises from the parties' own shortcomings. Both employers and unions often fail to prepare their cases as well as they should. Typically, they cover 80 or 90 percent of the matter. They overlook a crucial contract clause, they fail to see a significant line of argument, or they disregard an important fact which has been introduced in evidence. The arbitrator studies the record and discovers the missing 10 to 20 percent. To what extent, if at all, should his opinion rely on these missing points?

---

[4]The discussion in this paragraph assumes that the arbitrator is reasonably confident that his dicta are correct.

[5]Sometimes the parties describe this disease in terms of the arbitrator "giving the language to one side and the decision to the other."

No simple answer is possible. *Ignored facts,* where relevant, should be used in the opinion. That is what happens in practice. No one seems to be troubled by such arbitral behavior because the ignored fact is indeed part of the record of the proceeding.

*Ignored arguments* are troublesome. I have no problem placing such an argument in the opinion so long as it is closely related to what the parties have asserted, so long as it is consistent with the parties' theory of the case. The arbitrator, in these circumstances, is merely recasting the ideas before him in an attempt to provide a more realistic or more rational view of the dispute. His argument may be new, but it is a reasonable outgrowth of the materials the parties themselves have placed before him. The danger is that he will go further and develop an argument that has absolutely nothing to do with the parties' theory of the case.[6] Then he will be on questionable ground, for he cannot know what the parties' views would be on the new argument he is raising. He cannot know whether his argument could withstand the parties' probing. He acts without the benefit of the parties' guidance and, hence, substantially enlarges the possibility of making an error.

*Ignored contract clauses* pose a similar difficulty. My view is that such a clause ordinarily should not be used in opinions.[7] The arbitrator has no idea what the parties' interpretations of that clause might be. He knows nothing of the bargaining history. He knows nothing of the past practice with respect to the clause. All of us are familiar with contract language which seems clear on its face, but has been given strange and unexpected meaning by the parties. Should the arbitrator enter this thicket and rely on the ignored clause in writing his opinion, he increases the possibility of error, and this kind of error could turn out to be a serious and costly matter for the parties. The fact is that arbitrators are not omniscient. We do not know enough to make a definitive statement about an ignored clause. That could be

---

[6]The more sophisticated the parties and the more comprehensive their presentations, the less likely an arbitrator will attempt such a new argument. The less sophisticated the parties and the less comprehensive their presentations, the more likely an arbitrator will attempt such an argument.

I confess I have not followed the above admonition where the parties are so unsophisticated or poorly represented that their arguments fail to address the real issue in the dispute.

[7]The exceptions would, I suspect, depend on such considerations as the contract's restrictions on the arbitrator's authority, the submission agreement's reference to a specific contract clause, the adequacy (or inadequacy) of the parties' presentations, and the arbitrator's familiarity with the parties.

remedied, of course, by the arbitrator asking the parties for their views on the applicability of the ignored clause before he makes his decision in the case. But that approach also raises troublesome questions.

If the arbitrator can write a convincing opinion without these ignored materials, he should do so. The questions I have raised come into play only where the arbitrator believes his opinion will not be strong enough without the ignored argument or the ignored contract clause.

My comments on self-restraint can be translated into a simple message. Opinions should, to the greatest extent possible, attempt to honor the reasonable expectations of the parties. Those expectations can usually be gleaned from the evidence and arguments presented at the hearing and in the posthearing briefs. The theories we concoct in our opinions should flow from such evidence and arguments. They should not come as a total surprise to the parties. An opinion is far more likely to be accepted if we keep these expectations in mind as we write.

Acceptability is influenced by other factors as well. Behind many disputes there is a core reality unstated by the parties. Consider, for instance, the struggle in work-assignment problems between the union's interest in stability and management's need for flexibility. That reality may not be helpful in deciding the case, but its description in the opinion may serve to place the issue in sharper focus or provide the kind of background which will help to make the opinion more compelling.

Acceptability can be enhanced by the arbitrator's descriptive powers. Many disputes involve complex machinery or complex work processes or complex organizational relationships. To the extent the arbitrator can master this complexity and demonstrate his mastery in the opinion, he increases his chances of persuading the parties that he fully understood the problem. The better the description, the more credible his opinion is likely to be.

Acceptability is no doubt the reason why some arbitrators cite published awards extensively in their opinions. They seek to demonstrate through precedent that their views are consistent with what other arbitrators have said. Such behavior assumes, mistakenly I think, that published awards somehow represent a common law of arbitration. The fact is, however, that these awards arise from a bewildering variety of contracts, and each contract has its own distinct bargaining history and past practice. To say that a ruling in a farm equipment-UAW plant should be given weight in a basic steel-Steelworkers mill is nonsense, no matter how similar the cases may be. Moreover, the parties presumably hire an arbitrator for his judgment on the dispute before him. They are not getting what they contracted for if his opinion in the case is based largely on what other arbitrators have said in other relationships. Such an opinion, in Ben Aaron's words, "creates the impression that the writer did not trust his own judgment" and "is . . . [thus] self-demeaning and odious."[8]

None of this is meant to lessen the importance of precedent within a given relationship. Obviously, an arbitrator should honor previous awards for the same parties so long as those awards are in point and are not clearly in error.[9]

I turn now to matters of organization and style. To start with, far too many opinions begin with a statement of facts without any hint as to what the dispute is all about. Not until the middle of the opinion is the issue explained. This serves to frustrate the reader. The remedy is clear. Every opinion should begin with a brief introductory paragraph that sets forth the nature of the dispute.[10] One can then read the facts with some understanding of their significance.

As for the statement of facts, it can best be written after the decision in the case is fixed in the arbitrator's mind. The facts should nevertheless be couched in a neutral tone. But the choice of facts and the order of their presentation should relate in some way to how the arbitrator is going to decide the dispute. They should be shaped by what is to come. There is no point in reciting facts that have no bearing whatever on the parties' arguments or the arbitrator's ruling. There is no point in describing the facts at great length in this initial statement if the arbitrator intends to explore them in detail later in support of his decision.

As for the parties' arguments, they should be integrated into the arbitrator's discussion wherever possible.[11] Many opinions

---

[8]Aaron, *Arbitration Decisions and the Law of the Shop*, 29 Labor L.J. 536, 542 (1978).

[9]Where industry-wide bargaining exists and much the same language appears in every contract, an arbitrator may properly rely on previous awards within the industry.

[10]For example, the opening paragraph in a discharge case might be: John Doe was discharged on January 1, 1982, for insubordination. The Union insists that he was not insubordinate and that, even if he had been, the penalty imposed was excessive. It believes, accordingly, that his discharge was unjustified. It seeks prompt reinstatement with back pay.

[11]In the more important cases, it may be advisable to have the parties' positions fully described before the arbitrator's discussion.

contain a recitation of each side's argument and then a discussion, which often is little more than a rehash of the winner's argument. The reader is forced to cover the same ground twice. That is not a formula for capturing the reader's attention and admiration. A better approach, I believe, is to express the loser's argument and then discuss its flaws and weaknesses. No doubt that discussion will sometimes be a simple restatement of the winner's argument, but the opinion will read much better and the winner is not likely to complain about the failure to give equal space to its argument.

As for the arbitrator's discussion, the format will vary from case to case. His answer to a grievance can be constructed in many ways. He can mix fact, contract, and equity in a great variety of combinations. There is no one correct method. The materials themselves tend to dictate the arbitrator's choice of format. Whatever the choice, it is likely to be validated by an argument that flows smoothly and has an inner consistency.

Some other points are worth mentioning. The arbitrator's discussion should express his view of the dispute in his own words. He should not quote the winner's brief in responding to the loser's argument.[12] That kind of opinion-writing suggests that the arbitrator is incapable of independent analysis and can do little more than parrot the views of others. Moreover, he should respond to all of the loser's arguments. There is nothing more frustrating to the loser than having an argument ignored and thus rejected without reason. I realize that some arguments are so absurd that they cannot be answered without the arbitrator appearing to be equally absurd. In such situations, it should suffice to note briefly in the opinion that this argument lacks merit.

As for the award, the actual disposition of the grievance, there is no point in repeating what has already been said in the discussion. Ordinarily, it is enough to state simply that the grievance is granted, denied, or granted in part and denied in part. And, if granted, it is appropriate to describe what exactly the employer should do to correct the violation. Of course, in those cases which are submitted through a stipulated issue, it is enough to say that this issue is answered in the negative or the affirmative.

---

[12]However, there is nothing wrong with quoting from the parties' briefs at an earlier stage of the opinion in describing the parties' arguments. That is often useful when their arguments are difficult to paraphrase.

Our opinions tend to make dreary reading. A disinterested person would have to possess a strong will to wade through many of the opinions that cross my desk. I have sometimes wondered whether interested persons—the parties immediately involved in the dispute—take the trouble to read the entire opinion. And I admit I occasionally have trouble rereading my own decisions.

The drabness is, I suspect, attributable to several factors. First, the subject matter often does not lend itself to graceful exposition. Try preparing an opinion in a job-evaluation case which turns on the question of whether a widget-builder's responsibility for tools and equipment demands "*moderate* attention and care" or "*close* attention and care." Second, the arbitrator is not free to write as he wishes. He is given a set of facts, competing arguments, and contract language. He must ordinarily work with these materials, nothing more. Such limitations can stifle the writer's imagination. Third, an arbitrator who writes more than 100 opinions a year "usually lacks sufficient time to develop or to nourish an acceptable writing style. When opinion-writing becomes a dreary chore, grace and elegance of style cannot survive."[13] Finally, many arbitrators seem to believe that the parties view the quality of the opinion as a secondary matter. They feel the parties are concerned with the "bottom line," the result, and little else. This kind of cynicism, whether justified or not, serves to undermine the quest for excellence.

Drabness is not inevitable. Opinions ideally should have the balance and grace of a Mozart piano concerto, the strength and directness of a Rodin sculpture. But this is not an ideal world. Such perfection cannot be achieved with a mere two days of study time. Nevertheless, opinion-writing can be improved if we pay more attention to matters of style. My emphasis on style is not just a personal idiosyncrasy or an aesthetic interest. It is a conviction as to how arbitrators can best be understood. It is an appeal for simplicity, directness, and lucidity.

I recognize that each arbitrator develops his own unique style. I recognize, too, that there is no one best method of expression. Hence, my remarks are aimed more to what should be avoided than to what should be done. Let me point to some common failings.

It is not enough to write sentences that are grammatically

---

[13]Aaron, *supra* note 8, at 539.

correct. As Aaron has noted, ". . . one can ingest just so many pages filled with simple declarative sentences, unvaried by an occasional venturesome independent clause or a single felicitous phrase, before giving up and turning to what the writer of the opinion might well refer to as the 'bottom line,' that is, the award."[14]

It is not enough to paste together pieces of the transcript, the briefs, and the contract along with a few short personal observations and then leap to a conclusion. The arbitrator's presence should be felt. His opinion is supposed to involve the kind of careful analysis and reasoned argument that will convince the parties that he fully understood the problem.

It is not enough to list, briefly and numerically, the factors which led to a given decision. Such opinions have a sense of incompleteness. The arbitrator should consider the weight of these factors, and his opinion should reflect their relative importance. He should bind his ideas together through suitable transition phrases. His explanation should thus carry the reader forward, step by step, to the conclusion.

It is not enough to prepare an opinion which is merely contractually correct. The arbitrator must go further. He should be sensitive to the parties' needs and the practical impact of his words. For example, if he is deciding a credibility question, he may be accurate in stating that the foreman's testimony was a "pack of lies," but that statement might well destroy the relationship between the foreman and the employees he supervises. By muting his words, the arbitrator can make the same ruling without damaging the foreman's ability to function.[15]

An even better example is the arbitrator's choice between broad and narrow rationales for a given result. Both may appear to be perfectly sound, but because there is always the possibility of error, a decent self-restraint suggests the use of the narrow rationale.

Style demands an appreciation of shadings and subtleties. Arbitrators properly devote time to such questions as to whether an act should be described as "reasonable" or "not unreasonable." Style demands an appreciation of the uses of ambiguity. Arbitrators sometimes should not be explicit. We may be doing the parties and ourselves a favor by deliberately

---

[14]*Ibid.*
[15]Arbitrators' concern for their own acceptability results in their writing opinions in such a way as to avoid making the parties look bad.

placing an ambiguous phrase or argument into an opinion. Style demands an appreciation of those aspects of a case that are better left unmentioned. Arbitrators correctly ignore materials which have a potential for causing unnecessary trouble. The list is endless.[16]

Nothing I have said is meant to suggest that "art" is more important than substance. I am certain that the parties are more interested in a sound decision than an artful opinion. Arbitrators, faced with such a choice, would also opt for the right answer to the dispute. However, there is no reason why we cannot be both sound and artful. Opinions need not be dreary reading. We have the skills and experience to make our opinions more clear, more concise, and more compelling. What we have to do is to spend more time with the kinds of questions I have raised in this paper. Speed is not compatible with the high degree of selectivity necessary for good opinion-writing. Only those who are willing to spend extra hours at their drafting tables are likely to prepare *a quality product.* And that should always be our objective. We owe it to ourselves, no less than to the parties.

## Discussion—

MARK KAHN: I was very pleased to hear from some of the speakers, particularly the two partisan speakers on the essentially neutral subject, indications of the value of an opinion being reviewed by and with the parties through the medium of a tripartite board, or perhaps a discussion of the case by a tripartite board even before the opinion is written. I bring this up because I think most arbitrators prefer to operate as sole arbitrators. Because of the industries in which some of us arbitrate, we have had more exposure to tripartite boards, and in spite of the fact that the procedure is somewhat cumbersome, may cause additional delays, and so forth, I think it greatly enhances the quality of the product. I wonder if any of the speakers would think it appropriate to urge the parties who have not experimented with tripartite grievance arbitration boards to consider investing in that kind of procedure.

---

[16]One of my pet peeves is the impersonal reference to ourselves as "the arbitrator" or "the undersigned" instead of "I." It seems to me the arbitrator is a flesh-and-blood "I," not some disembodied presence.

MR. BERNSTEIN: I have worked with tripartite boards, and I have the view that they have been eminently successful. The problem, I suppose, with a tripartite board—and I've heard it expressed by others many times—is that all it does is drive you back to extend the arguments and the hearing to the executive session. The partisans find it very difficult to discipline themselves to the point where they can approach an executive session with the kind of objectivity that's implied in the concept of an award of a tripartite board. I'm not sure how you develop that discipline in new areas. Some parties have a long history of using tripartite boards and do not have to develop the discipline. Perhaps an alternative approach suggested by Syl Garrett might have some merit: not setting up a formal tripartite board, but simply testing on the parties an opinion which you suspect has some trouble with it, or may create some problems for them. That doesn't go the full way, but I think that would help solve some of the problems that Dick talked about and avoid what Sam described as the opinion's simply going too far because of the arbitrator's ignorance of what he is doing.

MR. CAMENS: I think the parties would all agree that we have had great success over the years with the U.S. Steel Board and now with the Iron Ore Range Board. We do not have a tripartite board arrangement, and I don't believe in it because it involves all kinds of rehashing of the case, minority opinions, and all the rest. What we have is an arrangement where a union member and a management member are liaison to the boards; they get draft opinions and they review them. In 50 to 75 percent of the cases, they telephone the arbitrator and say, "Fine. No comment." In, say, 15 percent there are a few generalizations that we think ought to be eliminated because they will get us into trouble later on, or we think a little tightening up or a little more explanation is needed. We find we're in dispute in maybe 5 percent of the cases where we think that either the determination of the facts or the application of the contract is not accurate. Then we might get into an executive-type discussion of these points—but with the understanding, of course, that the arbitrator is ultimately responsible for the opinion. The two people—the union member and the management member—are there in kind of an advisory capacity.

I want to mention here something we haven't discussed. Our system is the greatest training ground in the world for young new arbitrators because they're involved if there is more than one arbitrator on the board. They are associate arbitrators, and their opinions might be up for discussion and careful analysis; and then they hear why somebody thinks there ought to be some changes, for whatever reasons. I think that this exposure enhances the development of an arbitrator. One of the great problems is that an arbitrator can put out opinion after opinion and nobody ever says a word about whether they are good or bad—and he may be doing an awful job. Then suddenly he's not on the list anymore, and he doesn't know why. I think that the discussion process, with the collaboration of the parties, is most important in an arbitrator's development.

MR. MITTENTHAL: I think one can inject the parties into the opinion-writing process without a formal tripartite board. On rare occasions, for instance, I've had difficult cases in ad hoc situations where I have gone to the parties and suggested, in view of the seriousness of the issues involved, that I was not only willing, but would appreciate their reviewing the opinion with me prior to its formal issuance. And that offer has almost always been accepted, and the results of the discussions that I've had have been very fruitful and sometimes have resulted in the modification of the rationale or changes in important language. I think that the tripartite concept in terms of its influence upon opinion-writing is extremely important, and I don't think it has been fully explored by the parties.

ROBERT COULSON: Let me make the kind of radical proposal that one can make if one is not an arbitrator. I've read a number of arbitration awards, and I think it would be a great convenience to the parties and to others of us who are interested in your work product if you would get away from the traditional court-decision format—the mystery-novel format—of having to go to the very end to find out what the result is. You might summarize the decision early on in the first page. Then some of us wouldn't go on and read any more, but others of us would then be more interested in what your rationale was and how the facts looked to you. I know that's terribly radical, but even the court publishing companies do summarize the decision up front, and that saves a lot of time for many scholars and people interested in the common law. I think the same thing might be true in the labor arbitration field, and I say that with great diffidence and recognition that it's a radical idea.

PETER SEITZ: In the discussion of the art of opinion-writing, should we not include the art of no opinion-writing? There are certain cases—and I am not saying that there are very many of them—where no matter how much one writes, and no matter how carefully one writes, you're not going to persuade anyone because the decision comes out of the viscera. I know there are cases of that sort, and perhaps these 49/51 percent cases fall to some extent in that category. There is also a certain percentage of cases in which the parties are interested only in the result and not in an opinion. Now how did all of this opinion-writing happen to come about—simply because unthinkingly a number of arbitrators followed the course of common law judges and wrote opinions? I'm not saying that we shouldn't have opinions. Of course we need opinions to express the rationale of the decision. But it occurs to me that in a certain number of cases, at the end of the case the arbitrator could bring the advocates to the front of the table and say, "Do you really want an opinion in this case? How about just getting a decision—an award?" I have tried that in several cases. If delay and expense are two of the problems of arbitration, why shouldn't we try cutting down on opinions in cases where they can be dispensed with?

ELLIOT BEITNER: Mr. Mittenthal has expressed his judgment that quoting authority and citations is probably counterproductive and reflects someone else's thinking rather than the arbitrator's own decision-making process. Although I am over 50 years of age, I am referred to by many as "the kid," and being a "kid" without the national reputation of our speakers, I think perhaps that many parties require more than my own persuasiveness. While I agree, stylistically, that the purest approach may be to reason out an opinion and have your arguments support it, I also believe that the citation of authority or even of other cases that have similar facts can be of considerable persuasiveness for the parties.

DAVID FELLER: When I listened to Dick Mittenthal's description of the process of decision-writing, it sounded, almost word-for-word, like what I say to my students in appellate advocacy when I tell them how to write a brief. That raises a serious question, and I don't know the answer. What the argument seems to be is whether opinion-writing is advocacy-writing. You want to persuade the loser that he ought to have lost, which is very much the same as trying to persuade a court when you are writing a brief, and I'm not sure whether that really does serve the parties' interest. Now this gets back to the 51/49 percent kind of question. I have written opinions where I've said, "This

is a very close question—a question of contractual interpretation." After having set out fully my doubts about the question
and the reasons for the doubts, I say, "Although it is a very close
question, I find that this little bit of word here is the thing that
persuades me." This may not be very persuasive for the parties
who would prefer an argument which sets out the conclusion I
have reached in the strongest possible way. It seems to me that
that is really not the question where I think you and I differ, and
it's not the question which we ought to decide. I would like to
hear from the parties as to which kind of opinion best serves
their purposes because, after all, that's the reason we're in business.

MR. CAMENS: I think we're talking about instances where arbitrators, considering a given set of facts under the same contract
provisions, come out with different answers. What's important
in that type of decision is for the arbitrator to make clear that
under this particular set of facts, he is making this particular
decision, but under the same contract with another set of facts,
he might come out with a different decision. You have to be
careful in these cases to make it very clear that this one fact was
the basis for this decision, whereas if the facts were different,
your decision might be different. The important thing is to state
clearly the fact or facts that support the decision you make.

MR. BERNSTEIN: I would prefer that the arbitrator tell me
precisely what he had to go through, and if it was a tough
decision, I'd like him to tell me so. And I have a very pragmatic
reason. If I win, what's the difference, but if I lose, I want to tell
my client how close a case we had and that we really almost made
it.

THOMAS RINALDO: I have a more elementary question. In a
recent lengthy case, I asked the two attorneys to submit detailed
posthearing briefs, since I planned to eliminate citing or typing
out the contract clauses and the positions of the parties in my
opinion. When the final product came out of the typewriter, it
just seemed a little too skimpy, and I decided to reinsert the
contract clauses and the positions of the parties. I somehow had
this feeling that the quality of my opinion is directly related to
the quantity of pages. I would like to hear from the parties what
their views would be if they received a decision without all the
contract clauses and their positions recited.

MR. CAMENS: I have an aversion to all that recitation. Why did
we pay $500 or $1000 to have repeated what we already know

about our contract clauses? What we want from the arbitrator is for him to tell us precisely why he used this clause or that one. The worst opinions I've seen are those in which the arbitrator not only repeats and types out four pages of contract clauses, but he also types out three pages of verbatim evidence from the third-step minutes that are already attached to the record. Great costs are being incurred when, in a very short paragraph, you could have summed up the reasons why you relied on some fact in your award. You don't have to repeat what the foreman said. I've seen this create great problems because when the decision gets down to the grievant and he sees three pages of what the foreman said—what he didn't agree with in the first place—he begins to wonder about the fairness of the arbitration process. You've got to think about the grievant's reaction. For the process to work, he has to feel that he has had an honest day in court. Arbitrators are hired to dig out what they believe are the facts and to put in very concise and understandable language why they are relying on these facts and what sections of the contract are involved. I hope that along the way the arbitrator establishes his credibility so that everyone accepts his decision and the dispute is disposed of.

MR. BERNSTEIN: The problem you raise, I think, depends on the bargaining history. If my client is newly organized and is having his first arbitration, I would like very much for you to go into as much detail as you sometimes do—contract clauses, the arguments, the whole business—so that he understands that he has had his day in court. If I have a sophisticated client who has been through this over and over again, you can make the award one paragraph long and it's perfectly alright. And again, there's nothing wrong with your asking the parties themselves: What do you fellows want? Do you want a 20-page job, or do you want a half-page job? I have a situation right now where I hope I get a nice long one. I don't care how it goes, but I want that client to know that this is a very fair process. The fellow is in his first arbitration. He has the notion that arbitrators are all liberals, they're all crooked, and they never find for the employer, and if he's going to lose this one, I want him to know why he lost.

DALLAS JONES: I have been hearing in this discussion that we should explain our positions, and one position which always seems to me to be unexplainable is on what basis you decide a credibility issue. I must confess that I've given up trying to explain to the parties why I do it. I simply write that I accept one position. The testimony was credible or it was not. I wonder how you feel about that, Dick.

MR. MITTENTHAL: I think that there are cases in which one can explain in some detail why the credibility finding is going in one direction rather than another, and to the extent that you can do that, I think you should. But I agree that there are some cases in which it really is inexplicable. It's simply a reaction to everything that took place at the hearing and in your review of the testimony, and there's nothing wrong with simply concluding that A or B is not a credible witness.

MR. JONES: It seems to me that some of the strangest decisions I have read are those in which the arbitrator tries to explain why he decided that credibility issue. I am sure it must have been right; all arbitrators obviously are right. But if I were a party reading one of those, I would have real difficulty with it. I'd like to hear from the parties on that. When you have a real credibility issue, are you satisfied with our saying, "This is the decision"?

MR. CAMENS: I would have a real problem with it because, as I said, the whole discharge process is suspect because of its very nature. The great problem we have is to maintain the credibility of this process that is so important to us. All discharge cases are based on credibility, and when you are considering contradictory evidence and, without any explanation, you say that you have accepted one person's version rather than another's, I don't see how anyone can accept that as credible. In a discharge case there's got to be some basis for finding an employee guilty. There has to be, at least, a preponderance of the evidence or guilt beyond a reasonable doubt. We're talking about capital punishment in an industrial setting. If your decision is based on only a "gut feeling," then the grievant is not guilty. That's a principle of democracy that we don't take lightly. Arbitration is supposed to be a worker's forum that he accepts, and unless it is acceptable as democratic, it will be doomed and we will go back to the chaos that we used to have in these plants. If I leave no other message here today, it is this: We must begin to understand the great uneasiness over democratic principles that is rampant in these plants. We must begin to understand the feelings of this new generation of workers about this problem—their desires and their zealousness for freedom and the protection of their rights. Industrial plants are no different from all of society. And you who are involved in the arbitration process have got to understand, if you understand nothing more, that if arbitration is going to be a viable process, it has to be a viable process for the workers.

# CHAPTER 5

# ADMISSIBILITY OF EVIDENCE

This chapter consists of a collated set of excerpts from the transcripts of six separate workshops on "Admissibility of Evidence" in which members and guests of the National Academy of Arbitrators participated at their Washington meeting. Each portion of the discussion was preceded by a segment of a video-tape of a mock arbitration hearing, the script for which was prepared by Arnold M. Zack and Richard I. Bloch. The roles of company and union counsel were performed, respectively, by Norman White of Harrisburg, Pa., and George Cohen of Washington, D.C. The Academy acknowledges its deep appreciation for their participation and absolves them of all responsibility for the content of their presentations. Discussion leaders for the workshops were Academy members Dana E. Eischen, Joseph F. Gentile, Margery F. Gootnick, Emily Maloney, William P. Murphy, and Carlton J. Snow. Theodore J. St. Antoine prepared and edited this summary.

## I. Grievant's Prior Employment Record

GEORGE COHEN: Good morning, Madam Arbitrator. It's nice to see you again, notwithstanding your ruling the last time we were before you. My name is George Cohen. I'm counselor for the union. This is the grievant, Susan Low, whose discharge is the subject of the hearing today. We have done at least one productive thing this morning—counsel for the company and I have stipulated as to the issue. It is whether or not the termination for the alleged theft was for just cause and, if not, what would the appropriate remedy be. In a case such as this where a discharge is being alleged for a theft, the burden rests on the company, and the company counsel will have to proceed.

NORMAN WHITE: We accept that burden with great glee in this case, Madam Arbitrator, for we have a thief among us. The thief is sitting right here—Ms. Low, Susan Low, who has stolen some

$450 worth of the company's product, which is soap, as you know, in this case. We'd like to start the proceeding by introducing the prior work history, which includes her performance, absenteeism, insubordination, tardiness, and just about everything else . . . [interrupted].

COHEN: Stop! Hold on a second here! Let's not get carried away with ourselves. We agreed to an issue. It is *one* issue and *one* issue alone. Did she or did she not engage in an act of theft? If she did, we have acknowledged that, even though this is a first-instance discipline, she would be properly subject to discharge. What her past history is about, Counselor, is no more relevant than what your or my past history is about. Let's get on with the day. Have you got a case?

WHITE: It is going to be shown at this hearing that the theft engaged in here was part of a pattern of conduct on the part of this employee which is proven positively by the prior performance as I've indicated . . . [interrupted].

COHEN: Absolutely not, Madam Arbitrator! I think we have to have a ruling at the outset. None of this background, this past history, is relevant. None of it should be permitted into the case. Any of it that comes in may be prejudicial to my client. Therefore, we ask you to rule immediately on the preliminary matter.

WHITE: We agree with that, Madam Arbitrator. You rule.

*Discussion*

1. How would *you* rule?
2. In what kind of case would you allow the grievant's prior record?

DANIEL KATZ: I'm a union advocate. I heard Mr. Cohen say that, in terms of the remedy, there was a stipulation on behalf of the employee that if she were found guilty of stealing, discharge was the appropriate remedy. So he wasn't going to contest the appropriateness of the penalty if the arbitrator found that there was a theft and that the employee was responsible for it. The evidence therefore can't come in as part of the evaluation of whether termination was an appropriate punishment. It can't come in either to prove whether the theft occurred because all the specifics that the employer representative cited were instances of poor employee conduct, but nothing that would prove a theft. Absenteeism was one of those I heard mentioned, and the other misdeeds were equally unconnected with whether an employee is likely to steal or not. There was thus no pattern or practice of theft that was attempted to be proven. Because there was no indication that the evidence was going to be relevant to either of those two issues, the arbitrator has to reject all of that employment record.

JOHN LONGBARN: Let me make the other argument as a representative of management. While the company agreed that theft was one of the issues, they then got into the remedy. Did they not say, "What shall be the remedy?" My experience in these hearings is that you always end up, if the employee's record is good, with the argument that the remedy is inappropriate in the circumstances of a long, good record. It seems to me that when the record is bad, the company is entitled to put on the other side since clearly the remedy is opened by the framing of the issue.

RICHARD KANNER: I think "just cause" has two facets—that is, the substance of the charge and the remedy—and so the past record is ordinarily admissible on the issue of remedy. But you have an unusual twist in this case. When the union representative stipulated that the discharge was appropriate if the theft was found, the remedy was no longer an issue. I therefore don't think that the past record would be admissible because it is not probative of any issue before the arbitrator.

BARRY BROWN: I would allow the employer's submission of this evidence. There are several theories. First, although the employer seems to have agreed that the only issue is the question of theft, in his arguments he immediately went into a "last-straw" theory in which the cumulative overall employment record of this employee justified discharge. And it would seem that that's inconsistent with his supposed agreement that the only issue was one of theft. Secondly, an arbitrator is usually faced with the question whether reinstatement is even a possibility, and it would seem that an employee's total employment history would influence the arbitrator on whether this employee could be a productive and useful employee if reinstated. Finally, it would appear that the overall record of the employee might go to the question of her intent and possibly credibility on the issue of theft.

NED COHEN: I think the point is you may not find theft, but you may find gross misconduct in handling of material with no intention of thievery. Material is still lost, and therefore the grievant is guilty of some omission or commission of a wrongdoing and is deserving a disciplinary penalty. At that point, to determine the extent of the proper disciplinary penalty, the past record is very important. If it is an all-or-nothing deal and everybody has agreed to that, however, and if I'm not an activist arbitrator, I accept their premises and, of course, it's not admissible.

EDWARD PINKISS: This kind of evidence is sometimes offered as bearing on credibility. Some of it may be very remote on credibility, but suppose some of it really does have a bearing on credibility—for example, prior instances of dishonesty of one kind or another. The temptation could be to say, "Well, it has a bearing on credibility." If you follow that temptation, and I'm not advocating it, can you back out when you're then faced with trying six prior incidents, mushrooming the case into four or five days of hearing? If you go down that path, you may never turn back.

BRUCE WAXMA: I represent a union. The charges against the employee in a discipline matter ought to be precise charges. Many contracts so provide. One of the problems with admitting the prior record is that usually it would not have been part of whatever offense the employee would have been charged with coming into the arbitration. I presume she was charged with stealing 400-odd dollars worth of soap. To permit the employer in this instance to bring in the past record makes it extremely difficult for the grievant to defend herself because it's unlikely that there was any such expectation on behalf of the grievant or counsel. They would have to defend against what is in effect an open-ended charge, and so I think it should be outside the scope of the proceeding.

GEORGE LARNEY: I think the arbitrator ought to ask whether there is anything in the parties' agreement that provides for the introduction of a past disciplinary record, because some contracts do provide for that. It is also relevant to have a past record if you have a system of progressive discipline. Or there may be allegations of disparate treatment, and the past record would be appropriate under those circumstances.

DAVID KABAKER: What I want to point out is that we are on opening statements here. They haven't presented any evidence yet. I think the request for admission of the past record isn't in order at this point. They have stated what the issue is. Now they are ready for testimony. I don't think we have to treat this question of the disciplinary record or the rest of her past history. It may not even come in. I think you should hold off any ruling on that at this time.

ALLEN WEISENFELD: An arbitration is presumed to be different from the proceedings in the civil and the criminal courts with respect to the rules of evidence. In this case, while the past record seems to be of no evidentiary value with respect to the charge that led to her discharge, to make an issue at the onset of the hearing seems to me almost pointless. The arbitrator might well say, "Look, I don't think the record is of any value, but if you insist upon letting it go in, I'll accept it merely to avoid an argument—a protracted argument over admissibility."

LEO WEISS: Admitting a document which I presume I'm not going to consider because it's irrelevant or prejudicial, but will let into the evidence in order to avoid an argument, doesn't strike me as proper arbitral practice. While we do not apply the rules of evidence strictly, we don't throw them out the window. Where a document is allowed into evidence, the union advocate cannot say to himself or to his client, "Well, that's a useless document. They're not going to get anywhere with that." Because whatever you say at the hearing, who knows what you'll do when you get back to the office? The document is in evidence and the arbitrator may change his mind. And what happens is that the union advocate is in the position of defending against three past incidents of discipline which the arbitrator has said he's not going to consider. That is going to extend the hearing and bring in a lot of other irrelevant material. I think it's a responsibility of the arbitrator under such circumstances to make a ruling. He must admit it or he may exclude it, depending on how he looks at it, but I don't think he can admit it on the basis that was stated earlier.

## II. Spotters' Reports

WHITE: Madam Arbitrator, as part of our evidence, at this point we would like to introduce the report of an outside, independent detective agency. This report is the compilation actually of reports of spotters who watched the soap area and saw the grievant take the soap without authorization.

COHEN: Absolutely not, Madam Arbitrator, absolutely not! We are talking here about triple hearsay. We are talking about a report. First, you tried to introduce evidence about my grievant's past history; now you want to bring in a document like that. Inadmissible!

WHITE: We have a right to submit the material that we used to form our decision to discharge this grievant. There is absolutely no question that the people involved are proper, righteous, and upstanding individuals, all of whom produced truthful reports which we wish to introduce to you today.

COHEN: All right. Here is what we will do, Counselor. We will stipulate that the detective agency, in fact, sent this report in and that the report was the basis upon which you terminated my client.

WHITE: Madam Arbitrator, we expect to have to put these reports in because the first spotter no longer works for our agency. He has taken an excellent job with another employer. He's gainfully employed. The second spotter unfortunately wishes to have his identity kept secret. We all know the history of this union, the manner in which they handle the people in this plant, and we cannot have his identity revealed. The third spotter has retired to Hawaii and is doing well there. Of course, you understand the expense involved in bringing him here.

COHEN: Well, Madam Arbitrator, I would have thought that at least my worthy opponent would understand that even I cannot cross-examine a report. You know that and I know that. Your three spotters can be anywhere in this world doing anything they want. That is their business. But if they are not here, then the document doesn't come in and nothing is admissible. You don't have a case against us, and we'll pack up our bags and go home.

WHITE: These reports were prepared by upstanding and decent people who are trying to root out the theft and impropriety in the plant. Madam Arbitrator, we urge you to find this document admissible.

*Discussion*

1. Would you admit the whole report? For what purpose?
2. Would you admit the reports of Spotter No. 1 who's gone? Spotter No. 2 who's still in the plant? Spotter No. 3 who's in Hawaii?
3. Under what circumstances would you admit such hearsay declarations without the author being present for cross-examination?

JONATHAN LIEBOWITZ: I think the answer is clearly that the report should not be admitted, and the reason is that, while the rules of evidence need not apply in arbitration, there are times when they should indeed apply. This is one of them, because if you admit the reports and the investigators are not available to testify and to be cross-examined, it would deprive the grievant of a fundamental right to confront the evidence against her and to cross-examine the witnesses. True, it is also a fundamental part of the company's case against the grievant, which the company counsel stated earlier he had a right to present—namely, the reasons for the discharge. But that presentation has to be in a manner which can be met by confrontation and by cross-examination. The document is hearsay, but beyond that there are fundamental reasons to apply the hearsay rule here and not to admit the reports. The difficulty arising from the fact that the investigators are not available for what seem to be bona fide reasons outside the control of the company is simply one of the problems that the company confronts in presenting the case. It must have competent evidence available. If the arbitrator rules to the contrary, the union and the grievant would be prejudiced to an extent which should not be permitted.

NEIL BERNSTEIN: What we're trying to decide as an arbitrator is whether the company had just cause to do what it did. The company has established that it discharged this person on the basis of this report. If you want to talk about the hearsay rule, we don't have legally, in my opinion, a hearsay problem. This is a part of the res gestae. This is the actual evidence upon which the company acted. So, not only is it admissible, it's vital to the case because that's all that we're talking about: was this report sufficient basis for the company to do what it did? That really depends upon exactly what's in the report. And I don't care whether it's a spotter's report or a report from a fireman; I don't care whether the people are available or they're unavailable. But I certainly feel that it's crucial for the arbitrator to have the factual evidence upon which the company made its decision. You then get into the question as to what it says and how credible it is and the related issues. But the report is unquestionably admissible in my view.

WILLIAM E. SIMKIN: I'd let them all in for whatever they're worth. I'd like to see what the reports are. I may pay no attention to them in the end, but they are still part of the reason the woman was fired. Now I'd like to know why she was fired.

EVA ROBINS: Of course I'd accept the document. If the company wants to present that as the basis of its decision, I would take the reports and give them whatever weight I want. It seems to me I should know about the basis on which a judgment was made by the company. It may fall flat on its face, but it is the question of admissibility we are discussing. The report is admissible in my opinion.

PAUL ROTHSCHILD: I don't see the relevance of letting the report in for some other purpose. We started out in this case to resolve one issue—whether she stole the soap or didn't steal the soap. Now, what other purpose would you be allowing the report in for except for the truth of the matter? That's all that's at issue here.

JAMES E. JONES, JR.: The fact is that management said, "We are introducing the affidavits of these respectable people to show you the basis on which we made our decision." That seems to me to change the purpose from introducing them for the truth of what was asserted therein, with the cross-examination problem that would raise. Whether or not the company should have acted on the reports is a matter that comes out later. That is a different question, and I would reserve my answer on that point.

ELLIOTT GOLDSTEIN: The union stipulated that it knows why management acted. The question was: Was there just cause? And under those facts I think the reports and the basis of the company's action are irrelevant. If all you wish to do is show that something was said to the company, what was said has to have relevance. In light of the union's stipulation, that is no longer a relevant issue.

TED TSUKIYAMA: I think that these admissibility questions would become much easier for the arbitrator if he first steps back and examines his role in conducting these hearings. If he considers himself a finder of fact who is to examine this matter on a de novo basis, then I think the rules of evidence or analogies to them may be applied with some reason. On the other hand, there's an abundance of arbitral literature that arbitrations of disciplinary matters are really appellate in nature, that they're essentially a review of management's action. Now, when you're sitting in appellate review, you're not supposed to make rulings on what's admissible and what's not. The record I am looking for is what did management consider in making its decision. If management relied on triple hearsay or worse in making the decision, I myself have no problem that it's admissible. But then I think there should be considered the propriety, the just-cause aspect, of management's taking this type of disciplinary action, utilizing or relying on this kind of material.

JAMES MARKOWITZ: I guess I would accept the report into evidence, but I would tell the company point-blank that without the opportunity to cross-examine, I would not give it any weight. If they want me to give it weight, they should bring the witnesses in, because at this stage of the hearing the report seems to be a crucial part of the company's case. It is very important that the company understand what I am going to do. There is a problem with admitting evidence not for its truth, but for some other reason. If you don't have lawyers presenting the case, the parties might not have the foggiest notion of what you are talking about, and they may end up being very confused. I am concerned that if I take in the document and then later find for the company, the union is going to say, "What do you mean he didn't look at the truth of it? He read that and the so-and-so found that those detectives were right, and we never got a chance to cross-examine them."

HERBERT FISHGOLD: I think that if that report is the only evidence the company has to support its discharge, I wouldn't let it in. Normally, the argument made by companies for trying to submit reports and not the people is that they don't want to blow the cover. We have a situation here where there are apparently three spotters involved. Spotter No. 1 no longer works for the company and has another job. He may have another job in the same city. There is no reason why that person can't come in and offer testimony. As for Spotter No. 2 who still works there, I can see why the company wouldn't want to call that person, but that is their problem. And with regard to Spotter No. 3 who now has retired and lives in Hawaii, there could have been a request made prior to the hearing, or perhaps even at this time if it is the only evidence they have, for the opportunity to take a deposition with the right of counsel for the grievant to cross-examine.

RAYMOND GOETZ: Just to change the facts slightly, assume that only the second affidavit is offered—that of the detective who is still with the agency. I still would hold it inadmissible and would dismiss the management argument that this exposes the identity of the detective. Frankly, I don't think that is very realistic. I have had cases where they do bring in the detective and it does not destroy their effectiveness if you have a community of any size.

DONALD WECKSTEIN: Some arbitrators would put a shield between the spotter as a witness and the parties and let them examine from behind the screen. I had a recent case in which we had an affidavit that was offered and not admitted, but we did get a stipulation to examine and cross-examine the witness by conference telephone call. That could be done whether the witness was in Hawaii or in the next room. If revealing the identity of the witness would be harmful to that witness's future, while a telephone call is not as good as being able to observe the demeanor of the witness on the stand, it's certainly better than the written report. If the report was the basis of the management action, I think that's an acceptable compromise.

WAYNE HOWARD: I would disagree slightly. If the parties want to protect the spotter, it is incumbent upon them to put such procedures in their collective bargaining agreement. In the absence of those procedures, I don't think the spotter should be protected.

CORNELIUS PECK: What we ought to think about is that this grievant's reputation and her future job prospects are at stake. We must balance that against the company's concern for preserving the anonymity of the spotters. It isn't very difficult for me to decide which way that balance goes. I think, though, one could just tell the company that that's the way I look at it and if you still want to give me that sheet of paper, well, I'll take it. But I don't think much of that kind of evidence on a charge as serious as this.

### III. Decisions of Other Tribunals

WHITE: Madam Arbitrator, you certainly can't reject this next item that we are going to offer. That is the record from a criminal court that Ms. Low was found guilty of theft of $450 worth of soap. She was given a one-year suspension. You know that that is admissible.

COHEN: I sure can object, Counselor. Now let's just look at this. First, Counselor, as you know, different parties were in that proceeding. The union was not present. We did not cross-examine. A different burden of proof was applicable. This is not a criminal proceeding. You are here to prove a contract discharge and justify it under a collective bargaining agreement. That's an entirely different issue. The conviction is irrelevant, and we object to its admissibility.

WHITE: Even you know that the burden in a criminal case is

higher than that in this case under a collective bargaining agreement. Surely that fact plus the fact that the conviction rendered in that case is a public document, available for public inspection, ought to make it admissible.

COHEN: We are not in a criminal proceeding, Counselor. You had your day to do what you tried to do to this individual and you did it. We are here under the contract. We remain adamant and object to the admissibility of that document.

WHITE: Madam Arbitrator, we suggest that you take this for what it's worth.

*Discussion*

1. How would you rule on the admissibility of decisions of other tribunals? Judge or jury conviction? No plea? Guilty plea? Acquittal? Unemployment compensation ruling?
2. Does it make any difference that it's a public document if it's a public-sector or federal arbitration case?
3. If the employer later tried to get the court record in during an attempt to impeach the grievant, would you let it in?

MYRON JOSEPH: It seems to me that the arbitrator is employed by the parties to make a determination both as to fact and as to the relevance of that fact in light of their contract. I think that most arbitrators take the position that a determination by any other body cannot be considered by them and they should not be given any information about it because that would bias them and make it impossible for them to make an independent judgment. For that reason the finding of an unemployment compensation judge as well as the finding of a criminal jury or judge would be irrelevant and would not be admissible in the proceeding.

KATHLEEN JOHN: I wouldn't hold either one of them admissible because the issues are different in each case. For instance, in a criminal case you are seeking to prove the guilt or innocence of the defendant, whereas in the arbitration proceeding the essential issue is just cause. Similarly, in the unemployment compensation hearing, although the just-cause issue does come up, just cause is defined differently for unemployment purposes than it is in an arbitration proceeding.

HARRY DWORKIN: My own feeling is that an arbitrator is called upon by the parties to hear a case de novo and he should not be bound or hamstrung by the decisions of other tribunals that considered matters in accordance with their rules, their standards, and the evidence before them. If we are going to receive a conviction into evidence as res judicata or as determinative of an individual's guilt, what would you say to the converse? Suppose an employee is charged with possessing marijuana or another drug and he is found not guilty or is acquitted. Is that conclusive at the arbitration hearing? On the contrary, management may not have had much evidence at the criminal proceeding, but comes before the arbitrator armed with a lot of credible, substantial evidence. My view is that the parties would be better served and the arbitration process would be better served if you would not even entertain the results of other proceedings, but hear the case on the merits on the basis of the evidence and testimony and reasoning as it is presented before the arbitrator. I think that would be more in conformity with the arbitrator's responsibility to decide the case and issue an award in accordance with the parties' own agreement. I think it would be permissible, however, to offer into evidence or use in cross-examination a plea of guilty in another forum because that is an admission against interest on the part of the grievant. I think it would also be permissible to submit evidence either on direct or cross-examination as to what an individual may have said concerning the matter in the presence of another individual or in another forum. That is different from the conclusions or the determinations of the other tribunals.

BURTON KAINEN: As a management representative, I'll take up the invitation to argue for admission of the conviction. I was frankly flabbergasted when I heard three arbitrators flatly say that they would not admit it. I would not have thought that this was a difficult question. In the jurisdictions that I am familiar with, one of the grounds for vacating an arbitration award is the refusal of the arbitrator to consider relevant evidence. It seems to me that a conviction of a crime in the courts of the jurisdiction in which this incident occurred is relevant evidence in a civil trial; if, for example, the company were suing the grievant in a civil trial for restitution, the conviction would be perfectly competent, relevant evidence, and would be either res judicata or at least collateral estoppel as to some of the points. When the arbitrator says to me that he will not admit that into evidence, I think I have a very good ground for vacating that award. I think he has *got* to consider it.

DAVID FELLER: I would admit the fact of conviction. I would not regard it as binding on me because the question of whether there was just cause for discharge is a different question from what the jury and the judge had to decide. However, it is a fact that the individual was convicted. I would not take the testimony or the transcript. I would simply admit the fact of conviction and I would say that I will accept it as a fact unless the grievant denies there was a conviction. I would make it clear, however, that I don't regard the conviction as binding on me. Now, the answer to your second question is that I would allow statements that were made in the course of the earlier proceeding to be used to impeach the witness if the grievant testified. Those are statements that were made, whether made in a criminal case or to a neighbor or to anyone else as to which there is some evidence, and I am entitled to question the grievant about that. I would also admit the fact that there was a nolo plea or a guilty plea, with a recognition that many times people plead guilty in a plea bargain when they really think they are innocent. And I would allow the grievant to explain her plea if she wanted to—for example, to say that the district attorney threatened to send her up for 15 other offenses and her best way out of it was to plead guilty.

WILLIAM LUBERSKY: I'm a management attorney. First, I think we are missing something in the analysis. The real question is whether that record of conviction is relevant. Now what does the record of conviction prove? It proves that a judge did something or a jury did something. It doesn't prove that the grievant did or didn't do anything. The transcript is admissible. It can contain admissions against interest; it can be useful for credibility purposes. But very often what is brought out in a criminal trial is completely different evidence from that in the arbitration. There are also different parties, as the union representative said.

JOANN THORNE: It seems to have been stipulated at the beginning that if a theft had occurred, discharge was the only penalty that was permissible. What we're looking at now is not whether the penalty was correct, but whether or not in fact the theft took place. And if a court found beyond a reasonable doubt that indeed a theft took place, I think the arbitrator would look ridiculous to suddenly say, "No, a theft didn't take place." So, though I would agree that an unemployment compensation referee applies different standards, and I would agree that a court doesn't decide just cause for discharge if there was a question of penalty, here the issue is simply, did the theft take place or not. I don't see how you could not admit a court verdict that it did take place.

BENJAMIN WOLF: That would be an abrogation of the function of the arbitrator. The arbitrator is the one to make the decision. Sometimes the parties provide in their contract that it is cause for discharge if an employee is found guilty of theft in a criminal proceeding. That would be the only occasion an arbitrator should admit that kind of verdict. I don't know what might have gone in as evidence before the other tribunal. But certainly what the parties have bargained for is this arbitrator's judgment on the basis of what is presented to her. The admission of that kind of evidence not only removes the principal function of the arbitrator, but also seems highly prejudicial. You don't know in this case whether the employer is going to be able to produce the evidence which proves to you that the employee is guilty of the theft. It still is an adversary proceeding, and the benefits as well as the disadvantages of that kind of proceeding have to be recognized and respected by you because that's your function.

CARLTON SNOW: I suggest that you would do things differently on the federal level because the 1978 Civil Service Reform Act indicates that arbitrators ought to consider even the decision of that judge.

### IV. New Evidence at Hearing

WHITE: At this point, Madam Arbitrator, the company would like to introduce the printout on its soap shortages during the past period in question. It will show without question that the soap shortage coincided with the accused theft—in this case by that *thief.*

COHEN: Madam Arbitrator, I hate to keep objecting to everything counsel does, but I have to do it because everything he does apparently is going to be improper today. Now let's review where we are. In the first two steps of the grievance procedure, we asked the company specifically, "Do you have any documentation relating to shortages of this soap?" And we were told, "No, we do not." We took that at face value. What do the first two steps of this procedure mean if the whole effort between the parties isn't to resolve the dispute at the earliest point based on knowledge that both sides have equally available to them? Otherwise we're going to make a mockery out of the whole grievance procedure. Again, several weeks ago in anticipation of this hearing, just because I was concerned that someone from this company might come up with some last-minute information, I called you, Counselor, and I said, "Do you have any documentation that will relate to the shortages?" I was told once again that you did not. Where did you get these, Sir? When did they become available?

WHITE: Just as the grievant is entitled to counsel, so too is the employer entitled to counsel, Madam Arbitrator. If a document wasn't used before, that is not my problem, nor would it be the problem of Mr. Cohen if he sat on this side. We submit to you that we have the right to put before you such evidence as you need to determine this case.

COHEN: This is new evidence that was deliberately withheld from the union so that the union could not be properly prepared when it came to the hearing. In good-faith understanding, no such documentation exists. Madam Arbitrator, you rule.

*Discussion*

1. Would you receive such an exhibit if convinced that the company deliberately kept it from the union?
2. Under what circumstances would you accept new evidence to which the union (or company) did not have access during the processing of the grievance?

STEVEN GOLDSMITH: I think this one is easy. I assume that there is no requirement in the contract for that kind of disclosure in the course of the grievance procedure. I would take the evidence subject to an opportunity for the union to have a look at it.

CARL YALLER: I suggest that this is an exquisitely easy case— the other way. I think it's unusual in that the record in question was specifically requested by the union. A more typical situation is where management has documentation, unrequested by the union, which was also not presented during the steps below. My position in either case would be that the entire purpose of the grievance procedure is frustrated when either party presents evidence which was available earlier but which was withheld so it could be used to sandbag the opposition at the hearing. I don't think that an arbitration should be the industrial equivalent of a walk through a mine field. The idea is to ferret out whatever evidence one party has against the other, so an intelligent decision can be made whether the case warrants arbitration or whether it ought to be settled. When a party chooses not to share a germane piece of evidence which would aid the other party in making an informed and intelligent decision, or in preparing for arbitration if necessary, the penalty should be that they simply cannot introduce it. While that may impose hardship in the immediate case, the lessons learned for future labor relations and the effective functioning of the grievance procedure justify the exclusion.

I. B. HELBURN: I would give the union time to look over the material, but I think ultimately I would accept it. I have to assume that while the company's behavior is clearly tacky and possibly counterproductive, they have thought that issue through. If that is the way the parties want to conduct their relationship, then an ad hoc arbitrator is not likely to be in a position to reform them overnight.

WALTER GERSHENFELD: It is not my job to reform the procedure. I don't really want to know whether there was anything wrong in the withholding of the information. The proper course of action for the union, if there is such a belief, is the filing of a grievance complaining about the company's misuse of the grievance procedure and detailing what they might consider would be an appropriate remedy.

GIL VERNON: I think the big question here is the reason the evidence was withheld. I would think the union or the arbitrator would have the right to question the company in this case as to why it wasn't available. We have to recognize that both parties often get more thorough as the deadline for arbitration approaches and the investigation of the facts becomes more complete. Sometimes things are overlooked earlier or are unavailable. Sometimes new exhibits are prepared just before the hearing. But if there was a deliberate bad-faith attempt to keep the evidence from the other party, if it was withheld solely for ambush value, I would not admit it.

JOHN SANDS: The problem, in the first place, is that you've got a piece of evidence that is probative and relevant to the issue. In the second place, you do have a very important value at stake —the integrity of the grievance procedure in the earlier steps. Is the answer to protecting the integrity of the system excluding this evidence, which is material and competent and whose exclusion, in New York State at least, could conceivably be a basis for judicial vacatur of your award? When such a confrontation occurs, I find it useful to have a conference with the opposing counsel to make these points and say, "Well, look, if we are to preserve the integrity of the grievance procedure, perhaps the case ought to go back to an earlier step where it can be reviewed." The party responsible for the delay can pay any extra costs and then bring the grievance back up. But I really think it's a mistake to reject out-of-hand material, competent evidence on a point such as this.

EARL CURRY: I think we have to look at the purpose of the exclusionary rule. It seems to me that it's based in this scenario on whether or not the "new evidence" is in fact new evidence or is merely corroborative evidence. Does it only corroborate the charges that the company has already made, or is it really a new charge coming in against the grievant? If it's essentially a new charge, and particularly if the union has asked for the documentation, then I think it should be excluded. But if it's not a new charge, if it is simply something to corroborate testimony that the company has already put forward, then it seems to me that it ought to be accepted.

FRED WITTE: I certainly don't subscribe to a company's withholding a document, particularly when it's asked for ahead of time. However, there are steps that union counsel can take here. He can ask to receive a copy of the printout; he can ask for a day's adjournment or a week's adjournment so he can study it. Now, we management attorneys regularly see grievants change their stories. They'll come in and they'll confess, "No, it didn't happen that way. It happened this way." And this is after having an initial discipline meeting; this is after going through four or five steps in the grievance procedure and having benefit of counsel and also the benefit of their union representatives. But they still lied or withheld information or changed the story. Again, I don't subscribe to it, but if arbitrators take the testimony of grievants who change their story or come in with new facts, they should also take it from the company.

DAVID FELLER: In a discharge case I tend to be more liberal with a grievant coming in with a different story from what was told at the lower steps of the grievance procedure. I will allow the grievant to tell whatever his or her story is, and I will allow the company to cross-examine about how it was just the opposite at the earlier hearing. I will not say to a grievant that this is new information. A grievant will say he has an alibi witness, that he wasn't on the picket line. I will not say, "You can't put that in because you didn't say that at the second or third step of the grievance procedure." And so in a disciplinary case I would act a little differently toward the union side than toward the employer side. On the other hand, my general view is that you ought to exclude to the maximum extent possible material that was not introduced earlier. If you don't, you encourage the parties to withhold evidence and you destroy the grievance procedure.

## V. Grievant's Postdischarge Conduct

WHITE: Madam Arbitrator, at this point I would like to introduce a letter that we sent to the grievant following her termination concerning some conduct which she engaged in during the grievance proceedings in this case. While processing the grievance, we told her we were going to fire her anyway for what she did there. She threatened our personnel manager and started to get into a fight with him. Had we not been able to restrain her, it would have been a terrible situation.

COHEN: Madam Arbitrator, first of all, we all know this is a violation of the most fundamental proposition in discharge cases: *after-* discharge facts obviously cannot be introduced into evidence. Now, I would like the record to show, because my client's personality is being impugned, that she is 5'1" and weighs 111 pounds. Your personnel manager is a 6'4" graduate of Notre Dame and was a middle linebacker . . . . We stipulated that the issue is whether the discharge was for just cause. If not, what should be the remedy?

WHITE: Madam Arbitrator, in framing the remedy, you have the right, indeed the duty, to know her postdischarge conduct, particularly as it relates to her relationship with the personnel manager.

COHEN: This is trying what is left of my patience, Madam Arbitrator. The record has to reflect that there has never been one word of discussion at any point in the grievance procedure about this situation. This individual was already terminated. She was not an employee within the meaning of anything, Counselor, at the time in question. Therefore, we vigorously object to any such evidence coming in. It obviously prejudices my client's case. What you are trying to do is to try three cases here, aren't you, Counselor? One is her conduct as background; the other is the event in question, for which you apparently don't have any evidence; and the third is what she did on her way to her vacation after she was fired.

WHITE: If she did something that relates to her job on her way to her vacation after being fired, we can bring it in here. Now we are all part of the judicial system here. We understand the concept of judicial economy. If she wasn't going to be fired for the original theft of the soap, she would have been fired for this conduct. We've done it anyway. You might as well hear both of these situations today, Madam Arbitrator.

*Discussion*

1. Would you consider the "second" firing for threatening the personnel manager sufficiently related to the first, for theft, to make the second admissible?
2. If the second firing had not been brought up in the grievance procedure and was a surprise to union counsel, what would you do? Would you consider the union's refusal to consider the second termination during the grievance processing as a waiver and hear both terminations in arbitration?
3. Under what circumstances, if any, would you hear both terminations?

EARL CURRY: This is a new charge against the grievant. That's the major reason I would not accept the document. Secondly, the alleged incident occurred after the company made the decision to discharge the grievant for stealing soap. Her alleged threats to the personnel manager all occurred after the fact and have nothing to do with whether she did or did not steal the soap. That is the stipulated issue. And thirdly, I think it's manifestly unfair to hold an individual who has just been told that she's been discharged to the same standard of conduct that we normally hold people to regarding their demeanor and decorum in industrial society.

JAMES McMULLEN: It seems to me that the evidence is arguably relevant with respect to the remedy. It cannot be used by the arbitrator to determine the propriety of the employer's initial action in discharging the grievant, but I believe he can properly take it into account in determining the question of reinstatement —for instance, whether to return the grievant to that company.

Maybe the conduct in this particular case wasn't egregious enough to affect a remedy, but arguably it is relevant.

MARK KAHN: What you really have here is a problem of a second incident of misconduct which can't properly be brought into the case you are entitled to hear—the case that has gone through the grievance procedure and is properly in arbitration. If the grievant has subsequently done something for which she deserves to be discharged, that is a separate charge. The employer should discipline the grievant for her postdischarge misconduct, and that would be heard separately unless the parties agreed to consolidate it.

IDA KLAUS: I think this is a totally separate offense which has no bearing on the offense before the arbitrator. It should be kept separate. I do not believe that it comes within the realm of a remedy question. That is a special case. In my experience the parties pretty well understand that they may not bring up such evidence. They try it. When they are rebuffed on it, they accept it. They know what the procedures should be.

HOWARD LEBARON: I would accept the evidence as going to remedy, but not as going to whether the grievant was justly discharged. If she had so polluted the work environment by this conduct that her reinstatement would be a disturbing factor, I would consider that in deciding whether or not to reinstate her.

JAMES WHYTE: I had always thought that what went on during the grievance procedure was privileged. I would have a great deal of trouble admitting that if I were an arbitrator in this case.

LEO WEISS: It seems to me that there are things that go on in the grievance procedure that are not privileged and could be brought in. Not everything is part of settlement discussions, which are generally considered privileged. Suppose, for example, the grievant says at the first step of the grievance procedure, "Yes, I lost my temper and I hit so-and-so because of what he said." Or suppose there's an assault on someone—the supervisor or the personnel manager—or there are threats to witnesses: "If you come in and testify against me, I'll blow your head off." It's true that the company couldn't have considered that at the time of the discharge, but it seems to me that it's an appropriate consideration for the remedy. To put an employee back to work after you have heard evidence that he is threatening other employees, or physically assaulting the supervisors, is not performing your proper function as an arbitrator. I think that the arbitrator has a lot broader authority under the contract in formulating a remedy than he has in determining what the basic issue is, which is something that's normally decided between the company and the union.

## VI. Stolen Documents

COHEN: Madam Arbitrator, it appears that the union finally has an opportunity to introduce something into evidence. This is a letter from the plant manager to the personnel director. I would like to read into the record this very poignant paragraph: "Dear Larry: We've got the wrong person. Susan didn't do it. Norma did. But let's go forward against Susan anyway. Her record is so bad that she'd be fired for her next tardiness anyway."

WHITE: Where did you get that?

COHEN: I happened to find it in my file folder earlier today. It probably just arrived there.

WHITE: That is a stolen in-house company document. I demand that it be handed over, Madam Arbitrator. You cannot sanction that kind of conduct on behalf of a member of the bar or anybody who is part of the system of solving industrial relations cases.

COHEN: This document speaks for itself and makes it clear that what we have here in the soap industry is a railroad case. You are trying to railroad an innocent person by having her terminated for something she didn't do, Counselor.

*Discussion*

1. Would you admit such a stolen document?
2. Would you allow it to be used to impeach the testimony of the plant manager?

BRUCE BOALS: I would admit it, tainted as it is, simply because of the old fable of the dog and the rabbit. The rabbit is running for his life and the dog is running for a meal, and I'll leave it there.

ARVID ANDERSON: The charge in this case involves theft. If you sanction accepting a stolen document, you are sanctioning theft as a basis of defense. I find the reasoning unacceptable.

CHARLES REHMUS: Without regard to legal rules, I wouldn't admit it, assuming it can be shown that this was a stolen privileged or private company document. I think the potential dangers to the parties' relationship and to the collective bargaining process are so great if you start admitting documents of this kind, no matter what its weight might otherwise be, that I would keep it out.

ELLIOT BEITNER: I think the damage to the relationship of the parties is done. If the company indeed has this type of exculpatory evidence and withheld it and went forward with this termination in a hearing, it's very damning and damaging. It is so damaging and so probative that to deny admissibility because of the union's method of obtaining it might go to the basic guarantee of due process for a grievant. Certainly an arbitration hearing is not a criminal proceeding, but there is a duty imposed on a prosecutor to provide the other side with exculpatory evidence. While there may be no such duty in the collective-bargaining relationship, I think there is a tradition that would suggest not going forward in a case where there is this type of evidence. Without condoning the idea of stealing documents, I think you'd have to let the letter in.

IVAN RUTLEDGE: On the constitutional point, I don't see that the arbitrator has any responsibility to ride herd on private people. Both the Fourth and Fourteenth Amendments give rise to an obligation to safeguard the public from the lawlessness of the police. We don't have any instance here of a policeman having stolen something. But I do think that whether it comes from the U.S. Arbitration Act or from some sense of the *Steelworkers Trilogy,* there is a fundamental principle of procedural regularity that's germane to the arbitration process. On that I subscribe to Mr. Rehmus's doubts about participating in this kind of warfare.

MARSHALL ROSS: I sense a tendency on the part of some arbitrators to apply the exclusionary rule as if they had the obligation of policing the parties with respect to their bargaining relationship. I don't think an arbitrator really has the authority or can take upon himself that responsibility. I might point out to the parties informally that there's a danger of straining their relationship if this kind of conduct goes on. But beyond some such admonition I don't think an arbitrator has the right, by excluding good evidence, to attempt to regulate the bargaining relationship between the parties. I assume that in this case the document satisfies the hearsay rule as a business-record exception or as an admission against interest, or that some other foundation can be laid for it. On that basis it seems to me that an arbitrator must permit the document presented to be received into the record.

STEPHEN FORMAN: The rules of evidence which would prohibit the introduction of this kind of document in a criminal case are designed to prevent the police from becoming a bully. They are constitutional guarantees. Here you don't have that problem. It is true that there might be some reason to disfavor such evidence because you don't want to encourage stealing from the company. But anybody who broke into locked rooms or pilfered drawers, whether it be the grievant or other people, will doubtlessly be the subject of a separate future grievance. Break-ins and thefts are obviously against company policies and rules. The letter certainly goes to the truth which they are trying to get at in this case, but I don't think the purpose of the rules of evidence in a criminal case applies here at all. While I represent management, I think that if I were an arbitrator, I would admit the document.

DON WECKSTEIN: I agree with the conclusion that the mere fact that evidence is illegally obtained would not preclude its admission in an arbitration hearing. I have another problem here, though. There is one rule of evidence that I apply in addition to relevancy, and that is the rule of privilege. If the matter was part of the attorney's work product or part of an attorney-client privilege, I think I would exclude it on that ground.

PHYLLIS SENEGAL: In the final analysis, would anybody actually sustain the dismissal of an employee when that kind of letter is presented? The real problem I see with the letter is authenticating it. Suppose the plant manager doesn't testify and you can't use it to attack his credibility or prove that that's his signature on it. But otherwise how could anyone say, "Well, I am going to sustain this dismissal as a curb on union counsel's activity or as a curb on somebody else's activity"? You couldn't do that.

CHET BRISCO: I wonder if the question of admissibility here isn't really the wrong question. Even if the document is not admitted, it seems to me what the attorney for the union would do is simply call the apparent originator of that document as an adverse witness and ask him whether it was written or not. And then it would come in by virtue of impeachment.

## VII. Lie Detector Tests

COHEN: Madam Arbitrator, we'd like to have marked for identification as Union Exhibit No. 2 the results of a lie detector test which the grievant voluntarily underwent approximately one week after her termination. I have a memorandum of points of authority, Counselor, in case you are not familiar with those citations.

WHITE: How long have you been holding on to that? What kind of precedent is this? Are we going to allow the parties to hold things back until the last minute? If so, how are we going to solve these cases at the earliest possible point? You can't allow them to introduce that, Madam Arbitrator!

COHEN: You didn't even ask us whether we had taken a lie detector test, as we had asked you about your documents. The truth of the matter is, we just didn't think the company would believe the outcome of the test. But we are confident, when you review this document for its authenticity and validity, Madam Arbitrator, you'll recognize it supports our position—namely, that the grievant didn't commit this theft.

WHITE: Let me get serious, Madam Arbitrator. In this jurisdiction and in most jurisdictions in this country, lie detector tests are not admissible. I submit to you, aside from the fact that they are not scientifically reliable, you cannot show me a case where they have been admitted. They cannot be admitted here for the additional reason that you cannot have evidence held back until the crucial moment in the hearing where we have no time to prepare.

COHEN: As a matter of fact, Madam Arbitrator, this is an admissible document and it speaks to a vital issue in this proceeding. We ask that it be received.

*Discussion*

1. How would you rule on the effort to introduce data at the arbitration hearing which were held back throughout the processing of the grievance, but which were never specifically requested by the other party?
2. How would you handle the difference of opinion on the admissibility of the lie detector test results?
3. Under what circumstances, if any, would you admit the results of the lie detector test?

PETER FLOREY: On the first question, unless the contract specifically provides that there has to be disclosure of all information at one of the prior levels of the grievance procedure, I think either party can come in with whatever evidence they want to introduce at the arbitration. On the second question, I think this is a good example of a situation where the parties have to realize that rulings can work both ways. In one case one party makes a particular argument and in the next case it's the other party. Employers, especially in the retail industry, want to introduce lie detector tests to prove guilt or dishonesty on the part of employees. As a rule, arbitrators will reject the results of lie detector tests on the ground that they are unreliable. By the same token, if a union wants to submit the results of a lie detector test to prove the innocence of an employee, I think it should similarly be rejected on the same ground.

RICHARD HARTZ: Objection sustained to the polygraph test. It is a piece of hearsay. There is no opportunity for cross-examination. The polygraph operator is not present.

I. B. HELBURN: I would go further and say that even if the examiner were present to establish his own credentials and qualifications and be cross-examined, and even if he emerges clean as a whistle from that process, the results of the polygraph itself are too unreliable to be given any credence at all.

RAY GOETZ: I think you can change the facts a little, though, so it is not quite so obvious. For example, put the operator there to qualify himself and to be subject to cross-examination and assume the polygraph results are offered only after a question concerning the credibility of the grievant has been raised. I am troubled by questions of credibility, and I am always reluctant to rule out anything in a grievant's favor. It does seem to me that perhaps a polygraph (Ted Jones's article in our 1978 Proceedings to the contrary notwithstanding) is evidence of what happened to this grievant's blood pressure and respiration when she was asked these questions. I would never accept it as proof of the ultimate question of guilt or innocence, but I might accept it as some evidence on the question of credibility.

JAMES STERN: I am familiar with Jones's article. I also share his opinion. One of our distinguished colleagues, however, has given a good argument for an opposite conclusion. In a situation where the operator was present, his position was that the polygraph results should be admissible because management based its determination on the lie detector evidence and he, as an arbitrator, listens to all the evidence that management took into account in order to determine whether management had just cause.

SAMUEL CHALFIE: Under no circumstances would I admit a lie detector test unless it had been agreed upon by both parties prior to its administration.

CHARLES REHMUS: Suppose the company and the union stipulated that the grievant's responses to a properly administered lie detector test by an appropriate individual selected by the company would determine whether the grievant should be reinstated. Would you refuse to accept it?

PETER SEITZ: I always wait for an objection. If there is no objection and if they both stipulated that the lie detector test was going to determine the guilt or nonguilt of the person, I would under those very unusual circumstances take it. But I've never heard of such a case.

HOWARD LEBARON: My reading of the literature convinces me that polygraph tests are not reliable. It gives me considerable pause even if the parties stipulated that the polygraph test would not only be admitted, but would be considered as evidence of the truth of the statements made by the respondent to the test. I'm not so sure that the arbitrator should accept that kind of stipulation.

GEORGE NICOLAU: About eight years ago, when I was chairman of the labor committee of the bar association in New York, I was the principal author of a report called *The Lie Detector in the Search for Truth.* We did a great deal of research on the subject, and all of that research was leading me to the conclusion that I would not accept lie detector tests on the grounds of their utter unreliability. Then, during the course of a demonstration by the foremost polygraph expert in the New York City area, our estimable colleague, Tom Christensen, flunked the test, and I realized that our conclusions were right!

NATE LIPSON: There are various problems with a lie detector. In the first place, it only measures physical reactions—blood pressure, respiration rate, perspiration, things like that. Then an operator has to interpret the data. That is highly subjective. You can get results from people who are inexperienced as well as from those who have worked with the process over the years. These are among the reasons most jurisdictions don't admit this kind of evidence. It is also clear that there are certain people who are pathological liars and about whom it is impossible to determine anything whatsoever from an analysis of their responses. What we have at best is a method which may be indicative of credibility and may be a help in evaluating testimony, but certainly nothing that is conclusive. An arbitrator who accepts that kind of evidence and gives it substantial weight and uses it to determine credibility is, in my opinion, making a grave error.

BERT GOTTLIEB: I am an industrial engineer as well as an arbitrator. At one time I did extensive research into the whole lie detector area. I sat in on the examinations of about six different major lie detector companies, and I saw the sleaziest operations I have ever seen in my life. Even attorneys and medical people who were lie detector operators didn't follow the so-called "ethical practices of lie detectors." I also think arbitrators ought to know that today the laws of about 20 states forbid or limit the use of lie detectors in employment.

## VIII. Burden of Proof

COHEN: Madam Arbitrator, the union would like to sum up its case. The termination should be set aside and reinstatement with back pay should be ordered. There was no evidence whatsoever against the grievant other than that some company spies went into this parked car, while she was in the plant working at her job, and found some soap. That, plus the fact that she was located somewhere in the area of the plant where the theft supposedly took place, constitute the entire case that the company was able to bring forward here today. In a case such as this, Madam Arbitrator, where the company is claiming that this individual committed a crime on company property during the course of her employment, I need not remind you that the company has the heavy burden of establishing guilt beyond a shadow of doubt. The company, of course, fell completely short of that mark.

WHITE: Madam Arbitrator, our evidence speaks for itself. The thief has been unmasked. As you know, we don't have photographs of her taking the soap, but the circumstantial evidence demonstrates that we have met our burden. She is guilty. By the way, the burden is guilt by a preponderance of the evidence. This is a civil, not a criminal, case and the civil standard should apply. We urge that this grievance be denied.

*Discussion*

1. What is the appropriate burden of proof to sustain a termination action?
2. Is circumstantial evidence sufficient to meet that burden?

WILLIAM FALLON: My standard of proof in a case involving discharge for theft is proof beyond a reasonable doubt (not "shadow of a doubt") because if I have a reasonable doubt as to the guilt of that person, I have great difficulty finding that the discharge was for just cause. Circumstantial evidence is sometimes the most reliable evidence that arbitrators have available. The credibility questions presented by direct testimony are sometimes pretty rough. Circumstantial evidence, in my judgment, can satisfy the standard of proof beyond a reasonable doubt.

GERRY FELLMAN: First of all, with regard to circumstantial evidence, I agree that circumstantial evidence may very well be more reliable than evidence from eye witnesses whose memory may be faulty or whose perceptions may be faulty. There are eminent arbitrators on all sides of this question of burden of proof. I believe that an arbitration proceeding is not a criminal case and that it is improper to place upon management the reasonable-doubt burden of proof. Some famous criminal lawyer talked about the one drop of ink that falls into the bathtub full of water and that is the equivalent of reasonable doubt. If you have the slightest doubt, then you acquit. I think that is too demanding in arbitration. On the other hand, I believe that more than a preponderance of evidence should be required. I agree with those arbitrators who use the clear-and-convincing-evidence test. I realize that sometimes all of these tests are really irrelevant because the arbitrator weighs the evidence and makes up his or her mind, and the somewhat slight variations in the tests don't make a great deal of difference.

TIA DENENBERG: If I were to say what burden of proof I use, I guess it would be the preponderance standard, but personally I think arbitration is a common-sense proceeding. When the arbitrator is convinced, that is when the case is decided. We can try to make intellectual distinctions in theory; in practice, in each case when we are convinced, we are convinced. But I am firmly of the opinion that this is not a criminal proceeding; it is not a court proceeding. I object to creeping legalism coming into the proceedings and making us think we are in court when we are not. I think both parties should put on their best case, introduce substantial evidence, and then the man in the middle or the woman in the middle will make an honest call. I, for one, would certainly never impose a criminal burden on an employer in this situation.

PETER FLOREY: Essentially what Tia said is that the principles of burden of proof merely evolved as charges to the jury by the judge. What we have to decide is a completely different matter. In the last analysis we have to decide whether it was reasonable for management to impose discipline.

ZEL RICE: It seems to me that you have to use less than the beyond-a-reasonable-doubt standard unless you're going to require the employer to have an FBI to investigate every single situation that arises in his plant. I don't think that you can expect an employer to put together the kind of case to establish a basis for discharge that you expect the police to prepare when someone is facing the death penalty.

HERB SABGHIR: The State of New York in its contracts with some of its public employees does specifically provide that the test is a preponderance of the evidence. Now, regarding the last comment, some persons maintain that discharge is the industrial death sentence. What if the penalty is not discharge? It's suspension for a week, for two weeks, short of the death sentence. Would you all use preponderance? In the absence of any language in the contract specifying the standard of proof, would you want to apply beyond-a-reasonable-doubt if it's termination, but a lower standard if it's a suspension?

PAUL ROTHSCHILD: I think it's absolute nonsense to talk about death sentences unless you are really going to put somebody to death. That's not what's at stake in a discharge for theft. How many times are we going to put that guy back so he can take another shot at stealing company equipment?

C. B. ROSSER: There is, of course, some controversy on the standard of proof. It seems to me, however, that the body of arbitral case law is now flowing toward clear and convincing proof rather than proof beyond a reasonable doubt or a preponderance of the evidence. It seems to me that we're not talking about a criminal case here, and therefore beyond-a-reasonable-doubt is not appropriate in an industrial situation like this.

STEPHEN FORMAN: As a management attorney I have never understood why you should have a different burden of proof depending on whether you are being fired for absenteeism or some other infraction of the rules or for stealing. Now, a reason that proof beyond a reasonable doubt is required in a criminal case is that if you are found guilty, you are sent to jail, you are fined, and you are labeled with a conviction for criminal offense, whether it be a misdemeanor or a felony. If you are fired, you are fired! Some arbitrators say the difference is you are labeling this person a thief and by doing that you are presumably going to make it more difficult for her to find future employment. I always say that we are more than willing to respond to any employment inquiry that this person was discharged for cause. Period. We have no desire to prevent the person from getting a job in the future. We are simply firing this person for cause, and on that basis he is suffering a discharge for the reason he stole, the same as if he suffered discharge for any other rule infraction. I don't understand why we need a different burden of proof.

DAVID FELLER: I don't think anybody has made that kind of distinction here. I think that most of us have said, "I prefer not to use beyond-a-reasonable-doubt; maybe a clear-and-convincing standard," but that is just playing games with words. I don't distinguish between a discharge for failing to report to work for ten days or a discharge for stealing in terms of the burden of convincing me that what is charged in fact occurred.

WILLIAM FALLON: I agree that the same standard has got to be applied to any type of case and not just to one that is akin to a criminal case. It has got to be applied to a tardiness case, absenteeism case, or whatever. But if you leave the hearing room or finish the briefs with a reasonable doubt as to the guilt of the aggrieved, I don't see how you can be convinced that management has sustained its burden.

RUSSELL POWELL: On the subject of circumstantial evidence, they've done studies about the validity of eye-witness testimony and it's distressingly poor. Elizabeth Loftus of Seattle produced a book with several other scholars which shows that eye-witness testimony is very unreliable, generally speaking. People used to speak about circumstantial evidence pejoratively, and I think they should reexamine that position.

BRUCE FRASER: The book by Elizabeth Loftus is entitled *Eye Witness Testimony*. It contains a whole range of articles on the subject. Subsequent to that, *Psychology Today* carried several pieces. There's also a paper in the Proceedings of the National

Academy two years ago, authored by myself, that reviews a lot of this and other material about the dangers of eye-witness testimony.

PETER SEITZ: I'd like to know what else is new. I mean, the dangers of eye-witness testimony have been known for generations. Münsterberg at Harvard wrote all about it in the early years of the century. On this business of the burden of proof, I just have to be convinced. I look at the contract, which is my Bible, and it says that a man can be discharged or disciplined for just cause. The parties don't tell me what the burden of proof shall be, or to what extent I must be satisfied with the evidence. Yet I hear about me all of this learning which is taken from the criminal courts, which is taken from the administrative agencies, which is taken from the civil courts. This noon I listened to Ted Jones deliver his Presidential Address. Jones says, "Look at the contract," and I think Jones is right.

# CHAPTER 6

# PROCEDURAL RULINGS DURING THE HEARING

This chapter consists of a collated set of excerpts from the transcripts of six separate workshops for members and guests of the National Academy of Arbitrators at their Washington meeting. The discussion guide was prepared by Arnold M. Zack in collaboration with Theodore J. St. Antoine. Professor St. Antoine edited this summary. Discussion leaders for the workshops were Academy members Howard S. Block, Sanford Cohen, John E. Dunsford, William J. Fallon, Myron L. Joseph, and Edward B. Krinsky.

## I. Third-Party Participation

In a hearing on an allegedly improper promotion, the incumbent, a junior employee who was chosen for the position over the grievant on the basis of supposedly superior qualifications, appears with counsel and demands to participate. Either the union or the company objects.

1. If you were the arbitrator, how would you rule?
2. Under what circumstances, if any, would you permit such a third party to sit and observe?
3. Would your answer differ if it were a public-sector dispute or a state with an open-meeting statute?
4. Would you allow such an observer to take notes? Make a tape-recording? Have a stenographer transcribe the proceedings?

JOHN F. MORGAN: I'm a union representative. The union takes the position that the arbitration is initiated by the union against the company. They are the two parties to the process. There is no need for the incumbent to be a part of it. The union would investigate as to the incumbent's rights prior to choosing to go to arbitration, and they have made the decision to go ahead on the seniority rule and all the facts. The arbitrator should not permit any participation by the incumbent over the objection of the union.

EARLE BARTAREAU: I'm a management representative. We would object to an outside attorney representing this second employee in the dispute under any set of circumstances. It is a matter of principle. We don't want anybody except the correct representative, the union, in an arbitration case. We would not even want the incumbent's attorney to sit in and observe. The chances are that in some cases we would call the incumbent as our witness, but that is quite a different matter. I don't think we would object, however, to the incumbent employee—the one who got the promotion—sitting in and observing.

DAVID VAN OS: I am a lawyer who represents unions. I agree with the management representative who just spoke. We would object to the junior employee participating through counsel at the hearing. The union is not simply a legal-services mechanism for individual employees. The union is there upholding the integrity of the contract, whose terms and conditions apply to all employees equally. It is the union's statutory responsibility to apply the terms and conditions of the contract fairly to all employees, senior and junior, and all employees must bear both the privileges and the liabilities of that representation. That is the duty imposed upon unions by law under our system of exclusive representation. From my standpoint, we would object vehemently to an outsider's participation.

RAYMOND GOETZ: I take a kind of legalistic approach. I am there by virtue of an appointment pursuant to a collective bargaining agreement to which the union and the company are the parties. It is their agreement, and I am bound by what they agree on. I cannot compel them to do something beyond that agreement. My initial step, however, would be to take a little more affirmative action to induce the union to allow the incumbent to participate. If the union was not represented by counsel at the hearing, I would suggest that they take a short recess and check with their attorney to see whether legally they want to proceed in that manner. I would inform the union that if they insist, I will exclude the third party, but that they might have trouble down the road. The kind of participation I'd permit on behalf of the incumbent would depend on what the union's position finally was. At a minimum I would like to allow the incumbent's attorney to be there and to pass notes to the union if he wanted to;

that would at least allow the attorney to ask that a question be asked. I think, ideally, that the union should allow the incumbent's attorney to present the case with respect to his client.

WILLIAM E. SIMKIN: I would keep the incumbent out. The company took the action of promoting the junior man. I think it is the company's responsibility to present his case, and if he comes in and extols his own virtues, it just creates problems.

DAVID KABAKER: The incumbent has no place in this hearing. The incumbent has been selected for the job by the company. The protest is lodged by the grievant through the union. The situation might be different had the grievant asked to have his own personal representative there. But as it is, there is no reason whatsoever for the incumbent to be represented by separate counsel. I also think that each party, company and union, has a right to object to who is present at a hearing. I would rule him out if either party objected.

ROBERT NICHOLS: I am a union advocate from Chicago. First of all, I think it makes a great deal of difference as to who raises the objection. For example, there is a fairly strong suggestion from the Court of Appeals for the Eighth Circuit in the *Hussman* case that there might even be an affirmative obligation on the part of the union to produce counsel for each of the employees at the hearing. If the incumbent employee shows up with his own counsel and the union is silent, and only the company raises an objection, a strong argument can be made that the objection should be overruled. The individual and his attorney should be permitted to participate. On the other hand, if the union objects, I think great deference ought to be accorded that objection. While I recognize that the company may ultimately be a party to a lawsuit after the hearing if the union's objection is sustained, it is primarily the union that is on the firing line. It is their duty of fair representation that is at issue, and I assume they will have given some thought to that going into the hearing. I think the arbitrator in those circumstances ought to accord real deference to the union's views.

CAROL ZAMPERINI: I would ask the third party to leave in both cases. I think we are creating a dangerous situation when we ignore the fact that the contract is a contract between the two parties. I think it is dangerous, anyway, for us to start assuming that we have an obligation as arbitrators to take it upon ourselves to defend the interests of third parties in these situations. Here the grievant is being represented by the appropriate party and that is the union. The company has its representative there to defend its decision to promote the incumbent. I think if one side or the other objected to the presence of outsiders, both the incumbent and his counsel should be asked to leave. If the incumbent believes that he was improperly dealt with by the union, there is access to another forum. I think that is the forum he should utilize.

BENJAMIN WOLF: This question has been answered in New Jersey. I had a promotion case in which I decided that the incumbent was improperly appointed. He was not a party to the proceeding. The case went to the highest court in New Jersey, which held that where a person has a substantial interest at stake, such as a promotion or a possible demotion if he had been promoted, he must be impleaded with his counsel if he wishes. Contrary to what I would have expected, we have an answer now from a high tribunal that such a person has an absolute right to participate. You cannot deprive this person of his job or his property rights without his being present and having an opportunity to defend.

PETER FLOREY: I have found that most business agents know more about the duty of fair representation than the arbitrators, and I think it would be presumptuous for me to tell the union representative what he very well knows. If the junior employee appeared with his own counsel, I would say that I have been retained by the company and the union and any outsider can participate only with their permission. Preferably we would thresh it out not in the hearing room, but off the record somewhere. I'd let the parties try to work out what they wanted to do, but I don't think I would do anything against the wishes of the union rep because he knows better than I what the risks are.

BARNETT GOODSTEIN: I would make the opposite ruling as long as there is just one objection, and not objections by both parties. If the employee who got the job came in with his own counsel and wanted to be heard, I would grant him the right to be heard with the understanding that if the ruling went against him, he could not then file a grievance and come back for a second hearing. That would start the process all over again, which might even give this grievant the right to go into the second hearing and be heard. And where would it ever end? We would have a multiplicity of arbitrations over the same issue. It should be heard one time with all parties in interest present and be thoroughly aired with everybody given a chance to be represented and have his day in court—and then it is over.

DOUGLAS STANLEY: I am an arbitrator from Canada. Under Canadian law any third party who is likely to be affected by an arbitration has not only the right to be present, but also the right to receive notice prior to the hearing of the fact that his interest could be affected and that he has a right to appear and be represented by counsel just as the principal party. That is not a statute, but the result of a series of judicial decisions reviewing arbitrators' awards.

CHARLES FEIGENBAUM: In the federal sector, contrary to what you have in the typical private-sector situation, the incumbent who lost the promotion and was downgraded back to his old job has a right of appeal, not to an arbitrator but to an outside administrative body. There have been a number of cases in which, after an arbitrator ordered that the incumbent be removed from a position and the grievant be given the job, the incumbent appealed and won the appeal. The employing agency then had two orders before it—two perfectly conflicting orders. Thus the federal-sector procedures don't really tell you how to handle this kind of problem.

THOMAS RINALDO: Under the rules of the American Arbitration Association, an arbitrator has the right generally to regulate the hearing and decide on the procedure. Even in a state where there is an open-meeting law, therefore, I think an arbitrator would have the right to exclude any person or admit any person or otherwise regulate the hearing as he deems appropriate until some court tells him otherwise.

STEVEN GOLDSMITH: On the question of taking notes or making a tape-recording, once it is settled that a third party is permitted to stay at least as an observer, I would permit them to do that.

BARNETT GOODSTEIN: I always allow anyone who wants to take notes or to record the proceedings for his own purposes, or to have a reporter there to prepare a personal transcript, to do anything he wants to for his own purposes only.

RAYMOND GOETZ: If I allowed third parties to participate, I would very definitely let them also tape the proceedings.

STEPHEN RICHMAN: I don't know how you prevent people from taking notes. With respect to using either a stenographer or a tape-recorder, I think the answer to that is "No." I am aware of Labor Board precedent—the *Bartlett-Collins* case that was affirmed by a court of appeals—which prohibits the taking of a transcript by a stenographer or a tape-recording in collective bargaining over the objection of the other party. I don't see how a third person who is really not a party to the arbitration proceeding could come in and record it over the objections of a party, now that the Board and the courts have said that the presence of a stenographer or a tape-recording device may well stifle free and unfettered discussion of these issues.

PETER SEITZ: I conceive of the hearing as being conducted for one primary purpose, and that is to inform the arbitrator in a fairly conducted hearing of what he needs to know in order to make a just decision. He is supposed to control that hearing and its procedure, and keep order and decorum, and determine the order of proof so that he can understand what the case is about. Now, when you accept that as the purpose of the hearing, then you say to yourself: If somebody else is making a verbatim statement of stuff that may be off the record, is that outside person going to have a different record from the notes which the arbitrator takes or which the stenotypist takes (of course the stenotypist goes on or off the record as requested)? When you write your decision, you write it based on your notes. That other person has some other kind of record. What is the record in the case? This becomes confusing and raises all sorts of new problems. I think the kinds of questions posed here can only be answered by an inquiry as to the purpose of the whole arbitration procedure.

## II. "Due Process" Protections

During the arbitration of a discharge for theft, one party calls to the stand an alleged accomplice who has a case pending in criminal court for the same theft. The witness declines to testify. One party asks the arbitrator to direct the witness to testify; the other party objects.

1. If you were the arbitrator, how would you rule?
2. Under what circumstances generally would you extend the following "due process" protections to an arbitration proceeding in either the private or the public sector:
   a. Protection against self-incrimination, e.g., witness declines to testify or is absent from the hearing?
   b. Right to cross-examine one's accusers, e.g., written accusations from customers?
   c. Protection against unreasonable searches and seizure,

e.g., evidence has been uncovered by a search of lockers
or lunch pails, or through confiscation of an employee's
personal property (liquor, drugs, weapons)?

d. "Lawyer-client privilege" for internal communications,
e.g., one party has testimony (or a stolen document)
regarding communication between other side's representative and its witnesses that would clearly establish
that its case was a fabrication?

NATE LIPSON: An arbitrator doesn't have any contempt powers. You can't compel anybody to testify. But the arbitrator does
have an obligation to try to aid the parties to get a full and fair
case into the record. I would ask the witness to testify. I don't
think I could do much more than that. If the witness is a defendant in a criminal case, it would be understandable that the
witness would refuse to testify and might have a constitutional
basis for refusing to testify. The arbitrator is not that witness's
counsel. Somebody else might well advise the witness not to
testify. The arbitrator's obligation is to try to secure a full and
fair hearing. So, the arbitrator's duties are different from the
witness's rights.

DAVID KABAKER: I agree wholeheartedly with Nate Lipson. He
used the word "request," but I would say "order him to testify."

STEVEN GOLDSMITH: As I understand it, the constitutional
right against self-incrimination is one that can be invoked primarily in a criminal proceeding and it normally doesn't apply to
an arbitration proceeding. In any case, this is a right which
inures to the individual who is being asked to testify. If that
individual objected, I would recognize his claim because it is
quite clear that if he testifies with or without a transcript, he
would be putting his liberty in jeopardy, and I think that is much
more important than anything that I am hearing in the arbitration case.

WILLIAM G. MAHONEY: I would imagine that a person who has
been accused of theft is not present at the arbitration voluntarily. Let's assume, then, that he has been subpoenaed under an
appropriate statute. Now the question is the enforcement of the
subpoena. I believe that when you go to court to enforce the
subpoena, the matter is no longer private. You then have governmental action, and the constitutional privilege is applicable.

LARRY SCHULTZ: I don't agree that the Fifth Amendment
comes into play. True, you have no contempt powers. On the

other hand, the arbitrator is allowed to draw an adverse inference if somebody who is called doesn't testify. If an arbitrator
is faced with somebody pleading the Fifth, remind them that
arbitration is not a criminal proceeding. Even if it is not the
grievant who refuses to testify, I would feel entitled to draw an
adverse inference against the party that called this recalcitrant
witness. Unless they say they are calling the person as an adverse
witness so they can engage in cross-examination, you have to
assume that they are calling a witness who is going to support
their case.

PETER SEITZ: I don't use adverse inferences. I decide the case
on the evidence that is before me. If people refuse to testify,
including grievants, there is simply no testimony against them.
If the employer's evidence justifies a discharge—shows there is
just cause for a discharge—I will uphold a discharge. But I think
when you get into the question of adverse inference, you are
getting into a very sophisticated and complicated problem. I
frankly don't believe that I have the capacity to deal with it.

DAVID FELLER: If this kind of issue arose, I would advise the
witness to get a lawyer, because if he starts answering any questions, he may waive his privilege. I think the arbitrator has an
obligation in this situation, even if no objection is made.

JONATHAN DWORKIN: My respect for the distinction between
shop law and civil law or public law would impel me to instruct
the witness to answer questions with whatever power I might
have. I suppose in a state that has a uniform arbitration act the
question could be brought up in court on a citation for contempt.

CHESTER BRISCO: That matter is made rather simple for arbitrations in California. While the arbitration statute in California
declares that the rules of evidence do not apply, it is stated
elsewhere that privileges apply to all hearings. An arbitration is
defined as a hearing. Therefore, if a privilege against self-
incrimination is asserted in an arbitration, the arbitrator should
sustain the privilege.

TED TSUKIYAMA: I have assumed that we are dealing with a
private employer in this case. It may make a difference if the
employer is the state government or a city or other municipality.
The Fifth and Fourteenth Amendments would be inhibitions
against state action. That may provide a basis for distinction in
how an arbitrator might rule in this case.

GIL VERNON: To answer the question concerning written accusations, I have read awards that are quite old from the National Railroad Adjustment Board involving service employees with passenger contact whose discharges were upheld on the basis of written customer complaints. I don't agree with those awards, but there they are. The customers' written complaints were admitted under the hearsay exception of unavailability. The witness was unavailable and beyond the control of the employer. In a contemporary setting, I would admit statements if all the conditions were met under the unavailability exception; however, I would also stress that the employer could expect that no weight would be given to those written statements of persons who were not available for cross-examination.

JOANN THORNE: I am a labor relations officer of the Federal Railroad Administration. We shouldn't necessarily assume that we have an isolated incident like a patient or an airline rider who has a complaint and writes a letter. What if you have a person who gets repeated complaints? In the last three months, we have had 57 complaints on this particular person. In the federal sector where I work, the Civil Service Reform Act built in a provision that you could be disciplined for not being courteous to the public. Wouldn't it be appropriate in arbitration for management to walk in and say: "Here are 57 letters, Mr. Arbitrator. You can't expect us to bring in 57 people, but we feel by volume alone this is evidence of discourteous behavior."

THOMAS RINALDO: It seems to me that you have to afford due process to an employee who is being terminated from service. And due process means the right to cross-examine the accusers, and these are the complainants. I don't care if you have one or if you have a multitude of them. The burden of proof is on the employer before the employee can be discharged. That means they have to bring in good evidence. That means direct evidence, not hearsay evidence. You need witnesses. Their testimony has to be checked for accuracy through the process of cross-examination.

PETER SEITZ: Frequently in situations of this sort it is possible to get over the problem by agreement of the parties. I have had cases in which the parties agreed that I might talk to the complainant. I have had cases where the parties agreed that a deposition could be taken. For example, people come to New York and they have complaints about the hotel service. Then they go back to San Francisco. The arbitrator in such a situation has to be innovative in order to figure out ways of getting the facts. If you can't get agreement on it, it seems to me that you can't admit the statements.

CARL YALLER: There are contracts, as in the health-care industry, which forgive the lack of live complainants, like patients, to testify concerning something such as patient abuse and direct the arbitrator to draw no inference from the absence of the complainant. Where a contract does not so provide, I think hearsay problems would make their statements worthless. If employers desire to avoid that, they can seek to negotiate similar provisions in their agreements which would forgive the absence of a customer or other third party.

CHARLES FEIGENBAUM: On the search of an employee's locker, you might decide, based upon past practice or the parties' understandings, that the company does not have the authority to do that—that there is a privacy right which inheres in the locker. But the Constitution only forbids unreasonable searches and seizures by the government, not private employers. The first issue concerning self-incrimination did present a constitutional problem because there was a question of whether or not the witness was waiving a right that he had with respect to a forthcoming criminal trial. Here the constitutional guarantee does not apply.

MARSHALL ROSS: Due process in the sense of fundamental fairness does apply to arbitration proceedings, and cases can be reversed if the rights of due process are not recognized. But those rights are very limited. They would include the right to have notice of a hearing in which you are involved, the right to confront your witnesses, the right to be represented, and the right to present witnesses in your behalf. Now, the guarantee against search and seizure is not a right of due process. That is a special right found in the Constitution that applies generally to governmental agencies. If evidence is procured by an employer's breaking into a locker, that is not a violation of due process. That may be a violation of the rights between the parties as a matter of accepted industrial relations practice, but that does not taint the evidence.

IVAN RUTLEDGE: I agree with the previous speaker that if you have good evidence, you ordinarily use it no matter how tainted, although there may be a counter-grievance because of the manner in which it was obtained. But suppose we are talking about a document purloined by one party from another. It seems to me that the arbitrator is being asked to join in the misbehavior and to spoil the relationship between the two parties by allowing the arbitration process to be victimized by this kind of misconduct.

NEIL BERNSTEIN: In the courts, evidence obtained by unlawful searches or seizures is excluded solely as a device to discourage the police from engaging in such wrongful conduct. As an arbitrator, you have something of the same problem. The reason to throw it out, especially when you are talking about the case where the company finds something missing and they break open every locker in the plant and they find it in the grievant's locker, is that if you let the evidence in, what you are doing is telling the company: "Fine. Go ahead. Any time you have a problem, turn everything upside down and whatever you find is okay with me." I would be tempted to exclude it simply as a device to persuade the company to avoid this kind of action. I probably would be much more willing to do it if I were a permanent arbitrator. But, in any event, I think you have to keep in mind the value of deterrence.

SAM CHALFIE: I would recognize no privilege. I would let the employer search the locker, but he ought to have a member of the union—the steward or business agent or some rep—with him to help verify his credibility. If he did it without a union representative present, however, I still wouldn't keep that evidence from being introduced at the hearing.

JOANN THORNE: I have a problem with using internal documents of any kind. I constantly have dissent on my management team. I always have people saying: "You aren't really going to arbitrate this case, are you? It is a sure loser." If they put it to me in writing, and somehow the union got hold of it, I don't believe it should be admissible evidence. It is an opinion of one manager or perhaps input from one manager to another manager. It is a predecisional document. I don't think that such an internal communication, whether it be covered technically by the lawyer-client privilege or not, is appropriately introduced at an arbitration.

### III. Subpoenas

During the hearing one party insists that the other side has failed to produce a promised witness or certain promised documentation, and asks the arbitrator for a subpoena. The second party denies the promise and objects to the subpoena.

1. If you were the arbitrator, what would you do?
2. What if the second party says you haven't the legal authority to issue a subpoena, while the first party says you have?
   Or the first party says it doesn't know?
3. What if subpoenaed data are not provided, the disadvantaged party refuses to proceed without them, and the hearing has been arranged at considerable cost and inconve-
   nience?

TONY OLIVER: It seems to me, assuming the subpoena power
exists, that the fact of a promise is immaterial. If the arbitrator
has the power to issue a subpoena, he can issue a subpoena.

LARRY SCHULTZ: The subpoena power of an arbitrator is covered under the U.S. Arbitration Act, 9 U.S.C. § 7. Some courts
have held that this provision doesn't apply to labor arbitrators
because the Act excludes "contracts of employment" from its
scope. If you don't have the power there, you ought to look to
see whether the state has adopted the Uniform Arbitration Act,
which provides for subpoenas in Section 7. If you don't have
that, courts have upheld subpoenas under Section 301 of Taft-
Hartley in suits for specific performance of the labor agreement,
which includes providing a full and fair hearing under the grievance and arbitration provisions. The authority is generally
there.

JOHN F. LEAHY: Under the rules of the American Arbitration
Association as well as under the statutes of many states, the
arbitrator has the power of subpoena. I have also had the federal
courts on many occasions back up a subpoena. I wouldn't issue
it carelessly. I'd try to get the parties to work it out. But when
the chips are down, I would issue a subpoena.

PHILLIP LINN: I don't think that as arbitrators we are normally
operating under state law. And as one who moves from one state
to another, I certainly don't want to have to take the responsibility for determining what is state law. More important, I am
satisfied that we are under federal law. I am satisfied that we
have subpoena power under the U.S. Arbitration Act. And I
think we do ourselves a disservice if we look to state law. We
have power to subpoena both witnesses and documents under
the U.S. Arbitration Act. We have court decisions to support
that power. Indeed, in one federal case, the court went so far as
to say that, while the individual had attempted to subpoena
under state law, the federal court at that point would simply

accept the subpoena as though it had been requested as a federal subpoena.

DANIEL KATZ: The question of the legal authority of the arbitrator to have his subpoena enforced is really a red herring in terms of what an arbitrator should do. It seems to me that the arbitrator has to focus on the question of whether the testimony that is sought is necessary to the conduct of the hearing. If it is and somebody has been tricked into not having the witness available, or if he hadn't been tricked but it is still essential testimony, the arbitrator can then render a ruling saying, "With whatever authority I have, I compel you to produce this witness."

LAURENCE SEIBEL: It would seem to me the first thing that an arbitrator would have to do is say, "Will you demonstrate for me the relevance of the kind of information you are seeking?" Suppose the union says, "We don't know. We'd like to look at the company's records having to do with X, Y, and Z." They are not prepared to tell me what they expect to find or why the information they seek is relevant. It would seem to me that I would have to know all that and be convinced that what they are seeking would be relevant evidence, material evidence, probative evidence. If I conclude that the union is off on a fishing expedition, or that its request is unduly burdensome, I would not grant the subpoena.

JONATHAN DWORKIN: Signing the subpoena is a strictly administrative nondiscretionary obligation of an arbitrator in the assistance of the parties at a hearing. The arbitrator has no authority whatsoever to make a predetermination as to what is or is not relevant. In my view, he doesn't even have the authority to make a determination as to what is or is not burdensome. Where subpoenas are issued in states having uniform arbitration acts, the courts determine whether the subpoena has to be honored or not, not the arbitrator. In the absence of such statutes, the arbitrator still signs the subpoena and the court still determines whether the arbitrator had the authority to do so. I don't like to see arbitrators interfering, before you even get into a hearing, with the party's right to call for and produce what evidence they believe is relevant.

DAVID FELLER: A subpoena may look like something that somebody has to obey, but in fact nobody has to obey it until a court tells them they have to obey it. By itself it merely has a kind of *in terrorem* effect. I regularly get subpoenas, tendered to me by one party or another, several days before a hearing. I never ask what the witness is going to testify to and what its relevance is going to be. Now, I do think if somebody gives me a subpoena which I can see on its face is so burdensome that no court in its right mind would enforce it, I think, as a service to the parties, I'd say, "Look, if you insist that I sign this subpoena, I'll sign, but I'm telling you what I think. I suggest that you give me a more limited subpoena which would probably be enforceable and will much better serve your purpose."

BENJAMIN WOLF: I, too, think either side has a right to subpoena. It doesn't rest with the arbitrator to grant it or not to grant it. I think a subpoena ought to be signed as a pro forma matter. As a matter of fact, in many jurisdictions, you don't have to go to the arbitrator for a subpoena. An attorney just issues it. It seems to me that in every jurisdiction the attorney has some right of subpoena, whether he has to go to the judge or not. If he were to show me that I needed to sign the subpoena, I would sign it in every case. The other question which is posed is whether I should grant a continuance because of the late use of the subpoena. That would depend upon whether I thought the parties were entitled to it because of the circumstances. Here there may have been a promise that the material or the witness would be produced. That could have led the other side to omit the service of a subpoena. Consequently, the party who has been remiss ought not to benefit from that kind of practice.

CHARLES TRABAND: You can still continue with the hearing. There are things that are not going to be related to that one witness or piece of information which can be presented at your hearing, and then you can schedule another day.

JONATHAN DWORKIN: When an essential witness has not arrived at the hearing, I agree it's often better practice to receive whatever evidence is available that would not prejudice one side or the other. Then you make other arrangements. The Uniform Arbitration Act says an arbitrator must grant adjournments for good cause. Sometimes the parties will agree to complete presenting their evidence by affidavit, deposition, or conference telephone call.

PETER FLOREY: Suppose subpoenaed data are not provided, and the disadvantaged party refuses to proceed, asks for a continuance, and wants the other party charged for the extra day. The arbitrator doesn't have the power to fine one side or another for failure to do anything. The contract says that the fees and expenses of arbitration are to be split, so you have the obligation to split them. Of course, the parties can go to court if they claim damages under some kind of contractual right to fine or damages.

PETER SEITZ: When it is shown to my satisfaction that a party has delayed the hearing unduly and deliberately, I will assess the cost of that particular delay to the delaying party. I don't hesitate to do that.

WILLIAM E. SIMKIN: I have been amazed to hear so much about subpoenas. In thousands of cases over the years, I may have had a dozen requests for subpoenas, but I have always been able to talk the parties out of it one way or another without any ruling whatsoever. Is our process now getting so formalized that this is becoming a major problem?

TOM GREEF: One of the reasons you are seeing more subpoenas, particularly in disciplinary cases where you may have one bargaining-unit member testifying against another, is that the union wants them subpoenaed. They want the member insulated from any internal union charges of unbrotherly conduct or the like, so they won't be subject to fines or other discipline. I think you are going to see more and more of that.

PHILIP SCHEIDING: I'm from the Steelworkers. In our latest contract, the 1980 contract in the major steel companies, and in the aluminum and can contracts, we have provided that one side cannot subpoena witnesses from the other side. We did that for good reason. Under our international union constitution, a member cannot give testimony against a fellow member. We were getting into some embarrassing situations because of one member appearing against another member, sometimes at the behest of the company, sometimes pursuant to a subpoena. We cured that problem contractually. In the absence of this type of contractual clause, I think the arbitrator should attempt to use his powers of persuasion. He should try to avoid a confrontation between the parties and find other ways to get necessary evidence into the record.

## IV. Absence of Grievant or Key Witness

In the arbitration of a discharge for theft, the grievant is not present at the hearing.

1. If no one said anything, would you ask about his whereabouts?

2. When, if ever, would you request or demand that he be present?

3. When, if ever, would you call the grievant (or any other seemingly key witness) to the stand on your own initiative?

4. What if the union said, "We wanted the grievant here to testify, but he's in jail after a jury finding of guilt on a criminal issue in this case"? Would you grant a continuance for two years, or would you seek another approach?

CHRISTINE BARKER: It is my feeling that if the union wants to run the case without the grievant there, it is the union's right to do this. The company might bring up the fact that the grievant is not there, but I don't think I would open my mouth as the arbitrator and ask where the grievant is.

EARLE BARTAREAU: As a management representative, if I had a discharge case and the grievant wasn't there, I think I would inquire why he wasn't there.

CHARLES TRABAND: I totally agree with that position. If you saw what happened to Anchor Motor Freight in the *Hines* case on the duty of fair representation, you know an employer could end up being liable for millions of dollars on a joint and several liability theory. I think if you are doing your job as a management representative, you should get it on the record: What is going on? Why isn't the grievant here?

BENJAMIN WOLF: I would hate to feel as an arbitrator that I was being used by the employer and the union to drop some employee who didn't even know about the hearing. Just for my own satisfaction, I would have to know that I had a genuine case, not one contrived between management and the union. I certainly would inquire as to the circumstances of the grievant's absence.

DAVID VAN OS: I'm a union advocate. There may be cases where the arbitrator ought to inquire, at least off the record, whether the grievant has been notified of the hearing. But I would not go any further than that. I do not think that it is the arbitrator's place to determine what sort of case the advocates should be attempting to present to him.

DAVID KABAKER: I certainly would ask where the grievant is and whether or not he was notified and why he isn't present. Even in industries where it isn't customary to have the grievant present, some courts have held that he is entitled to be present and to be represented by counsel.

ELLEN ALEXANDER: I would ask the person who had claimed to have given notice to state what that notice was. I would get into the record whether it was personal contact, like a conversation, or a certified letter, or whatever. But if I was satisfied that the notice had been adequate, I would probably proceed, although there are many arbitrators who would not. I think due process is always left up to the arbitrator even though fair representation may primarily be a matter for the union. Even though the parties were ready to proceed, I would still want to satisfy myself from the due-process viewpoint that there had been notice.

GEORGE NICOLAU: In a particular case, I have required counsel to contact the grievant on that very day and to come back and represent to me that the grievant had authorized him to proceed in his absence. It was done without any difficulty.

STEVEN GOLDSMITH: In an arbitration case where both sides are ready to proceed and there is no objection to the proceeding, but the grievant isn't there, I ask the union to state on the record what efforts they have made to get in touch with the grievant—telephone calls, letters, other efforts—and whether they have sat down with the grievant to discuss the facts, if they want to tell me about that. I will put that on the record to show in effect that the union is not at fault. We are going ahead after due notice to the grievant.

MARK KAHN: There are two distinct situations. One is where the union and the employer are equally surprised by the failure of the grievant to be on hand. I think there it would be a mistake to proceed. Obviously, the grievant could have been taken ill or been involved in a traffic accident, or whatever, and he would not be getting due process. I think the situation calls for a continuance and an investigation of the reasons for the grievant's not having appeared. An altogether different situation is where the union does take the position that we advised the grievant not to appear or he advised us that he wasn't going to appear and we want to go ahead. I think you go ahead.

IRVING BERGMAN: Around the New York area, the state designating agencies, e.g., the New Jersey State Board of Mediation and the New York Board, will advise the arbitrator on what to do if the grievant is not present. We are cautioned not to proceed, but to automatically grant a request for postponement. That will generally be made by the union in order to cover the possibility of that bugaboo we now have about lawsuits. After the automatic adjournment is granted the first time the grievant doesn't show up, I make it a practice to insist the union give me copies of their receipts for certified mail and an affidavit of whoever it was—such as a business agent—who contacted the grievant and who said he would be there for the second hearing. I put that right in the award when I dismiss the petition or the demand for arbitration, as an explanation of the grievant's absence. That is done now to cover yourself against lawsuits because the agency doesn't want to be sued either.

WILLIAM GLINSMAN: When a grievant doesn't appear, I too require the union to provide proof that they have notified him. If they have such proof, I render an award that says that the grievant upon due and sufficient notice is entitled to show good cause why he was not available at the hearing. He may apply for a reopening within 30 days, and if he does not, I discharge him. You instruct the union in your award to send a follow-up telegram. They use a mailogram that is certified that they did notify the employee at the last address of record. Consequently, there is proof that the award is final and binding.

MARSHALL ROSS: I have had the situation more than once where the grievant was served proper notice but failed to appear, and at first the union wanted a continuance. Then there was an objection from the company on the ground that an employer has the right to refuse to have the matter withdrawn. If they insist, I think they have a right to go forward with the hearing because they may have engaged in a lot of expense and trouble, and they are entitled to be heard even though it wasn't their grievance.

WILLIAM FREDENBERGER: Sometimes the employer will move that the grievance should be summarily denied if the union does not produce the grievant. In this regard, it seems to me that it is a fundamental proposition that the union has both the burden of proof, in the usual nondisciplinary case, and the right to prove, in any case. If they can make that proof without the grievant being present, at least they should be given the opportunity to do so. So I would not grant the employer's motion in these circumstances.

RALPH NORTON: I'm a union advocate. In a discharge case the union may have concluded that the grievant was not properly terminated. Now they come to the arbitration proceeding and the union does not call the grievant. But the company still has not made its case. I think the arbitrator in this instance can't draw an adverse inference. He has to make the determination on the basis of the evidence presented. It is the employer that has the burden of proof, that has to establish the case.

I. B. HELBURN: Just two observations: First, in the rare instance where the grievant has not appeared or has appeared and not testified, it was painfully obvious to me that the only thing the grievant could do by appearing on the stand was to weaken his or her case. Second, I am not sure that the matter is one of drawing adverse inferences so much as it is that the absence of the grievant's testimony either eliminates or severely diminishes the union's opportunity to rebut the case made through the evidence presented by management. Both approaches, of course, may lead to the same conclusion—the grievant loses.

WILLIAM E. SIMKIN: If the discharged person is at the hearing and does not testify, I have never called that person as a witness. But almost invariably at the tag end of the hearing, I'll turn to the grievant and say, "Look, do you have anything to say for yourself?" And usually they say something and then I may have a few questions I want to ask, but I don't officially call them as a witness. Sure, I have drawn adverse inferences from the grievant's failure to testify. But that is why I usually ask those questions. I want to give him a chance.

JAMES MCMULLEN: I would not call the grievant. If I thought that I needed additional evidence, I would indicate privately to counsel what it was I thought I needed. I would give counsel the opportunity to make that decision himself. That is his decision.

CAROL ZAMPERINI: I think the arbitrator should just be satisfied to know that the grievant is there and not make any move to call the grievant. I don't think that the arbitrator should put himself or herself in a position where they are going to conduct the case for either party.

MORRISON HANDSAKER: While I do not disagree with that position in general, I have called the grievant when the union made no attempt at all to put in any defense for the grievant. It seemed to me that maybe he was being railroaded.

ZEL RICE: I don't think I would call a supposed key witness either. I think I would let someone know that there was some information that I would be interested in hearing, but I don't think I would call him myself.

PAUL ROTHSCHILD: I think you indicate to the parties what you need. Then it is up to them to decide whether they are going to risk your displeasure and not provide you with the information for whatever it is worth. But I don't call witnesses.

Richard Mittenthal: I think the arbitrator does have some larger obligation to find out the facts in the controversy which the parties, for one reason or another, unknown to the arbitrator, have not bothered to bring out. I remember a knife fight in which two employees were discharged because the company was unable to determine who initiated the fight. A third person was there throughout the fight whom the union and management had attempted to question without success because the man was afraid to testify. I worked out an arrangement with the agreement of all parties to preserve the confidentiality of his testimony. He came in and testified, and it became perfectly clear which of the two grievants was lying.

Jerome Greene: The last hypothetical, where the grievant has been found guilty and is in jail, is relatively easy. Most of the time they throw in the towel before they get to arbitration. Otherwise, it depends upon how long the grievant is going to be in jail. If he is going to be in for only six months or even a year, I would put it up to the parties as to what they want to do.

## V. Witnesses From Opposing Sides

In the arbitration of a discharge for insubordination, the employer calls a bargaining-unit member as a witness and the union objects.

1. As the arbitrator, how would you rule?
2. Suppose the employer calls the grievant as its first witness?
3. Would it make any difference if the union indicated it was going to call the grievant anyway—but on the assumption that the employer would previously have completed its case?
4. Would you allow the union to go first if it insisted on doing so as the party appealing to arbitration, even if it wished to start by calling company officials?
5. How would you rule if one party called the other party's lawyer or representative to testify as to nonprivileged matter, e.g., an observed incident? What if a lawyer offered himself as a witness for his own side?

Horace Williams: I'm with a union. I don't think there is any justification for the company's calling a bargaining-unit witness. If that witness is going to testify, the company would have an opportunity to cross-examine later anyway. The company has the burden of proof and should start with its own witnesses. If they need something from a union witness, they could get to that part of it when the union is presenting its case. If the union presented its case without calling that person, then I think an arbitrator would take another look and exercise some judgment on the need for that witness's testimony.

WILLIAM LeWINTER: As a general principle, reserving the question of the grievant, each side has the right to subpoena or call any witness they want. I permit that. I have even held against a party, relying on the burden of proof, that failed to call a witness from the other side. I presumed that the witness would have testified against them. They obviously knew of him. They had the right to call him, and they knew they had the right and they didn't call him.

GEORGE NICOLAU: In the broadcasting industry and a number of other industries, the parties have a rule that they do not call each other's witnesses. In other areas, again leaving the grievant aside, a party has the right to call anyone they want. There would be no problem with that.

PHILIP SCHEIDING: Suppose the company desires to call a union witness and the union representative reminds the arbitrator and also the man whom the company wants to call that if he testifies, he opens himself up to possible charges under the union constitution for giving testimony against a fellow member.

WILLIAM E. RENTFRO: This happens today with some frequency. Under the facts you described, I would allow the company to call the union member. If the international representative made such a threat in the hearing, I would admonish him against that kind of threatening. I would allow the witness to take the stand, and if he chose not to testify because of the problem he had with his constitution, that would be a privilege for him to assert. If he didn't want to testify, I wouldn't compel him. I couldn't.

MARSHALL ROSS: We are not here to enforce the union's constitution any more than we are here to enforce the federal constitution. If the company wants to call a union member to testify, I think they have a right to do so. Under the circumstances, it would be easy to accommodate the member by simply suggesting that the company obtain a subpoena. I also think that the employer has a right to call the grievant as its first witness. But as a practical matter, I call the parties aside and point out that this might cloud their future industrial relations. I urge the company to refrain from calling the grievant until they make out a prima facie case. I never fail to obtain their assent to that method.

WILLIAM E. SIMKIN: I have no recollection of ever ordering an adverse witness to testify. I have had a number of cases where the request has been made. I have never granted that request. The only thing that I have ever done that even approaches it is that I may ask a few questions of my own at the end of the hearing. Fundamentally, it is the responsibility of each side to put on its own case with its own witnesses. Of course, they can cross-examine whoever shows up on the other side. But as to ordering someone to appear as an adverse witness, I am vigorously opposed to the whole notion.

MARK KAHN: I think it is bad practice for the employer to call the grievant as its first witness. If the union objects, I would uphold the objection. I think that the employer is under an obligation to present the employer's case, and the employer certainly should have witnesses and evidence to show why it discharged the person. I would, however, make some effort to ascertain whether the union intends to call the grievant as its witness. Receiving such assurance, I would certainly be firm on the fact that the employer can cross-examine the grievant later. The grievant will clearly be on the stand. If the union hedges and says that they don't know yet, I would say that we will see what happens. I have under such circumstances sometimes permitted the company to call the grievant last.

DANIEL BRENT: The hypothetical fact pattern mentioned that this was a case of insubordination. By definition, I suppose insubordination requires someone giving an order and someone refusing to carry that order out. So, in this particular situation, I think that it would be appropriate to have the person whose order was refused outline the basic facts for the arbitrator before requiring either observers or the grievant himself or herself to participate in the hearing. In the event that only bargaining-unit employees observed the fight or theft or other event and the supervisory personnel arrived on the scene or became involved at a later time, one can expedite the hearing by requesting the supervisor who meted out the discipline merely to set forth the facts to the limit of his or her knowledge. That seems to satisfy both parties, and we can proceed without becoming unduly bogged down in highly technical arguments that we have heard in regard to this situation.

TERENCE CONNOR: As a management advocate, there are numerous occasions on which I would call the grievant first. For example, you may be in the situation where the grievant has made up at least two or three stories along the way through the grievance process, and you know that that person is capable of making up still another story to fit the facts that are presented by the management witnesses. What I am most concerned about, though, is how a group of arbitrators can come up with this exclusionary rule without any legal basis for it. There is nothing but the loosest kind of reasoning that it is not fair to ask someone to testify first in a termination case. It is a civil proceeding and a private law system, and I don't know the source of this right not to be called.

GABRIEL ALEXANDER: I was brought up in this business between two powerful institutions—the UAW and General Motors —and they were sophisticated and they had pioneers in the umpiring system, and they taught me what the expectations of this private tribunal were. It is really a question of the expectations of the parties. It comes back to the feeling of the shop. Now, I should qualify that because, as I got away from autos and arbitrated elsewhere and some management lawyer called the grievant or bargaining-unit witnesses, there was dead silence. Down in the rubber industry in Dayton, it was commonplace, and no one raised an eyebrow and I didn't open my mouth. If that was the way they were going to go with their system, it was of no concern to me. But the minute I heard a union sound incensed—"What are you trying to do to us?"—I knew I would be defeating the expectations of equal participants. From my experience, there isn't one in 95 management representatives who would do this.

RALPH HANNABURY: It bothers me considerably as a company advocate that so many arbitrators feel that they should dictate how a company should present their case. I firmly believe that nobody owns a witness and that either party should be able to put their case in through whomever they wish. If a company wants to call a grievant first, whether or not an arbitrator likes that, I don't think he should try to block it.

VICKIE HEDIAN: I'm a union representative. My point is that there are two sides and there are two cases to be presented. The employer may want to call the grievant, and the union may not want to or may want to reserve the right to make that decision once it hears the employer's case. If you let one person put on the case they want, you may be denying the other person the chance that they want. When you are balancing those two things, remember that the burden of proof is on the employer. We are entitled to have the grievant not testify at all if we don't think they have put in enough evidence to prove their case.

ROBERT J. MUELLER: I am going to be in the minority, but I will let the employer call the grievant or anyone else adversely, provided that they don't have restrictions in their contract or understandings or past practice not to call members of the union to testify against each other. The grievant is the one who is asking for a remedy and is invoking the process. Many times when it is a contractual issue the union will call a company witness adversely to start their case out. I see no problem either way.

PETER FLOREY: Just a matter of statistics: This question was discussed at a regional meeting of the Academy recently, and the arbitrators were split about 50-50, almost evenly, on the question of whether or not management can call the grievant as its first witness.

THOMAS RINALDO: The same principles apply to calling the other party's lawyer or representative to testify as to non-privileged matters. I think you can call anybody as long as you are not talking about privileged information.

CHARLES TRABAND: Sometimes the union's representative, usually a business agent, will have been party to negotiations and will offer a statement as proof and subject himself to cross-examination. Calling the other side's attorney is often an exercise in futility as a practical matter because he certainly is not going to say what you want him to say. You can get into some technicalities about calling a witness and about when you are bound by what your witness says and when you can treat him as an adverse witness. I think we have to be aware that we're in arbitration and not in court and try not to get caught in those technicalities. Let's get the facts on the record. That's all we're trying to do.

DONALD WECKSTEIN: The problem with calling a lawyer as a witness is that the code of ethics that governs lawyers says that a lawyer shall not be a substantive witness, at least on a nontechnical matter, where that person is also counsel. I doubt whether that would apply to a labor arbitration. Certainly it's quite common for business representatives serving as counsel in the absence of a lawyer to be witnesses as well—sometimes giving narrative statements, sometimes having someone else examine them. They are obviously not subject to the lawyer's code of professional responsibility. Why should it be any different unless there's something inherently unethical about a lawyer testifying as a witness? As I see it, the reason for that prohibition is two-fold. One, the lawyer might destroy his independence of judgment. I figure that's something for the parties to judge, not for me. The other is that in a court trial the jury might be confused as to whether the lawyer is playing the role as advocate or as witness. Arbitrators, of course, are superior to juries at keeping such things separate. So I would say that that ethics rule probably does not apply to labor arbitration.

## VI. Medical Affidavits

At the hearing, one of the parties produces a letter from a board-certified physician detailing the results of a hospital examination of an employee, with the conclusion that the employee was "disabled" and unfit for work during the disputed period. The other party objects to the report as hearsay.

1. As the arbitrator, how would you rule?
2. If either the board-certified physician or the company plant doctor were "on call" and ready to come and testify, would you call him if neither party did?
3. Would you accept the report of an examination by the company's physician or nurse if the employee's counsel objected on the grounds of doctor-patient privilege?

ED TEPLE: I much prefer to have doctors testify, but I've had few experiences with that. They're expensive, and the parties don't see fit to bring them in as witnesses as a normal rule. Obviously, the doctor's letter is hearsay, but I usually accept it strictly as that and give it appropriate value. Often I have the same thing from both sides, and you have different doctors making different statements about the same matter. You have to judge. But if that's all a party has, I certainly wouldn't keep it out of my record.

HOWARD LeBARON: Sometimes these physicians' reports can be dispositive of whether, in fact, the employee was absent because of an illness on the pertinent date. If that is so, this note is of great value. Now we come to the next question with respect to medical notes or letters or extended documents from a doctor, a diagnosis and prognosis, where we don't require the doctor to be present since they are so busy and so expensive. This is still a document which cannot be cross-examined. It is of dubious probative value, in my mind. There may be a different opinion. Most of us have had a lot of cases where you have a document from the union and a different document from the company, and they are in direct conflict. On occasion I have suggested to the parties that they bring the doctors in. And the testimony has also been in direct conflict. You have to resolve that conflict just like any other.

WILLIAM LeWINTER: Suppose the company has received the medical form we are talking about in the grievance procedure. The company has not told the union that they were going to contest the use of it, and they reasonably could expect it would be presented in an arbitration. Now, in that situation, I am prone to accept the document. If it shows me that there has been some form of diagnosis, some form of treatment, I am going to give it weight. I am not going to let the other side start to contest it on the basis that doctors do this and doctors do that. I now have evidence in front of me, and if you don't have sufficient conflicting evidence, you are going to find that I accept this as a valid, substantive piece of evidence in the case.

ROLAND STRASSHOFER: There is a practical solution to the problem that arises when there is a substantial question about the authenticity of the document. I have found that the parties will usually agree to a phone conference. I call the doctor immediately. I ask him when we can arrange for a discussion. As long as everyone can hear what is going on in the phone conversation, that seems to suffice, unless, of course, a serious issue does emerge during the phone conversation. In that event we may have to adjourn until we can have the doctor come in personally.

GERRY BOYLE: I am a labor advocate. It is my experience that these reports routinely come in under the business-record exception to the hearsay rule. But in talking about privilege, one thing we ought to keep in mind is whom the privilege belongs to. The privilege does not belong to the lawyer or doctor. It belongs to the patient or client. I have had several situations where there was some medical information in the file that the grievant didn't want disclosed, so they wouldn't give a release to get the medical records. In those situations I have indicated to them that we can't go forward with the case until they sign that release. They get to make their own decision on whether we go forward or not.

BARRY BROWN: What the advocate just said is true except that most people, when they have applied for insurance benefits, disability benefits, absence pay, or something similar, have usually filed a waiver or a release with the company in order to take the physical examination or submit to some doctor's review. If there is such a release, I would receive the document. However, if the patient—the grievant in the case or whoever it is that this doctor's statement is about—objects and exercises their privilege, then I would refuse to receive it on the basis of the doctor-patient privilege. The question then is, can an arbitrator draw any conclusions from the grievant's objection to the admission of the document. I am sure the advocate for the side trying to propose the document would raise the argument that some conclusions should be drawn. I think it would be dangerous to do that, but at least that would be the argument.

ANTHONY BALDWIN: In your hypo regarding the privilege, I can't conceive of a situation where an employer wouldn't have the employer's doctor or the staff doctor examine the employee. In that situation, especially if there was an industrial accident, it would seem to me that we wouldn't have the problem of the privilege.

## VII. Closing Arguments, Briefs, Remedies

In a discipline case the union suggests that, to save time and money, the parties dispense with briefs and rely on closing arguments. The company says it will agree only if it is allowed to close last, since it had to open first.

1. As the arbitrator, how would you handle a dispute over the order of closing arguments?
2. How do you respond to a disagreement between the parties about the need for briefs? Do you ever express your own preference in a particular case?
3. If neither party raises a remedy issue, do you?
4. Under what circumstances, if any, would you grant a union's request for interest on back pay? At what rate?

SAMUEL CHALFIE: It has been my policy to tell the parties at the close of the hearing that if they want to make oral argument or if they want to file briefs, it is for them to agree between themselves. It's utterly amazing, but I have had a party say that he wanted to give an oral argument and file a brief, and the other one wisely says that he will just file a brief. On closing arguments, again I give them all the leeway they want. But the one who opens the case will open the closing argument, followed by the other. If they want to rebut, they each rebut in the same manner.

ZEL RICE: I handle it almost exactly as a court does. The party that opens gets to close. They give the final argument. They also go first. In between the other party gets a chance to make their own points and respond to the points of the first speaker.

ED TEPLE: On the question of who gives the oral summation first, I would simply say, "Look, you can both have rebuttals, so it doesn't matter who goes first and who goes last. I'll listen to you all until you're both satisfied that you've got everything before me the way you want to do it." That usually handles it very nicely.

THOMAS RINALDO: I always give the parties an opportunity to submit briefs if they want to submit briefs. If it is a particularly difficult case, involving complex language of the contract or shop, I may request briefs.

CAROL ZAMPERINI: If one side or the other requests briefs, then I would allow briefs. I might argue against them and say they may not be necessary. I might point out that the only thing they're likely to include in those briefs are statements that have already been made at the arbitration. But if either side wants them, then I think it's a privilege that should be extended. Whether the other side wants to file a brief or not at that point is up to them, although it probably behooves them to do so.

DALLAS YOUNG: I have suggested to the parties that short summaries rather than formal briefs are very valuable. They ensure that the arbitrator does not miss a point which has been developed by one of them. They can be extremely helpful if he must summarize the respective positions of the parties without any briefs. Short summaries can also be money-saving.

GERRY FELLMAN: An arbitrator may assume that the authority to provide an appropriate remedy is implicit in the submission, but you could be buying trouble. It's so easy, when the parties give you the submission agreement, to say, "Oh, by the way, am

I correct that you meant to include a line, what shall the remedy be, after, was the discharge for just cause?" I would recommend that everyone, as a matter of course, ask the parties that at the start of the hearing. You may save a lot of hassle. I've seen the question briefed heavily, and it's a waste of time that could be avoided at the hearing.

PHILLIP LINN: We have the strangest rule in the Tenth Circuit. If there hasn't been a remedial issue put before the arbitrator, the arbitrator may not fashion an enforceable remedy. You may find there was a contract violation, but you cannot provide a remedy without clear authorization. That is not true in other circuits.

JOANN THORNE: I would like to add something from the federal sector's standpoint. A lot of times in our arbitrations the remedy is more complex than the merits, and we've gotten into some very detailed arguments on the applicability and permissibility of remedies. If an arbitrator who has a federal case doesn't ask for and hear argument on remedy, they're doing themselves a disservice and are likely to get appealed.

ROGER SCHNAPP: As a management advocate, I think remedy can be very important. Often what appears to be crystal clear is not crystal clear. What if the grievant has been working, or has received unemployment compensation benefits, or has had a period of disability? Then the remedy can be critical. I would like the arbitrator in the award to deal as specifically as he can with the remedy that he believes to be fair.

BEN GILLINGHAM: I raise the remedy issue if the parties don't. I am surprised at the number of times in which the parties will get so involved over the question of the substantive issue that the matter of the remedy may get overlooked entirely. Often I find by asking, "What is the union proposing as a remedy in the event that it prevails?" we get a lot of clarification on the substantive nature of the issue and the union's theory of the case. Or you may discover that the problems of remedy that were already running through your head are greatly simplified by learning the remedy which the union seeks.

ZEL RICE: If you are going to do that, it is a good idea to do it at the start of the hearing, whenever possible, because of the inference that the employer might otherwise get that you have already made up your mind.

EDWARD PERELES: I would raise the question in a very neutral way. But I don't want to ask the parties about the remedy until they have clarified the issue. So where the issue is cloudy in the beginning, I wouldn't ask for the remedy early.

SOL YAROWSKY: There is a great reluctance on the part of arbitrators to allow interest, first, because it is an element of damages over and above back wages, and because in a majority of cases other arbitrators would frown upon the addition of interest to a back-pay award. It is practically never requested in the grievance. It is only an afterthought, possibly even in the posthearing brief. But if an arbitrator concludes that the violation of the contract was rather grievous, interest should be allowed. You ask at what rate. A number of arbitrators, and I include myself in that group, follow the lead of the NLRB. They have a very definite rule of allowing interest on their back-pay awards. It is a fluctuating rate. It is not a constant rate, like 6 percent in the old days. It varies with the market. It is subject to revision at the end of every six months.

IRVING BERGMAN: The NLRB has a right to fashion a remedy, and they justify their interest charge on that ground. It is an appropriate remedy to make whole. Absent anything in the contract, the only remedy that an arbitrator has on reinstatement with back pay is to give the man the hourly rate of pay that he would have earned if he had worked. There are arbitrators who have granted interest nevertheless. I don't know that it has been contested. In my view, the arbitrator probably has no right to do it. The contract doesn't say anything about making him whole.

THOMAS RINALDO: I have awarded interest in a very limited case, and that is where there was a flagrant violation of some employee's rights. I granted interest at the rate of 4 percent two years ago.

PHYLLIS SENEGAL: If you are going to allow interest, I think you should use the interest rate that the state allows you to attach to any judgment. I think in some states it is 8 percent; in others it is 12 percent. I think I might grant a union's request for interest under certain circumstances, where there was a tremendous abuse and the employee suffered a tremendous amount of damage in terms of his income or lost his house.

JOHN SHEARER: I'm not an attorney; I'm an economist. I have no trouble at all with the concept of interest in a back-pay award. I do not understand how an award can be a make-whole remedy without taking into account the changing value of the dollar. My attorney friends have yet to convince me that interest is in any way punitive damages or anything of the sort. As to the rate of interest, except for extenuating circumstances, I generally use an approximation of the Consumer Price Index for the relevant time period.

HOWARD COLE: If the contract is silent or merely speaks generally of remedy, I think it is fair to say that the parties have negotiated for the arbitrator to have the right to issue what in his judgment is an appropriate remedy. In reaching their bargain, they presumably had in mind a long history of collective-bargaining practices throughout varying relationships, including their own. The general collective-bargaining practice has been not to award interest, but to rely upon the rough justice approach. Is it really fair to expect the arbitrator to plow that new ground against years of the no-interest practice, or is the burden on the party desiring interest on back-pay awards to seek that change in negotiations?

## VIII. Token Presentations, Agreed Awards, and Disqualification of the Arbitrator

During the hearing the representative of one of the parties says to the arbitrator, in the presence of the other party's representative but out of the hearing of the grievant, "The union is only taking this case to arbitration because of fear of a lawsuit."

1. If you were the arbitrator, how would you respond? Specifically, should you disqualify yourself?
2. Would your answer differ if the grievance involved a contract interpretation rather than discipline?
3. Would your answer differ if the statement were made at or near the end of a long hearing rather than at or near its beginning?
4. What if the representative told you the parties had agreed that the grievance should be denied? Would it make a difference if they had agreed that the grievance should be sustained?

BARBARA DOERING: I would consider disqualifying myself if the union said they were going to arbitration because they feared a lawsuit. If the company said it, I'd say they were entitled to their opinion. I would, of course, disqualify myself if I felt the union was really telling me they wanted to throw the case.

MARK KAHN: I think you should disqualify yourself. There

could conceivably be exceptions, especially if the union representative were to agree to have the grievant made aware of this observation and if the grievant were to agree to go ahead. That would take something extremely unusual. The hypothetical may be more difficult if you have just completed three full days of hearing and, as bags are being packed, the union representative says that. Once the hearing is over, I think you are in a position at least to make a judgment as to whether the grievant was well represented. You can be well represented in a losing case. The simplest situation, of course, is where you determine that the grievant has a winning case in spite of that remark. The remark becomes irrelevant. But if you feel that the grievant has been well represented, that the union hasn't taken a dive, it is not trying to sabotage the grievant, it is just a sincere but improper remark, I think I would probably say that I have heard the case and that I thought a good case was made for the grievant. The parties have a big investment now—three days. I'd be likely to ignore it.

WILLIAM E. SIMKIN: We have got a ruling of the Ethics Committee bearing on this, which I disagree with. As I read it, it says that in this kind of situation, you have two alternatives: one is to resign; the other is to go to the grievant and tell him what has happened and ask the grievant whether he is willing for you to proceed to decide the case in view of what has happened. That second point of going to the grievant and telling him the story, I think, is a serious mistake. That creates all kinds of problems in the relationships of the parties and is something that an arbitrator under no condition should do. I do agree completely that we have the obligation to press continually to make sure that there is no improper collusion.

DAVID KABAKER: Even if the union said it feared a lawsuit, the union has a right to assume that they can pursue any grievance to avoid a lawsuit. That wouldn't bother me, but it would bother me if the union says that they know they have a losing case. That is entirely different, and I would consider withdrawing. I think I would be inclined to disregard the statement at the close of the case.

MIRIAM MILLS: I think it makes a difference whether the union's action is overt or covert. If they engage in dreadful eye-rollings and give you that sort of message, I think then that the arbitrator is permitted to be more intrusive in the case and to permit more latitude in questioning the witnesses, because my own feeling would be that the grievant is not being well represented. If, however, they were to say it straight out, regardless of the costs, it becomes improper. I also think it doesn't make any difference whether the grievance involves a contract interpretation rather than discipline. Whether it is a person or a principle, the union shouldn't throw the case.

IDA KLAUS: If the company and union approached the arbitrator and said that this is a loser and we fully expect the award to be for the company, that is a fix. They are telling you that it is a fixed case and they want you to render a decision for the company, and I would immediately disqualify myself. I would do the same if they said they wanted me to sustain the grievance. Either way, I would disqualify myself in those circumstances.

DAVID KABAKER: I think the last question presents two different possibilities. Where they want an award without your hearing any testimony, that is a fix. I think the other situation is where the company and the union representatives come and say that they recognize the merits of the grievance. At that point you say to them, you are proposing to withdraw and settle the grievance. And they say that they would like to have a stipulation of settlement, and they would like to have that incorporated in the award. That is an entirely different situation.

CHARLES FEIGENBAUM: My own reaction is that it's a very different situation if they both agree that the grievant should be reinstated with back pay as opposed to their both agreeing that the termination should be upheld. In the first instance, the grievant certainly isn't being harmed, the union isn't being harmed, and the company isn't being harmed, as opposed to the other situation where clearly the grievant is being harmed. I think any theoretical abuse of the arbitration process is offset by whatever the needs of the parties were that made them feel they had to go through this charade. I guess I would go along. It may be collusion, but it's a benign collusion in this situation.

GEORGE NICOLAU: The Code of Professional Responsibility says that prior to the issuance of an award, the parties may jointly request the arbitrator to include in the award certain agreements between them concerning some or all of the issues. The parties may say, "Please put in, too, the fact that the grievance is sustained." The Code goes on to state that if the arbitrator believes that a suggested award is proper, fair, sound, and lawful, it is consistent with professional responsibility to adopt it.

* * *

*Program Chairman's Note and Acknowledgment:* The foregoing comments in Chapters 5 and 6 reflect the spontaneous reactions of the participating arbitrators and advocates. If my own experience is any guide, no one should be held bound forever by the views expressed. People respond differently to the dynamics of live situations, to the needs of particular parties, and to small and not-so-small variations in the facts. Opinions change over time.

I should like to acknowledge an enormous debt of gratitude to all the program participants, especially to the discussion leaders whose own wise observations were ruthlessly excised in accord with my perhaps perverse notions of fairness. Finally, deep appreciation is due my secretary, Nan Druskin, and her colleagues on the secretarial staff of the University of Michigan Law School, for patiently transcribing over 36 hours of recorded tapes, and for carefully organizing the resulting mass by subject matter so as to facilitate my selection process.

T. J. S.

# NATIONAL ACADEMY OF ARBITRATORS
# OFFICERS AND COMMITTEES, 1982–1983

I. *Officers*

Byron R. Abernethy, President
Alfred C. Dybeck, Vice President
Thomas T. Roberts, Vice President
Martin Wagner, Vice President
Dallas M. Young, Vice President
Richard I. Bloch, Secretary-Treasurer
Mark L. Kahn, President-Elect

II. *Board of Governors*

Howard D. Brown
Martin A. Cohen
Walter J. Gershenfeld
Marcia Greenbaum
James Harkless
John Kagel
Edward E. McDaniel
Milton Rubin
James J. Sherman
James L. Stern
Ted T. Tsukiyama
Marian K. Warns
Edgar A. Jones, Jr. (ex officio)

III. *Past Presidents*

Ralph T. Seward, 1947–49
William E. Simkin, 1950
David L. Cole, 1951
David A. Wolff, 1952
Edgar L. Warren, 1953

Saul Wallen, 1954
Aaron Horvitz, 1955
John Day Larkin, 1956
Paul N. Guthrie, 1957
Harry H. Platt, 1958

G. Allan Dash, Jr., 1959
Leo C. Brown, S.J., 1960
Gabriel N. Alexander, 1961
Benjamin Aaron, 1962
Sylvester Garrett, 1963
Peter M. Kelliher, 1964
Russell A. Smith, 1965
Robben W. Fleming, 1966
Bert L. Luskin, 1967
Charles C. Killingsworth, 1968
James C. Hill, 1969

Jean T. McKelvey, 1970
Lewis M. Gill, 1971
Gerald A. Barrett, 1972
Eli Rock, 1973
David P. Miller, 1974
Rolf Valtin, 1975
H. D. Woods, 1976
Arthur Stark, 1977
Richard Mittenthal, 1978
Clare B. McDermott, 1979
Eva Robins, 1980
Edgar A. Jones, Jr., 1981

IV. *Appointments and Committee Rosters*

(a) *1983 Annual Meeting*

*Arrangements Committee for the
Thirty-Sixth Annual Meeting—1983*

John F. W. Weatherill, Chairman

Harold D. Brown
Claude Lauzon

Thomas T. Roberts
Roland Tremblay

Nicholas H. Zumas

*Program Committee*

Frances Bairstow, Chairwoman

George William Adams
Joseph F. Gentile
Gladys Gershenfeld
Matthew A. Kelly
Harold H. Leeper
Edward E. McDaniel

Robert B. Moberly
Charles M. Rehmus
Zel S. Rice, II
Owen B. Shime
Carlton J. Snow
Roland Tremblay

(b) *The Standing Committees*

*Executive Committee*

Byron R. Abernethy, President

Richard I. Bloch
Alfred C. Dybeck

Edgar A. Jones, Jr.
Mark L. Kahn

*Membership Committee*

Arvid Anderson, Chairman

| | |
|---|---|
| Joseph F. Gentile | Lawrence T. Holden, Jr. |
| J. B. Gillingham | Edward B. Krinsky |
| Alan B. Gold | J. Joseph Loewenberg |
| Margery F. Gootnick | William E. Rentfro |
| Theodore K. High | John C. Shearer |

*Committee on Professional Responsibilities and Grievances*

Howard A. Cole, Chairman

| | |
|---|---|
| Gerald A. Barrett | Richard Mittenthal |
| Frederick H. Bullen | Eli Rock |
| William J. Fallon | Ralph T. Seward |
| Dallas L. Jones | Arthur Stark |
| Bert L. Luskin | John F. W. Weatherill |
| Thomas J. McDermott | Sol M. Yarowsky |

*Committee on Law and Legislation*

Ivan C. Rutledge, Chairman

| | |
|---|---|
| Benjamin Aaron | Raymond Goetz |
| Reginald Alleyne | Jacob D. Hyman |
| James B. Atleson | James E. Jones, Jr. |
| David L. Beckman | Emily Mahoney |
| Merton C. Bernstein | Cornelius J. Peck |
| Tim Bornstein | Paul Prasow |
| Howard M. Fitch | Marshall Ross |
| Robert W. Foster | James P. Whyte |

*Committee on Research and Education*

Anthony V. Sinicropi, Chairman

*Planning Section*

Anthony V. Sinicropi, Chairman

| | |
|---|---|
| Dana E. Eischen | Howard G. Foster |
| Charles L. Mullin, Jr. | |

*Subcommittee on Continuing Education: Seminars*

Dana E. Eischen, Chairman

Thomas F. Carey      Paul E. Fitzsimmons
Jonathan Dworkin      William Levin
Joel M. Douglas      J. Earl Williams

Arnold M. Zack

*Subcommittee on the Development of Arbitrators:*
*Intern and Training Liaison*

Charles L. Mullin, Jr., Chairman

Lewis R. Amis      Marlyn E. Lugar
J. D. Dunn      Walter E. Maggiolo
Alice B. Grant      Joseph A. Sinclitico

*Subcommittee on Research*

Howard G. Foster, Chairman

Elizabeth Benz Croft      Philip K. Kienast
Sherman F. Dallas      Joseph Krislov
Julius G. Getman      Charles A. Myers
James A. Gross      Cornelius J. Peck
James E. Jones, Jr.      Paul H. Sanders

Foster Jay Taylor

*Auditing Committee*

Seymour Strongin, Chairman

Alfred C. Dybeck      Clare B. McDermott

*Committee on Future Meeting Arrangements*

Thomas T. Roberts, Chairman

Alfred C. Dybeck      Anthony V. Sinicropi
William J. Fallon      Rolf Valtin
John Phillip Linn      John F. W. Weatherill
Clare B. McDermott      Nicholas H. Zumas

*Committee on Legal Affairs*

Howard S. Block, Chairman

| | |
|---|---|
| Bennett S. Aisenberg | George R. Fleischli |
| William Belshaw | J. Ross Hunter, Jr. |
| John F. Caraway | John Kagel |
| Donald Daughton | Walter N. Kaufman |

Roland H. Strasshofer, Jr.

*Committee on Legal Representation*

P. M. Williams, Chairman

| | |
|---|---|
| Gabriel N. Alexander | Nathan Lipson |
| Howard S. Block | Robert G. Meiners |
| Peter DiLeone | Milton Rubin |
| Alex Elson | John E. Sands |
| James Harkless | Howard M. Teaf, Jr. |

*Committee on Overseas Correspondents*

Charles J. Morris, Chairman

| | |
|---|---|
| Mario F. Bognanno | James C. McBrearty |
| Gerald Cohen | Samuel S. Perry |
| Alvin L. Goldman | Herbert V. Rollins |

Jack Stieber

*Committee on Public Employment Disputes Settlement*

Helen M. Witt, Chairwoman

| | |
|---|---|
| Robert J. Ables | Barnett M. Goodstein |
| Robert F. Barlow | Paul D. Jackson |
| Howard S. Bellman | Harold D. Jones, Jr. |
| Irving T. Bergman | Ruth E. Kahn |
| George E. Bowles | William J. LeWinter |
| Thomas F. Carey | Leonard E. Lindquist |
| Paul J. Dorr | Walter H. Powell |
| Jonathan Dworkin | Julius Rezler |
| Walter L. Eisenberg | Thomas N. Rinaldo |
| Paul J. Fasser, Jr. | Herman Torosian |

L. Reed Tripp

*Editorial Committee*

James L. Stern, Chairman

Tia Schneider Denenberg                    Walter J. Gershenfeld
Dana E. Eischen                                   James J. Sherman

*Future Directions Committee*

William P. Murphy, Chairman (1981–82)
John E. Dunsford, Chairman (1982–83)

Frances Bairstow                                   Lewis M. Gill
Richard I. Bloch                               Edward E. McDaniel
Howard S. Block                                 Jean T. McKelvey
Mario F. Bognanno                            Thomas T. Roberts
Howard D. Brown                                     Eva Robins
Martin A. Cohen                                 James J. Sherman
Tia Schneider Denenberg                   Anthony V. Sinicropi
Alex Elson                                          Edwin R. Teple
Julius G. Getman                                     Rolf Valtin

Arnold M. Zack

*Nominating Committee*

Alexander B. Porter, Chairman

Edgar A. Jones, Jr.                                  Eva Robins
William E. Rentfro                              James L. Stern

*Special Committee on Policy Handbook*

Martin Wagner, Chairman

Richard I. Bloch                                     Eva Robins

Dallas M. Young

*Special Committee on Archives*

Peter Seitz, Chairman

Richard I. Bloch                                    Arthur Stark
Charles M. Rehmus                              James L. Stern
Anthony V. Sinicropi                            Martin Wagner

*1982–1983 Regional Chairpersons*

Edwin R. Teple, Coordinator of Regional Activities

| | |
|---|---|
| Region 1, New England | Paul J. Dorr |
| Region 2, New York City | Jesse Simons |
| Region 3, Eastern Pennsylvania | William M. Weinberg |
| Region 4, District of Columbia | Robert J. Ables |
| Region 5, Southeast | James J. Sherman |
| Region 6, Upstate New York | Milton M. Goldberg |
| Region 7, Canada | Howard D. Brown |
| Region 8, Western Pennsylvania | Helen M. Witt |
| Region 9, Ohio | Arthur R. Porter, Jr. |
| Region 10, Michigan | Nathan Lipson |
| Region 11, Illinois | Martin Wagner |
| Region 12, St. Louis | Gladys W. Gruenberg |
| Region 13, Southwest | Raymond L. Britton |
| Region 14, Rocky Mountain | John Phillip Linn |
| Region 15, Northern California | Joe H. Henderson |
| Region 16, Southern California | Leo Weiss |
| Region 17, Pacific Northwest | J. B. Gillingham |

# REPORTS OF OVERSEAS CORRESPONDENTS*

## The End of Australian Incomes Policy

### J. E. Isaac**

My 1975 report on Australia outlined the introduction by the Arbitration Commission of a package of principles based on the assumption that uniform national wage adjustments related to consumer price and national productivity movements would constitute the bulk of wage increases. These adjustments would be determined quarterly in relation to the consumer price index movement and annually in connection with productivity change. Increases beyond these adjustments would need to be, in overall terms, small and related to local issues pertaining to job reevaluation (known here are "work value" adjustments), special allowances, and the like. These would be determined in accordance with narrowly prescribed principles. There was also a special provision to deal with "anomalies and inequities."

The Commission was persuaded to embark on this concept because of the inflationary and self-defeating effects of sectional (by industry or occupations) wage adjustments which, by the pressure of coercive comparisons (known here as "comparative wage justice"), tend to be generalized. The indexation package was intended to provide a "more orderly, more rational, more equitable and less inflationary" approach to wage fixation. In embarking on this approach, the Commission laid the basis for the development of an incomes-policy package: it would prescribe general and particular wage movements along the lines indicated, provided that appropriate "supporting mechanisms" were in place. These included the continuation of price surveil-

*Members of the Committee on Overseas Correspondents are Benjamin Aaron, Monroe Berkowitz, William B. Gould, Alvin L. Goldman, Joseph Krislov, Charles J. Morris, Herbert L. Sherman, Jr., and Jack Stieber, chairman.
**Deputy President, Australian Conciliation and Arbitration Commission, Melbourne, Australia.

lance by the Prices Justification Tribunal, sensitivity of the federal government on the relationship between taxation levels—direct and indirect—and wage claims, and the willingness of state wage-fixing tribunals to follow the lead of the federal tribunal—the Arbitration Commission.

The consensual approach taken by the Commission was not only dictated by the lack of legal powers to enforce the principles, but more importantly by the recognition that the success of a wages or incomes policy depends substantially on the willingness of major parties—unions, employers, and governments—to abide by prescribed rules.

The concept embarked upon in April 1975 came to an end in July 1981. During this time, the principles were altered marginally: six-monthly adjustments took the place of quarterly consumer price adjustments, and various principles were extended and clarified. For the first three years the indexation package approach, as it came to be called, worked reasonably well. The rate of inflation, which had peaked at about 17 percent, came down to just over half that rate, despite the effect of increases in indirect taxes and exchange-rate depreciation on the consumer price index. Strike activity also fell markedly. These results were noted in my 1976–1977 report. But thereafter the concept came under increasing pressure and moved from crisis to crisis. The state of the economy and the monetary and fiscal measures applied by the federal government dictated the granting of less than full indexation in order to ease the growing unemployment problem. In the eyes of the government and many employers, the Commission did not go far enough in restraining wages, while the unions and their members became increasingly discontented with a system which did not at least ensure that real wages would be maintained. The increasing weight of taxation added to the workers' disenchantment. Strike activity began to rise, fuelled in part by the concerted move in the metal industry and elsewhere for a reduction in the standard working week from 40 to 35 hours.

In June 1979 the Commission announced that it was on the brink of abandoning the "centralized orderly system based on indexation" essentially because "one side wants indexation without restraints while the other wants restraints without indexation." The Commission asked the parties to show why the system should not be discarded. A conference and lengthy hearing disclosed that all the parties wanted an orderly centralized system to continue. In the circumstances, the Commission persisted with the system, but ordered a fuller debate on the principles in 1980. It made a number of observations about "certain essential requirements for the survival of such a system" in the following terms:

"1. The quest for perfection is illusory and counter-productive. Ideal solutions as seen by each side must be adjusted for what is economically necessary and industrially workable. Alternative economic options may have to be taken in the interest of more acceptable industrial requirements. Inflation cannot be brought to heel too quickly by wage decisions without adverse industrial effects and consequential adverse economic effects. On the other hand, wage and conditions claims must be based on realistic expectations of what the country can afford. In short the preferred choices of employers, unions and governments may have to give way to what is necessary if a centralized system is to exist at all.

"2. The operation of a centralized system must be subject to rules to be applied and observed consistently at all levels of the system. Experience has shown that actions which breach the letter and spirit of the rules are contagious and lead to the breakdown of the system.

"3. Costs to the economy arising from stoppages and bans threaten not only improvements in real wages and conditions but even the maintenance of existing standards. This is not a moral judgment but a matter of hard economic reality.

"4. There may be no workable method in a centralized system which will allow the cost of breaches of the rules to be borne only by those responsible for such action. The problem of finding disincentives for industrial action may, therefore, be vital to the equitable operation of a system.

"5. The power of the Commission to compel compliance is limited. It relies on the effective support of all those who wish to see an orderly system survive. Tacit approval is not enough. Unless the level of industrial disputes is contained and the processes of conciliation and arbitration accepted as the means of resolving issues in dispute, there does not seem much point in searching for a centralized system."

The inquiry which followed resulted (April 1981) in a reframing of the principles which provided for two half-yearly reviews every year. The first would apply 80 percent of the consumer price index increases of the preceding two quarters semi-automatically; the second review would consider the remaining 20 percent of this increase together with the subsequent two quarterly CPI increases and national productivity increases for the years.

However, subsequent events provided that the concept of a centralized system of wage fixation was not sustainable. More and more claims were made at company and industry levels and often settled outside the principles. In abandoning the system in July 1981, the Commission said:

"Since April 1975 the Commission has operated a centralized system of wage fixation based on indexation. It was expected that such a system would be more orderly, more rational, more equitable and less inflationary and would therefore reduce industrial disputation.

"The essential feature of such a system was the need to regulate and limit wage increases outside National Wage to allow high priority to be given to the maintenance of real wages. It was accepted by all that a set of rules would be necessary to achieve this priority.

"The viability of the system depended on the voluntary cooperation of all participants in industrial relations including those not directly represented at National Wage hearings. Monitoring of sectional claims through the processes of conciliation and arbitration was fundamental to its operation.

"From time to time since 1975, the Commission has pointed to the fragility of the package and in June 1979 the Commission came to the brink of abandoning the system. A decision about whether we should persist with the system was given as recently as April this year. The Commission refashioned some of the principles to strengthen the priority for the maintenance of real wages but the essential requirements of the package were otherwise unaltered.

"The events since April have shown clearly that the commitment of the participants to the system is not strong enough to sustain the requirements for its continued operation. The immediate manifestation of this is the high level of industrial action in various industries including the key areas of Telecom, road transport, the Melbourne waterfront and sectors of the Australian Public Service. In many cases action was taken on the pretext that the claims could not be processed because of the principles. Some of these disputes have resulted in substantial increases being agreed without regard to the test of negligible cost or the implications of flow-on.

"To accommodate these strong pressures the ACTU and the Commonwealth proposed widening the safety valve provided by the principles dealing with anomalies and inequities. The belief that the answer lies in greater flexibility of the kind proposed is illusory. Such flexibility would resolve sectional claims at the expense of national adjustments and destroy the priority expected of a centralized system. It cannot be otherwise.

"For these reasons we have decided that the time has come for us to abandon the indexation system.

"Now that we have taken this step the guidelines will no longer apply in proceedings before the Commission or the Public Service Arbitrator. The Commission will deal with applications as filed,

members of the Commission will sit alone or on Full Benches and
the various provisions of the Conciliation and Arbitration Act will
apply. For instance the concept of the 'interests . . . of society as a
whole' (section 4) will still permeate activities of the Commission
and of course Full Benches will still be required pursuant to section
39 to have regard to the state of the economy with special reference
to likely effects on the level of employment and inflation.

"Any application for adjustment of wages or conditions on economic grounds will not be heard before February 1982."

My 1976–1977 report concluded as follows:

"As in other countries, the question whether it is possible to engage
reflationary measures while keeping prices on a downward path has
been the center of public controversy. In Australia, this controversy
assumed special significance because wage-fixing institutions have
established a sense of unity and coherence of wage principles which
some believe could well withstand the pressure of economic recov-
ery on cost. This is especially so, in view of the prospects of tapping
the unit-cost advantages of fuller capacity use."

The Australian experiment was not sustainable for several
reasons—unwillingness by unions and employers to accept the
necessary degree of rigidity in the application of wage-fixing
rules, unwillingness by state tribunals to continue to follow the
lead of the federal Commission, and unwillingness of the government to trade off the taxation needs of demand management
in favor of taxation requirements of wage restraint.

Since the abandonment of the indexation system, collective-
bargaining-type settlements have taken place in a number of key
industries, including the metal industry which has traditionally
been a pattern-setter for the rest of the workforce. The metal-
industry 12-month agreement included an immediate wage increase of about 11 percent, a wage increase of about 6 percent
effective from 1 June 1982, and a reduction in standard hours
from 40 to 38. An important feature of the agreement was an
undertaking given by the unions that no further claims would be
made for the 12 months except in the event of "an unforeseen
change of an extraordinary nature in the economic circumstances." In such an event, the parties have agreed to abide by
arbitration should they not be able to settle the issue agreement.

The metal-trades agreement has become a model for many
other agreements, though not all have included a reduction in
hours. These agreements have been taken to the Commission
for ratification to give them the legal force of arbitrated awards.
Although the size of the wage increase in these agreements

could accelerate inflation if generalized, in ratifying them the Commission has been moved by consideration of industrial peace flowing from ratification. It has also been influenced by a general climate of opinion, generated principally by the federal government, for greater decentralization in wage-fixing, including more collective bargaining on American or Japanese lines. And it should be remembered that the Commission is, after all, a Conciliation *and* Arbitration Commission and that one of the objects of the Act under which the Commission operates is "to encourage, and provide means for, conciliation with a view to amicable agreement, thereby preventing and settling industrial disputes."

The analogy with America and Japan is, of course, simplistic. The very presence of arbitration tribunals affects the style and nature of collective bargaining in Australia,[1] which, in turn, affects the claims before arbitration tribunals. Thus, the unions which have not been able to secure agreement on wage increases on the metal-industry standard have applied for a catch-up by arbitration at a national wage hearing currently in progress. What the outcome will be remains to be seen. The state tribunals, which are independent of the Commission, have in many cases awarded increases commensurate with the metal-industry standard. These developments have occurred despite rising unemployment, currently at a postwar record of 7 percent, and accelerating inflation, now over 10 percent. The next 12 months will show whether in a deteriorating economic climate the metal-industry standard can be resisted in the rest of industry. In the Australian context, as distinct from the American or Japanese context, an interaction between wage-fixing tribunals and collective-bargaining units has in the past been a fact of life. Whether it will continue to be so in the present circumstances will be clear in the next few months.

In my 1976–1977 report, I outlined legislation introduced by the federal government directed at greater control of union power. Some four years later it is difficult to discern any tangible results of this legislation. The same government has recently foreshadowed further laws directed to the same end.

First, the government proposed to stop the granting of union preference in awards of the Commission. The present Act con-

---

[1]See my paper, *The Coexistence of Compulsory Arbitration and Collective Bargaining*, in Essays in Honour of Kingsley Laffer, ed. W. A. Howard (London: Oxford University Press, 1982).

tains a provision for the award by the Commission of union preference. It is in line with one of the objects of the Act "to encourage the organization of representative bodies of employers and employees and their registration under this Act." Some may say that a denial of a discretion available to the Commission to award union preference is inconsistent with this object of the Act. The issue is not easily resolved. On the one hand, arbitration depends on the existence of unions to process claims and grievances on behalf of individual or groups of workers. It would be clumsy, if not unworkable, otherwise. On the other, arbitration does not depend on 100 percent union membership.

A further point to be borne in mind is that the strong and militant unions do not rely on the preference provision of the Act to ensure a union shop. They ensure it by dint of their industrial power. It is generally the weaker unions in the white-collar areas who have sought union preference as an award entitlement in order to bolster their finances. The proposed legislation may not in the end achieve the intention of weakening the power of the stronger and more militant unions.

The second piece of proposed legislation is to encourage the development of industry and enterprise unionism, the latter presumably by providing for something like the American bargaining-unit concept. This move is partly inspired by the face of American and Japanese unionism. But it may underrate the weight of history against any forced change in union structure. The Australian Council of Trade Unions (the Australian equivalent of the AFL-CIO, but with more authority over its affiliate union members) has had among its objectives the establishment of industry-based unions since 1927 when it was formed. But little has changed over the years. Union amalgamations have occurred, but they have largely been the consolidation of occupational unions *across* industries. Inertia, vested interests, political and personal differences have stood in the way of industrial unionism. It is difficult to believe that the legislative initiative foreshadowed by the government will change this situation. Any forced-draft approach, especially coming from a government which is not regarded generally by the trade union movement as sympathetic to it, may have destabilizing effects on industrial relations. Experience suggests that perceived threats to union security may encourage militancy, and it is not clear whether employers generally would welcome any forced change in the current structure of unions despite its many shortcomings.

The third piece of legislation to be introduced relates to the right of an employer to stand-down (lay off) its employees as a result of a strike either of its other employees or employees elsewhere. At present, awards may contain a stand-down clause or they may be varied to include such a clause in the event of a strike. The employer is thereby given the right to stand-down (i.e., not to pay wages to) any employees who cannot be usefully employed because of "any strike or through any breakdown in machinery or any stoppage of work by any cause for which the employer cannot reasonably be held responsible." But the continuity of employment is not interrupted by a stand-down.

The rationale of such a clause in a weekly contract of employment is obvious: the employer is not obliged to terminate employment on a week's notice and incur the extra cost of such notice, and the employee's accrued rights with respect to paid leave (annual, sickness, long-service) are not ended by being stood down.

Where no such provision exists in an award, an employer may seek at very short notice to have one inserted. The Commission does not grant the application automatically. It must be persuaded that there is a real prospect that the workers concerned cannot be usefully employed and that, in consequence, the employer will suffer economically. This procedure has worked reasonably well in the past and can be set in motion quickly. Many employers do not invoke their rights under the clause or seek its insertion in a hurry, partly from fear that it may provoke strike action subsequently. Thus, the Waterside Workers' Federation (our longshoremen's union) has a policy that a stand-down in any port will result in a strike at all ports.

Legislation to confer on employers the right to stand-down without resort to the Commission may be effective where unions are weak, but may not make any real difference where unions are strong and resist the stand-down. Furthermore, an attempt to impose what may be regarded as the doctrine of "collective responsibility" on unions generally may not necessarily stay the hands of strong unions. But it could create bitterness among those who are stood down because other workers, for whose cause they may not have any sympathy, are on strike.

The dilemma often facing the employer is understandable. And while the legislation will generally not make his lot any easier, it may assist the employer in those cases where a union resorts to filibustering before the Commission—calling evidence and dragging proceedings out virtually until the strike is settled.

I should finally record my pleasure at meeting a group of a dozen or so members of the NAA, led by Arnold Zack, who visited Australia in May 1981 for a week. It was a pleasure also to have enjoyed the company of Ben Aaron on his rather longer stay in Australia. I hope they found the highly concentrated experience of comparative labor relations rewarding.

## Arbitration—The Changing Scene in Great Britain

### Sir John Wood*

Those unfamiliar with the structure of industrial relations in Great Britain, or merely familiar with some of its idiosyncracies, must find it difficult to understand the apparently unstructured and haphazard use of arbitration. Even those working within the system find it difficult to say why arbitration still lacks a clearly established role.

Two general characteristics of the system add to the complexity. It is well known that no clear distinction is made between disputes of right and disputes of interest. This lack of clarity will remain so long as collective agreements are not regarded as legally binding. Each dispute about the interpretation of an existing agreement takes on the character of a fresh negotiation. This is felt by some to be a foolish, indeed amateurish, lack of formality and precision. To others, and they appear to be in the majority, the system is beneficially flexible and stresses "mutuality"—that is to say, the joint regulation of problems. Whatever the merits of that majority view, and it appears to be receiving increased criticism, it means that the arbitrator has failed to secure a regular place in the system as interpreter of disputed collective agreements. That is to be regretted.

More confusing still is the other important characteristic—the existence of a somewhat distinct type of arbitration, usually referred to as unilateral arbitration. In classical voluntary arbitration, the two parties agree to submit their difference to an arbitrator, usually promising to accept his award. Unilateral arbitration allows one party to insist upon arbitration. This form

*Professor, Faculty of Law, Sheffield University, Yorkshire, England.

is usually found in legislation where not only is one side able to
force arbitration, but the award is also legally binding. It is very
occasionally to be found in collective agreements, usually in the
public sector where the pressure of striking was rarely resorted
to (times have indeed changed). For example, the Railway Staff
National Tribunal has an interesting provision by which a joint
submission to the tribunal leads to a binding award, a unilateral
submission to an advisory award.

These two characteristics—the use of arbitration in interest
disputes and the existence of unilateral arbitration—have inevitably made the process of arbitration itself the subject of warm
political debate. It is arguable that arbitration flourishes best
quietly and unsung, though this may be a somewhat British
reaction. Certainly the opposite is true. Where arbitration is
used to settle major pay disputes or to resolve a collective-
bargaining dispute which had led to disruptive strike action,
then the full glare of publicity is inevitable and can so easily give
a false impression of the whole process. Opinions are formed
from one well-publicized, but badly understood, instance. Hostility to the process can easily take root.

Like so much else in democratic politics, these attitudes seem
to swing violently from time to time. Just now arbitration is
definitely out of general favor. The U.K. government has
adopted a philosophy based on the market economy, not unknown, we are given to understand, in universities on the shores
of Lake Michigan. Intervention, especially enforced intervention by a third party into wage determination, is regarded now
with some hostility, especially by the government as employer
itself.

The recession has added greater weight to this criticism. Several of the usual devices of the interest-dispute arbitrator—
comparability is the strongest example—have been fiercely criti-
cized. The process is said to have ignored important factors, of
which "ability to pay" is the most frequently mentioned. An
argument such as that is difficult to refute, in part because in the
public sector the wage fund drawn from rates and taxes can
never be as finite as that available to the commercial employer.
He has always used the inability-to-pay argument, and it is easier
—though by no means easy—to test his sincerity. Since, in the
mixed economy, the government is a major employer either
directly (the civil service) or indirectly as contributor to the wage
fund in areas ranging from local government and hospital ser-

vices to subsidized nationalized industries, and even grant-aided private industry, its attitude is crucial. Since the government has as one of its primary functions the overall regulation of the economy, it is inevitable that its political stance in that field will be strongly reflected in its role as employer. Thus the boundary between the economic arguments (can't afford) and the political (the government has willed the end, so must provide the means) is never clear and, in this context, is virtually nonexistent.

So, since the election of the Conservative Government in 1979, the criticisms of arbitration have grown. The government has made public its adverse view of unilateral arbitration machinery in the public sector and has started to dismantle it. Pay-fixing generally is regarded as primarily to be based upon market forces, and arbitration is obviously in that context an irritant. It follows that while there is an increasing growth of third-party resolvement of rights disputes, arbitration generally is in decline. It is possible to illustrate this by looking briefly, but in more detail, at the changing pattern.

*I. Individual Rights and Industrial Tribunals*

The growth of individual rights has depended largely upon a steady legislative program, begun in 1963. It started with the establishment of minimum periods of notice for all employees, gained a great boost with the regulation of dismissal by the Industrial Relations Act of 1971 (now repealed, but these provisions were reenacted in the new legislation), and by 1976 had covered a wide area including points such as time-off for trade-union activity and maternity leave. These statutory rules supplemented collective agreements, which had never been able to establish such an advantageous position overall. It was welcomed by the trade unions; indeed, they persuaded the Labor Government to make the advances of 1974–1975. The obvious disadvantage appears to have been overlooked. The existence of the statutory provisions lessened the need to press for strengthened collective agreements. The gains still appear to many to outweigh the loss. Yet many would argue that the easy option of legislation has provided yet another excuse to the trade unions who lack real professionalism.

The real interest to arbitrators is the emphasis now placed on dispute resolution outside the collective agreement. The statutory rules are enforced by the industrial tribunals—a system

outlined in the 1980 report by my colleague, Professor John-
ston. The growth in the number of complaints made to the
tribunals was remarkable, and there has been little sign of a
diminution. The annual figure of about 40,000 is a surprise, but
there is a conciliation step, so the majority of cases never reach
a hearing.

The reasons for surprise are twofold. The acceptance of a
legalized tribunal system firmly linked, through the Employment Appeals Tribunal, to the ordinary courts is such a marked
change from the staunch independence of those in industrial
relations. It may well be that the indirect impact of tribunal
decisions on the concept of a fair-employment contract was not
fully appreciated. So far little has been written, other than by
academic lawyers, about the creation of a plethora of rules which
amount to a "standard form" of contract. The second ground
for surprise is the apparently acceptable loss of control, and
even power, by the trade unions as the legal rules come to
regulate more and more. Obviously, in an area as untilled and
unstructured as the law of employment was until the 1960s, any
development of rules is likely to be an improvement of rights—
certainly for those working in areas without a history of collective bargaining. This perhaps obscured the previously clear
disadvantages of legal regulation—a loss of flexibility and an
artificiality as abstract rules replace individual settlement of
difficulties. Again, some academic voices are being raised on this
point, too. But the system flourishes.

The current development will be of real danger only if there
is a move towards legally binding collective agreements. This is
still stoutly resisted by both sides of industry. However, as so
often happens, pressure for reform comes on a different wind.
The current political cry is for a reassessment of the power and
position of our trade unions, secured under the common law by
means of statutory immunities. Already in the Employment Act
of 1980 and the current proposals (Employment Bill of 1982),
the process is in train. One major step would be to make immunities depend upon "failure of due process" under the collective agreement. This proposal, in line with the present government's political views, has not found favor, largely perhaps
because of practical difficulties. For it to be workable, the status
of the collective agreement would have to be more firmly established—the very groundwork that would be needed before, and
therefore might lead naturally to, the status of being legally
binding.

Were that to occur without deliberate thought, the likelihood would be that supervision of legally binding agreements would become the responsibility of the tribunals. Although at first sight this is logical, it has one very important drawback. The close integration via the Employment Appeals Tribunal would tend to bring to bear on the handling of a collective-agreement dispute the methods of documentary interpretation developed by the courts. This has a very legalistic flavor, very foreign to usual industrial relations practice. It is to be hoped that this development does not occur unnoticed. Attention at some stage will need to be given specifically to whether arbitration along the U.S. lines would not provide a more fruitful advance.

## II. Unilateral Arbitration in Pay

The period 1974–1979 was notable for its use of unilateral arbitration, by which is meant provisions enabling one party to insist that the other submits an issue to binding arbitration. It is secured by statute. The use of the device has its roots in attempts to prevent industrial strife during the Second World War. It allowed the employee who felt he was being paid less than the established rate—that is, the rate fixed by a national or local collective agreement—to claim an increase.

In the Employment Protection Act of 1975, the trade unions persuaded the government to extend this process to a worker who could show that his rate fell below the "district level." The law was, surprisingly, put into operation at the beginning of 1976, a moment when the government was establishing a pay policy that year-by-year attempted to reduce the permitted wage increases. The juxtaposition of the pay policy and the procedure —usually referred to as Schedule 11, where the rules were to be found in the 1975 Act—meant an inevitable use of the machinery.

Thus the body to which the machinery was entrusted, the Central Arbitration Committee (once known as the Industrial Court), found itself inundated with cases. The figures speak for themselves: 1976, 54; 1977, 742; 1978, 529; 1979, 346. It was not merely the low-paid who used the system. Since it was based on comparative levels, highly paid workers who felt they had fallen behind those of similar skill in the same industry and district were able to bring a case. Employers who found that they were unable to attract labor because their wage rates were out of line encouraged their trade unions to bring such a case.

Indeed, on occasion the government as employer or, through public ownership, the paymaster encouraged raises to be sought by this route so that the annual increase would remain within pay-policy limits.

The result of this phenomenon was that the process of arbitration boomed as it never previously had done. Techniques had to be developed and members of the panels had to gain experience. For four years the amount of work was unprecedented.

The Conservative Government, elected in 1979, had policies strongly opposed to the social-democratic approach. The concept of solidarity of wages—that is, the rate for the job—were replaced by a faith in competition. The whole system was swept away, leaving wage-fixing as far as possible to market forces and to collective bargaining. No doubt if the pendulum swings back again to where comparability and solidarity predominate, a very uneven wage pattern will be found giving scope, under a political philosophy so minded, to another bout of consolidation of rates.

It is interesting to note, too, that when the Labor Government found itself under pressure from public employees for "catching-up" raises, it set up a standing committee on pay (called the Clegg Committee after its chairman). It was not, of course, in form an arbitration body, yet in reality it had many of the same features. It received written evidence from the parties, held discussions with them, and produced a report which had much the same effect as an arbitration award. Obviously it differed from arbitration chiefly in that the committee itself did a great deal of research in comparative levels of pay, either itself or by means of commissioning consultants. This body, too, fell under the axe of the market-oriented Conservative Government.

This relatively brief period of pay-determination by unilateral arbitration, or the Clegg Commission, is typical of the U.K. scene. A process or a new body is launched, and before its techniques can be properly refined or its longer-term impact evaluated, it falls to a political change of wind. This not only changes the principles, but does considerable institutional damage.

*III. Voluntary Arbitration*

The failure to regard the collective agreement as even a quasi-legal document means that voluntary arbitration remains a fitfully used instrument in industrial relations. Its use is not monitored, so it is impossible to give adequate statistics. Arbitration services are offered free by the public, but independent, Advisory Conciliation and Arbitration Service (ACAS). Its establishment, with a tripartite council—employer, trade union, and independent members—led to a marked increase in the use of its services. A complete guess will be that it arranges at least half and probably three-quarters of the arbitration work. The statistics are:

| | 1975 | 1976 | . . . | 1979 | 1980 |
|---|---|---|---|---|---|
| Boards (three-member arbitration) | 32 | 31 | | 44 | 34 |
| Single arbitrators | 260 | 265 | | 304 | 237 |

The pattern is relatively steady with a workload in the 375–475 range. It seems clear that there is a need for arbitration under the present arrangements, but the need, like so much else in the system, is not institutionalized; it is an ad hoc reaction to current problems.

To summarize: There are two areas of tension which will determine future development. The first is political. Both the Labor Party and the new, and as yet not provenly established third force, the Social Democratic Party, will undoubtedly turn to more institutional and formalized procedures. It is inevitable that the pendulum would then swing back towards the concept of unilateral arbitration in one form or another. The current Conservative Party, although itself containing differing attitudes, is at present firmly wedded to laissez-faire views which do not regard arbitration as other than an emergency escape, to be used sparingly. The political battle is likely to be resolved next at a general election in 1984 or thereabouts. Arbitration will not be an issue! But its short-term future will be at stake.

The second is more subtle and would need expanded consideration to be fully explained. There is, however, a relatively unnoticed conflict between the legal approach, epitomized by the industrial tribunals, and the more traditional informal approach. Arbitration is flexible enough to live in either camp, but its real role should be as the formalism of the informal system. Yet there are signs that, despite a great deal of opposition, the legalization of industrial relations is gathering momentum. The result should make an interesting report in two to three years' time.

# CUMULATIVE AUTHOR INDEX*
## 1973–1982

---

*For the Cumulative Author Index covering the period 1948 through 1972, refer to
Labor Arbitration at the Quarter-Century Mark, Proceedings of the 25th Annual Meet-
ing of the National Academy of Arbitrators, eds. Barbara D. Dennis and Gerald G.
Somers (Washington: BNA Books, 1973), 355 et seq.

# TOPICAL INDEX